Cottage, Cabin & Vacation

HOME PLANS

D1472104

SUNSET BOOKS

Vice President, General Manager:
  Richard A. Smeby
Vice President, Editorial Director:
  Bob Doyle
Production Director:
  Lory Day
Director of Operations:
  Rosann Sutherland
Retail Sales Development Manager:
  Linda Barker
Art Director:
  Vasken Guiragossian

Cover: Pictured is plan 574-CHP-1642-A-10 on page 151. Design by Chatham Home Planning. Photograph by Chris A. Little.

10 9 8
First printing May 2003
Copyright © 2003 Sunset Publishing Corporation,
Menlo Park, CA 94025.

Library of Congress Catalog Card Number:
2003105040
ISBN: 0-376-01061-4
Printed in the United States.

For additional copies of *Cottage, Cabin & Vacation Home Plans* or any other Sunset book, call 1-800-526-5111 or visit our web site at **www.sunsetbooks.com**.

*E*scape-that's what cottages, cabins, and vacation homes offer. Whether nestled in a stand of pines, edging a mountain lake, or basking in the desert sun, these homes provide a retreat from hectic city life. For many people, nature's attraction is so great that they spend nearly as much time in their vacation home as in their city home. For some, it eventually becomes their permanent residence.

Most of today's vacation homes are not very different from primary residences. Although they may be smaller in scale and highly space efficient, they usually offer the same construction and many of the same amenities. Perhaps the biggest difference is in appearance-vacation homes often look more rustic, blending into natural settings. And many are designed to cope with harsh weather, unusual sites, difficult access during construction, and fewer available conventional utilities.

Choosing the Right Plan for You

As you look through this book, many of the homes will appear to be just what you're looking for. But are they? Consider some of the following questions for determining your dream home.

One way to find out if the home is right for you is to analyze what you want. Though it's not always easy, it's an important first step because of the investment you are about to make and the satisfaction and enjoyment you will receive from building your dream home.

Overall size and budget. Generally, the size or square footage of living area in a home establishes the cost. How large a house do you want? Will the house you're considering fit your family's requirements? It is often better for the house to be a little too big than a little too small, but remem-

ber that every extra square foot will cost more money to build and maintain.

Number and type of rooms. Consider your family's lifestyle and how you use space. Do you want individual bedrooms or a large, dormitory-style room? Will one large great room suffice or do you want a separate living room, dining room, and kitchen? Would you like lots of windows to capture nature's beauty?

Room placement and traffic patterns. Where do you want to place the bedrooms? Do you prefer a kitchen that's open to family areas or private and out of the way? Is it important to have easy access to the outdoors?

Architectural style. With a vacation home, especially one that's tucked away in a picturesque spot, it's particularly important that the style of the home be in harmony with its surroundings. Moreover, climatic conditions may make certain demands on style, such as a roof designed for snow in a heavy snowfall area. Be sure to choose a style that's appropriate for the location.

Site considerations. Site topography and size is a consideration of floor plan development. For example, if the lot is shallow in depth, a sprawling ranch may be the ideal design. If the lot is narrow, you may want to consider a narrow lot design allowing you to maximize the site space. Also, slopes (both gentle and steep) will affect the home design you select.

Check the orientation of the site as well. Note trees, rock outcroppings, slopes, views, prevailing winds, direction of sun, and other similar factors. All will have an impact on how a house design works on a particular site.

Although we've only scratched the surface, we've tried to present key considerations that will help guide you in selecting the home plan that's right for you.

QUICK AND EASY CUSTOMIZING
MAKE CHANGES TO YOUR HOME PLAN IN 4 STEPS

HERE'S AN *AFFORDABLE* AND *EFFICIENT* WAY TO MAKE CHANGES TO YOUR PLAN.

1 Select the house plan that most closely meets your needs. Purchase of a reproducible master is necessary in order to make changes to a plan.

2 Call 1-800-367-7667 to place your order. Tell the sales representative you're interested in customizing a plan. A $50 refundable consultation fee will be charged. You will then be instructed to complete a customization checklist indicating all the changes you wish to make to your plan. You may attach sketches if necessary. <u>If you proceed with the custom changes the $50 will be credited to the total amount charged.</u>

3 FAX the completed customization checklist to our design consultant at 1-866-477-5173 or e-mail blarochelle@drummonddesigns.com. Within *24-48 business hours you will be provided with a written cost estimate to modify your plan. Our design consultant will contact you by phone if you wish to discuss any of your changes in greater detail.

4 Once you approve the estimate, a 75% retainer fee is collected and customization work gets underway. Preliminary drawings can usually be completed within *5-10 business days. Following approval of the preliminary drawings your design changes are completed within *5-10 business days. Your remaining 25% balance due is collected prior to shipment of your completed drawings. You will be shipped five sets of revised blueprints or a reproducible master, plus a customized materials list if required.

4 *Terms are subject to change without notice.

BEFORE
Plan 2829

Customized Version
of Plan 2829

AFTER

MODIFICATION PRICING GUIDE

CATEGORIES	Average Cost from... to
Adding or removing living space (square footage)	Quote required
Adding or removing a garage	$400 $680
Garage: Front entry to side load or vice versa	Starting at $300
Adding a screened porch	$280 $600
Adding a bonus room in the attic	$450 $780
Changing full basement to crawl space or vice versa	Starting at $220
Changing full basement to slab or vice versa	Starting at $260
Changing exterior building material	Starting at $200
Changing roof lines	$360 $630
Adjusting ceiling height	$280 $500
Adding, moving or removing an exterior opening	$55 per opening
Adding or removing a fireplace	$90 $200
Modifying a non-bearing wall or room	$55 per room
Changing exterior walls from 2"x4" to 2"x6"	Starting at $200
Redesigning a bathroom or a kitchen	$120 $280
Reverse plan right reading	Quote required
Adapting plans for local building code requirements	Quote required
Engineering stamping only	$450 / any state
Any other engineering services	Quote required
Adjust plan for handicapped accessibility	Quote required
Interactive illustrations (choices of exterior materials)	Quote required
Metric conversion of home plan	$400

Note: Any home plan can be customized to accommodate your desired changes. The average prices specified above are provided only as examples for the most commonly requested changes, and are subject to change without notice. Prices for changes will vary according to the number of modifications requested, plan size, style, and method of design used by the original designer. To obtain a detailed cost estimate, please contact us.

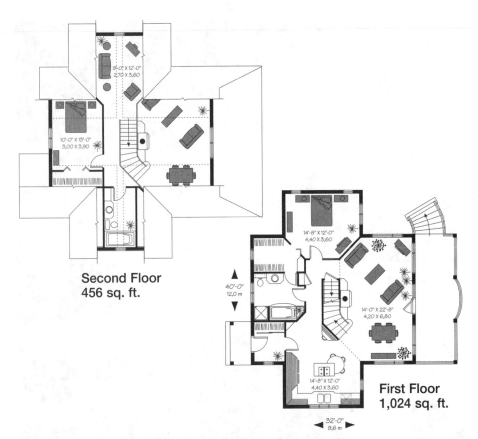

Second Floor
456 sq. ft.

9'-0" X 12'-0"
2,70 X 3,60

10'-0" X 13'-0"
3,00 X 3,90

14'-8" X 12'-0"
4,40 X 3,60

40'-0"
12,0 m

14'-0" X 22'-8"
4,20 X 6,80

First Floor
1,024 sq. ft.

14'-8" X 12'-0"
4,40 X 3,60

32'-0"
9,6 m

Covered Porch Adds Appeal

Total Living Area:	1,480 sq. ft.
Blueprint Price Code:	A
Rear porch:	195 sq. ft.

FEATURES

- Energy efficient home with 2" x 6" exterior walls
- Cathedral ceiling in family and dining rooms
- Master bedroom has walk-in closet and access to bath
- 2 bedrooms, 2 baths
- Basement foundation

Plan 574-DR-2939

Summer Home
Or Year-Round

Total Living Area:	1,403 sq. ft.
Blueprint Price Code:	A
Drive under garage:	595 sq. ft.
Front porch:	32 sq. ft.

FEATURES

- Impressive living areas for a modest-sized home

- Special master/hall bath has linen storage, step-up tub and lots of window light

- Spacious closets everywhere you look

- 3 bedrooms, 2 baths, 2-car drive under garage and second bath on lower level

- Basement foundation

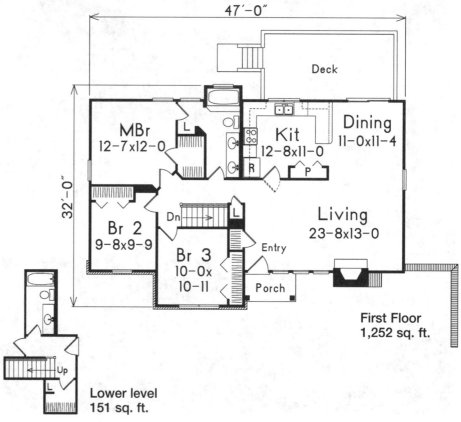

47'-0"

32'-0"

Deck

MBr
12-7x12-0

Kit
12-8x11-0

Dining
11-0x11-4

Br 2
9-8x9-9

Dn

Living
23-8x13-0

Br 3
10-0x
10-11

Entry

Porch

First Floor
1,252 sq. ft.

Up

Lower level
151 sq. ft.

Plan 574-0484

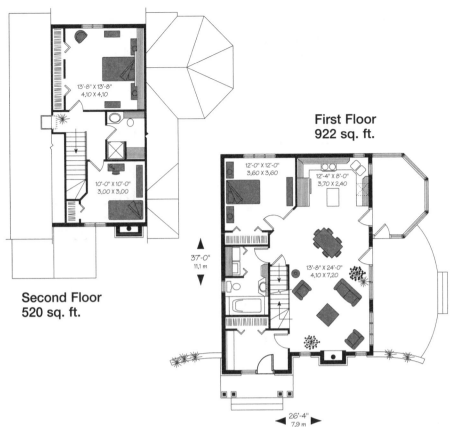

Second Floor
520 sq. ft.

13'-8" X 13'-8"
4,10 X 4,10

10'-0" X 10'-0"
3,00 X 3,00

First Floor
922 sq. ft.

12'-0" X 12'-0"
3,60 X 3,60

12'-4" X 8'-0"
3,70 X 2,40

13'-8" X 24'-0"
4,10 X 7,20

37'-0"
11,1 m

26'-4"
7,9 m

Charming Screened-In Gazebo Porch

Total Living Area:	**1,442 sq. ft.**
Blueprint Price Code:	**A**
Front porch:	48 sq. ft.
Screened porch:	118 sq. ft.

FEATURES

- Energy efficient home with 2" x 6" exterior walls

- All bedrooms on second floor for privacy

- Open living area makes relaxing a breeze

- 3 bedrooms, 2 baths

- Basement foundation

Plan 574-DR-3906

Spacious A-Frame

Total Living Area: 1,769 sq. ft.
Blueprint Price Code: B

FEATURES

- Living room boasts elegant cathedral ceiling and fireplace

- U-shaped kitchen and dining area combine for easy living

- Secondary bedrooms include double closets

- Secluded master bedroom with sloped ceiling, large walk-in closet and private bath

- 3 bedrooms, 2 baths

- Basement foundation, drawings also include crawl space and slab foundations

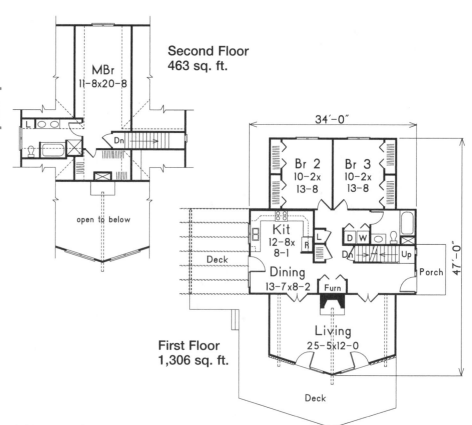

Second Floor
463 sq. ft.

First Floor
1,306 sq. ft.

Plan 574-0539

TO ORDER BLUEPRINTS USE THE FORM ON PAGE 256 OR CALL **TOLL-FREE 1-800-367-7667**

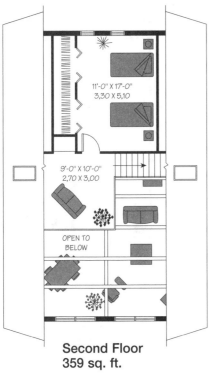

First Floor
945 sq. ft.

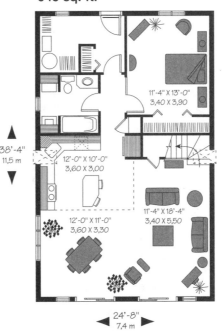

11'-0" X 17'-0"
3,30 X 5,10

9'-0" X 10'-0"
2,70 X 3,00

OPEN TO
BELOW

Second Floor
359 sq. ft.

11'-4" X 13'-0"
3,40 X 3,90

12'-0" X 10'-0"
3,60 X 3,00

11'-4" X 18'-4"
3,40 X 5,50

12'-0" X 11'-0"
3,60 X 3,30

38'-4"
11,5 m

24'-8"
7,4 m

A-Frame Has It All

Total Living Area: 1,304 sq. ft.
Blueprint Price Code: A

FEATURES

- Energy efficient home with 2" x 6" exterior walls

- Second floor features a sitting area outside the bedroom creating a relaxing retreat from the living area below

- Large dining area combines with living area for maximum comfort and space

- 2 bedrooms, 1 bath

- Basement foundation

Plan 574-DR-2925

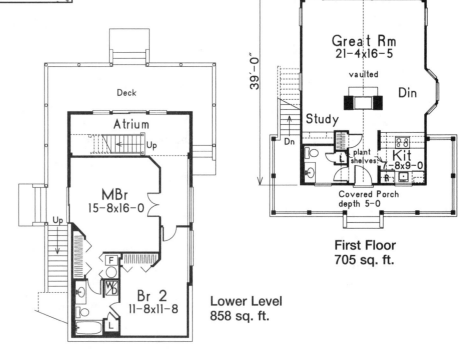

Rear View

Irresistible Paradise Retreat

Total Living Area:	1,563 sq. ft.
Blueprint Price Code:	B
Front porch:	265 sq. ft.

FEATURES

- Enjoyable wrap-around porch and lower sundeck

- Vaulted entry is adorned with palladian window, plant shelves, stone floor and fireplace

- Huge vaulted great room has magnificent views through a two-story atrium window wall

- 2 bedrooms, 1 1/2 baths

- Basement foundation

Deck

Atrium

Up

MBr
15-8x16-0

Up

F

W

Br 2
11-8x11-8

L

Lower Level
858 sq. ft.

22'-0"

Atrium below

Dn

39'-0"

Great Rm
21-4x16-5

vaulted

Din

Study

Dn

plant shelves

Kit
7-8x9-0

Covered Porch
depth 5-0

First Floor
705 sq. ft.

Plan 574-0653

TO ORDER BLUEPRINTS USE THE FORM ON PAGE 256 OR CALL **TOLL-FREE 1-800-367-7667**

10'-0" X 11'-0"
3,00 X 3,30

11'-0" X 15'-8"
3,30 X 4,70

Second Floor
597 sq. ft.

First Floor
691 sq. ft.

12'-0" X 19'-0"
3,60 X 5,70

14'-0" X 20'-0"
4,20 X 6,00

12'-8" X 15'-8"
3,80 X 4,70

40'-0"
12,0 m

◄ 28'-0" ►
8,4 m

Cathedral Ceiling
In Family Room

Total Living Area:	**1,288 sq. ft.**
Blueprint Price Code:	**A**
Garage:	253 sq. ft.
Front porch:	416 sq. ft.

FEATURES

- Energy efficient home with 2" x 6" exterior walls

- Convenient snack bar in kitchen

- Half bath has laundry facilities on first floor

- Both second floor bedrooms easily access full bath

- 2 bedrooms, 1 1/2 baths, 1-car rear entry garage

- Basement foundation

Plan 574-DR-2937

Distinguished Styling For A Small Lot

Total Living Area:	**1,268 sq. ft.**
Blueprint Price Code:	**A**
Garage:	380 sq. ft.
Front porch:	70 sq. ft.

FEATURES

- Multiple gables, large porch and arched windows create classy exterior

- Innovative design provides openness in great room, kitchen and breakfast room

- Secondary bedrooms have private hall with bath

- 3 bedrooms, 2 baths, 2-car garage

- Basement foundation

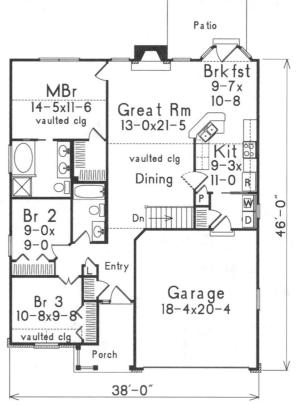

Plan 574-0717

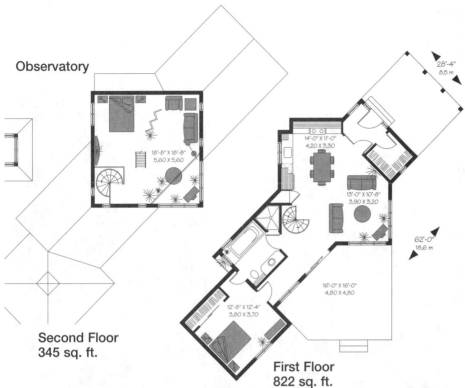

Observatory

Second Floor
345 sq. ft.

18'-8" X 18'-8"
5,60 X 5,60

28'-4"
8,5 m

14'-0" X 11'-0"
4,20 X 3,30

13'-0" X 10'-8"
3,90 X 3,20

62'-0"
18,6 m

16'-0" X 16'-0"
4,80 X 4,80

12'-8" X 12'-4"
3,80 X 3,70

First Floor
822 sq. ft.

Stunning Contemporary Home

Total Living Area:	**1,167 sq. ft.**
Blueprint Price Code:	**A**

FEATURES

- Energy efficient home with 2" x 6" exterior walls
- Bedrooms separated for privacy
- Unique observatory perfect for mountain, lake or seaside views
- Second floor bedroom includes large sitting area
- 2 bedrooms, 1 bath
- Basement foundation

Plan 574-DR-2905

Small Home Is Remarkably Spacious

Total Living Area:	**914 sq. ft.**
Blueprint Price Code:	**AA**
Drive under garage:	373 sq. ft.
Front porch:	102 sq. ft.

FEATURES

- Large porch for leisure evenings

- Dining area with bay window, open stair and pass-through kitchen creates openness

- Basement includes generous garage space, storage area, finished laundry and mechanical room

- 2 bedrooms, 1 bath, 2-car drive under garage

- Basement foundation

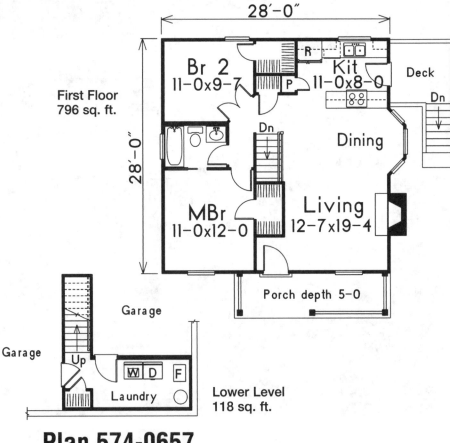

First Floor
796 sq. ft.

28'-0"

28'-0"

Br 2
11-0x9-7

Kit
11-0x8-0

Deck

Dn

Dining

Dn

MBr
11-0x12-0

Living
12-7x19-4

Porch depth 5-0

Garage

Garage

Up

W D F

Laundry

Lower Level
118 sq. ft.

Plan 574-0657

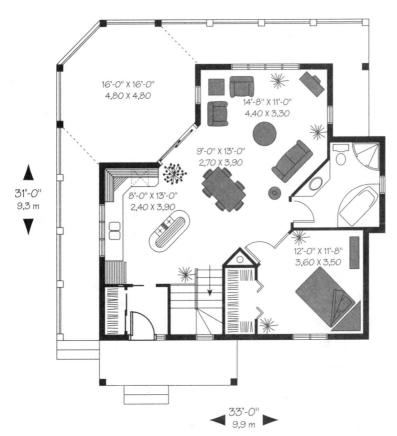

16'-0" X 16'-0"
4,80 X 4,80

14'-8" X 11'-0"
4,40 X 3,30

9'-0" X 13'-0"
2,70 X 3,90

8'-0" X 13'-0"
2,40 X 3,90

12'-0" X 11'-8"
3,60 X 3,50

31'-0"
9,3 m

33'-0"
9,9 m

Casual
Open Living

Total Living Area:	**840 sq. ft.**
Blueprint Price Code:	**AAA**
Front porch:	80 sq. ft.
Covered deck:	466 sq. ft.

FEATURES

- Energy efficient home with 2" x 6" exterior walls

- Prominent gazebo located in the rear of the home for superb outdoor living

- Enormous bath has corner over-sized tub

- Lots of windows create a cheer-ful and sunny atmosphere

- 1 bedroom, 1 bath

- Walk-out basement foundation

Plan 574-DR-3900

Trendsetting Appeal For A Narrow Lot

Total Living Area:	**1,294 sq. ft.**
Blueprint Price Code:	**A**
Garage:	254 sq. ft.
Front porch:	91 sq. ft.

FEATURES

- Great room features fireplace and large bay with windows and patio doors

- Enjoy a laundry room immersed in light with large windows, arched transom and attractive planter box

- Vaulted master bedroom with bay window and walk-in closets

- Bedroom #2 boasts a vaulted ceiling, plant shelf and half bath, perfect for a studio

- 2 bedrooms, 1 full bath, 2 half baths, 1-car rear entry garage

- Basement foundation

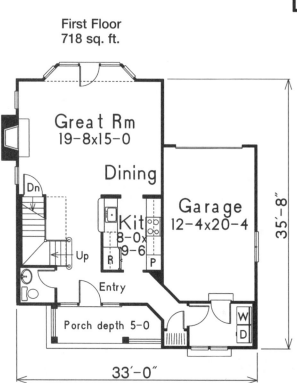

First Floor
718 sq. ft.

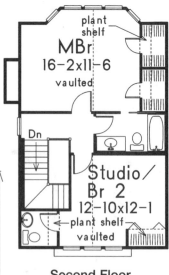

Second Floor
576 sq. ft.

Plan 574-0479

Loft
9-0x9-6

Br
11-6x9-6

Dn

open to below

Second Floor
275 sq. ft.

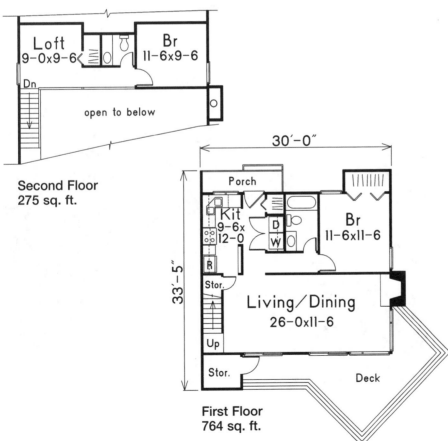

30'-0"

33'-5"

Porch

Kit
9-6x
12-0

D
W

Br
11-6x11-6

Stor.

Living/Dining
26-0x11-6

Up

Stor.

Deck

First Floor
764 sq. ft.

A Vacation Home For All Seasons

Total Living Area:	1,039 sq. ft.
Blueprint Price Code:	**AA**
Storage:	34 sq. ft.

FEATURES

- Cathedral construction provides the maximum in living area openness
- Expansive glass viewing walls
- Two decks, front and back
- Charming second story loft arrangement
- Simple, low-maintenance construction
- 2 bedrooms, 1 1/2 baths
- Crawl space foundation

Plan 574-0101

Simple Rooflines And Inviting Porch Enhance Design

Total Living Area: 1,389 sq. ft.
Blueprint Price Code: A
Garage: 505 sq. ft.

FEATURES

- Formal living room has warming fireplace and a delightful bay window

- U-shaped kitchen shares a snack bar with the bayed family room

- Lovely master suite has its own private bath

- 3 bedrooms, 2 baths, 2-car garage

- Slab foundation

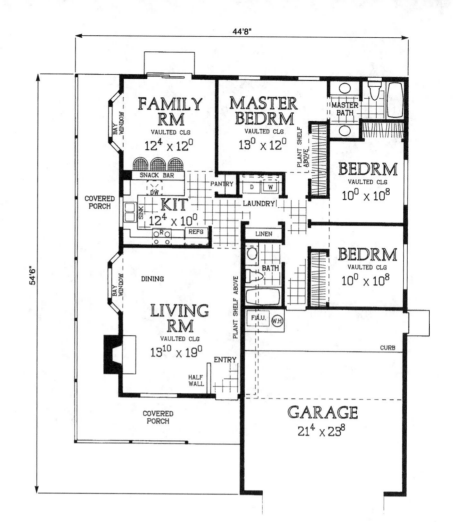

Plan 574-HP-C460

TO ORDER BLUEPRINTS USE THE FORM ON PAGE 256 OR CALL **TOLL-FREE 1-800-367-7667**

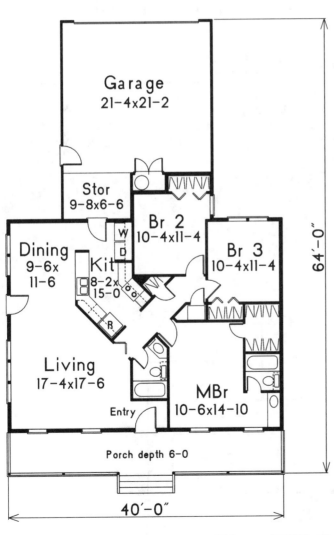

Garage
21-4x21-2

Stor
9-8x6-6

Br 2
10-4x11-4

Br 3
10-4x11-4

Dining
9-6x11-6

Kit
8-2x15-0

W D

R

Living
17-4x17-6

Entry

MBr
10-6x14-10

Porch depth 6-0

64'-0"

40'-0"

Compact, Convenient And Charming

Total Living Area: 1,266 sq. ft.
Blueprint Price Code: **A**
Garage: 473 sq. ft.
Storage: 65 sq. ft.
Front porch: 240 sq. ft.

FEATURES

- Narrow frontage is perfect for small lots

- Energy efficient home with 2" x 6" exterior walls

- Prominent central hall provides a convenient connection for all main rooms

- Design incorporates full-size master bedroom complete with dressing room, bath and walk-in closet

- Angled kitchen includes handy laundry facilities and is adjacent to an oversized storage area

- 3 bedrooms, 2 baths, 2-car rear entry garage

- Crawl space foundation, drawings also include slab foundation

Plan 574-0192

Covered Porch Highlights This Home

Total Living Area:	1,364 sq. ft.
Blueprint Price Code:	A
Optional garage:	528 sq. ft.
Optional front porch:	96 sq. ft.

FEATURES

- Bedrooms separated from living area for privacy
- Master bedroom has private bath and large walk-in closet
- Laundry area conveniently located near kitchen
- Bright and spacious great room
- Built-in pantry in kitchen
- 3 bedrooms, 2 baths, optional 2-car garage
- Basement foundation

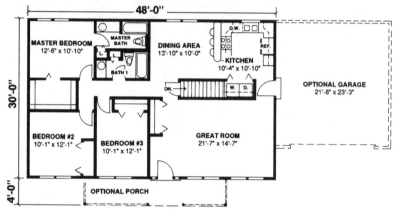

Plan 574-1329

Front Porch Adds Style To This Ranch

Total Living Area:	1,496 sq. ft.
Blueprint Price Code:	A
Drive under garage:	747 sq. ft.
Front porch:	162 sq. ft.
Back porch:	77 sq. ft.

FEATURES

- Master bedroom features coffered ceiling, walk-in closet and spacious bath
- Vaulted ceiling and fireplace grace family room
- Dining room adjacent to kitchen and features access to rear porch
- Convenient access to utility room from kitchen
- 3 bedrooms, 2 baths, 2-car drive under garage
- Basement foundation

Plan 574-0239

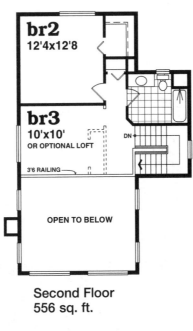

br2
12'4x12'8

br3
10'x10'
OR OPTIONAL LOFT

DN

3'6 RAILING

OPEN TO BELOW

Second Floor
556 sq. ft.

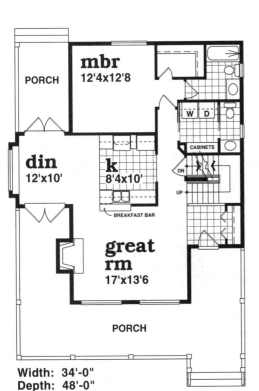

PORCH

mbr
12'4x12'8

W D

CABINETS

din
12'x10'

k
8'4x10'

DN

UP

← BREAKFAST BAR

great rm
17'x13'6

PORCH

First Floor
1,012 sq. ft.

Width: 34'-0"
Depth: 48'-0"

Country Accents Make This Home

Total Living Area:	1,568 sq. ft.
Blueprint Price Code:	B
Front porch:	464 sq. ft.
Back porch:	104 sq. ft.

FEATURES

- Master bedroom is located on first floor for convenience

- Cozy great room has fireplace

- Dining room has access to both the front and rear porches

- Two secondary bedrooms and a bath complete the second floor

- 3 bedrooms, 2 1/2 baths

- Basement or crawl space foundation, please specify when ordering

Plan 574-SH-SEA-400

Old-Fashioned Comfort And Privacy

Total Living Area:	**1,772 sq. ft.**
Blueprint Price Code:	**C**
Detached garage:	576 sq. ft.
Front porch:	235 sq. ft.
Back porch:	229 sq. ft.

FEATURES

- Extended porches in front and rear provide a charming touch

- Large bay windows lend distinction to dining room and bedroom #3

- Efficient U-shaped kitchen

- Master bedroom includes two walk-in closets

- Full corner fireplace in family room

- 3 bedrooms, 2 baths, 2-car detached garage

- Slab foundation, drawings also include crawl space foundation

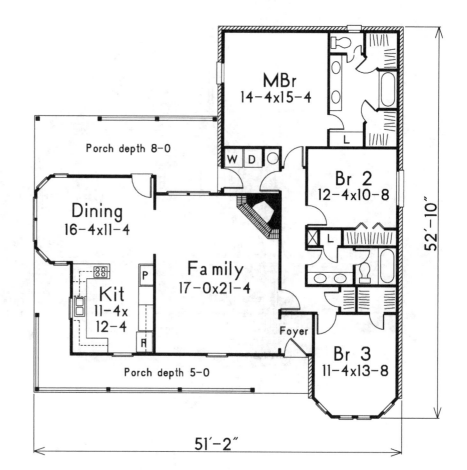

Plan 574-0163

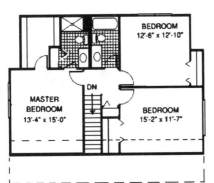

Second Floor
868 sq. ft.

Inviting
Home With
Country Flavor

Total Living Area:	**1,948 sq. ft.**
Blueprint Price Code:	**C**
Garage:	535 sq. ft.
Front porch:	216 sq. ft.

FEATURES

- Large elongated porch for moonlit evenings

- Stylish family room features beamed ceiling

- Skillfully designed kitchen convenient to an oversized laundry area

- Second floor bedrooms all generously sized

- 3 bedrooms, 2 1/2 baths, 2-car garage

- Basement foundation, drawings also include crawl space foundation

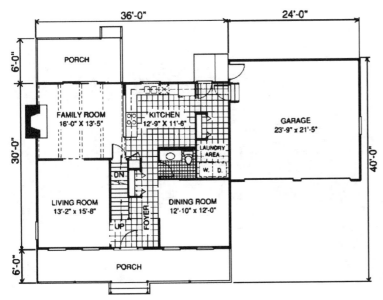

First Floor
1,080 sq. ft.

Plan 574-1347

Roomy Two-Story Has Screened-In Rear Porch

Total Living Area:	1,600 sq. ft.
Blueprint Price Code:	**B**
Garage:	462 sq. ft.
Storage:	110 sq. ft.
Front porch:	232 sq. ft.
Rear porch:	160 sq. ft.

FEATURES

- Energy efficient home with 2" x 6" exterior walls

- First floor master suite accessible from two points of entry

- Master suite dressing area includes separate vanities and a mirrored make-up counter

- Second floor bedrooms with generous storage, share a full bath

- 3 bedrooms, 2 baths, 2-car side entry garage

- Crawl space foundation, drawings also include slab foundation

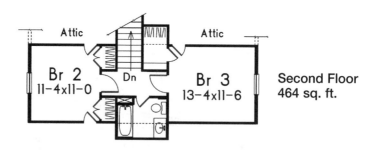

Second Floor
464 sq. ft.

Br 2
11-4x11-0

Dn

Br 3
13-4x11-6

Attic   Attic

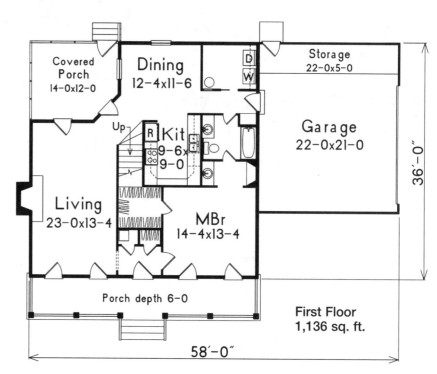

Covered Porch
14-0x12-0

Dining
12-4x11-6

Storage
22-0x5-0

Garage
22-0x21-0

Up

R Kit
9-6x
9-0

Living
23-0x13-4

MBr
14-4x13-4

Porch depth 6-0

First Floor
1,136 sq. ft.

36'-0"

58'-0"

Plan 574-0291

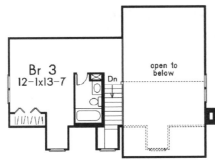

Br 3
12-1x13-7

open to
below

Dn

Second Floor
360 sq. ft.

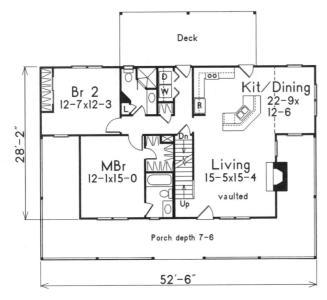

Deck

Br 2
12-7x12-3

L

D
W

R

Kit/Dining
22-9x
12-6

28'-2"

MBr
12-1x15-0

Dn

Living
15-5x15-4

vaulted

Up

Porch depth 7-6

52'-6"

First Floor
1,259 sq. ft.

Wrap-Around Porch Adds Country Charm

Total Living Area: 1,619 sq. ft.
Blueprint Price Code: B
Front porch: 612 sq. ft.

FEATURES

- Private second floor bedroom and bath

- Kitchen features a snack bar and adjacent dining area

- Master bedroom has a private bath

- Centrally located washer and dryer

- 3 bedrooms, 3 baths

- Basement foundation, drawings also include crawl space and slab foundations

Plan 574-0221

Cozy Front Porch Welcomes Guests

Total Living Area:	**1,393 sq. ft.**
Blueprint Price Code:	**B**
Garage:	528 sq. ft.
Front porch:	97 sq. ft.

FEATURES

- L-shaped kitchen features walk-in pantry, island cooktop and is convenient to laundry room and dining area

- Master bedroom features large walk-in closet and private bath with separate tub and shower

- Convenient storage/coat closet in hall

- View to the patio from the dining area

- 3 bedrooms, 2 baths, 2-car detached garage

- Crawl space foundation, drawings also include slab foundation

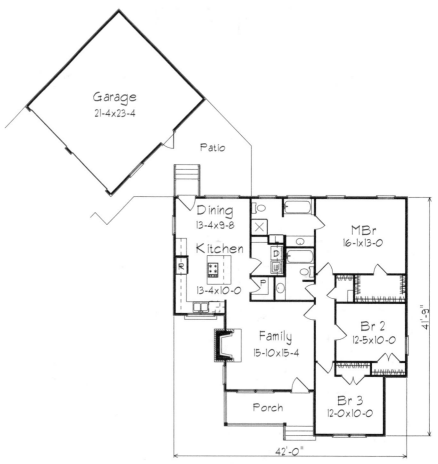

Plan 574-0447

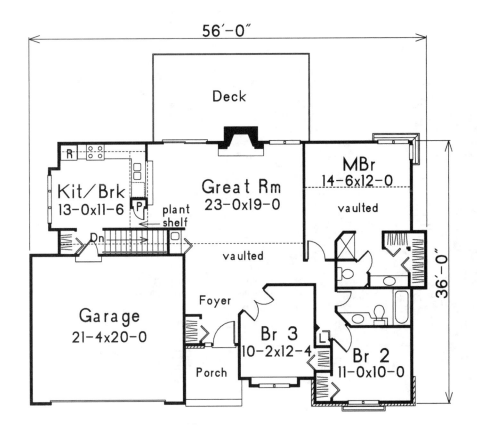

56'-0"

Deck

Kit/Brk
13-0x11-6

Great Rm
23-0x19-0

MBr
14-6x12-0

vaulted

R

P

plant shelf

Dn

vaulted

36'-0"

Garage
21-4x20-0

Foyer

Br 3
10-2x12-4

Br 2
11-0x10-0

Porch

Distinctive Ranch Has A Larger Look

Total Living Area:	**1,360 sq. ft.**
Blueprint Price Code:	**A**
Garage:	455 sq. ft.
Front porch:	50 sq. ft.

FEATURES

- Double-gabled front facade frames large windows

- Entry area is open to vaulted great room, fireplace and rear deck creating an open feel

- Vaulted ceiling and large windows add openness to kitchen/breakfast room

- Bedroom #3 easily converts to a den

- Plan easily adapts to crawl space or slab construction, with the utilities replacing the stairs

- 3 bedrooms, 2 baths, 2-car garage

- Basement foundation

Plan 574-0105

Perfect Home For Escaping To The Outdoors

Total Living Area: 1,200 sq. ft.
Blueprint Price Code: A
Front porch: 224 sq. ft.

FEATURES

- Enjoy lazy summer evenings on this magnificent porch

- Activity area has fireplace and ascending stair from cozy loft

- Kitchen features built-in pantry

- Master suite enjoys large bath, walk-in closet and cozy loft overlooking room below

- 2 bedrooms, 2 baths

- Crawl space foundation

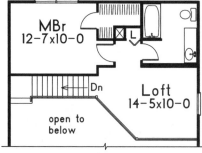

MBr
12-7x10-0

Loft
14-5x10-0

Dn

open to below

Second Floor
416 sq. ft.

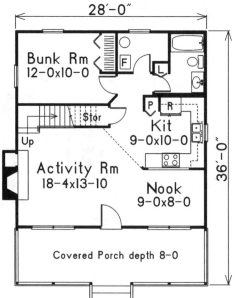

28'-0"

Bunk Rm
12-0x10-0

F

Stor

Up

P R

Kit
9-0x10-0

Activity Rm
18-4x13-10

Nook
9-0x8-0

36'-0"

First Floor
784 sq. ft.

Covered Porch depth 8-0

Plan 574-1293

REAR VIEW

A Charming Home Loaded With Extras

Total Living Area:	**1,997 sq. ft.**
Blueprint Price Code:	**C**

FEATURES

- Screened porch leads to a rear terrace with access to the breakfast room

- Living and dining rooms combine adding spaciousness to the floor plan

- Other welcome amenities include boxed windows in breakfast and dining rooms, a fireplace in living room and a pass-through snack bar in the kitchen

- 3 bedrooms, 2 1/2 baths

- Basement foundation

ROOF • ROOF
WALL BELOW
RECESSED ROOF
UPPER BREAKFAST RM
BEDROOM 11¹⁰ x 11⁴
BEDROOM 11⁴ x 11⁴
WALK-IN CLOSET
LINEN
BATH
WHIRLPOOL
DN RAILING
BATH
OPEN BELOW
DRESS. RM
UPPER FOYER
MASTER BEDROOM 12⁴ x 16⁰
WALK-IN CLOSET
RECESSED ROOF
ROOF • ROOF

Second Floor
886 sq. ft.

32'8"
TERRACE
UP
UP
50'0"
BREAKFAST RM 16⁸ x 10⁶
SCREENED PORCH 11¹⁰ x 11²
SNACK BAR
RANGE
DESK
DINING RM 12⁰ x 12⁸
FLOWER BOX
KITCHEN 16⁸ x 11²
DW
REF'G
PANTRY
PDR RM
DN DN
UP
FOYER
OPEN ABOVE
CL
CURIO
CURIO
LIVING RM 18⁴ x 14⁰
VERANDA
RAILING
RAILING
UP

First Floor
1,111 sq. ft.

Plan 574-HP-C316

©Alan Mascord Design Associates, Inc.

Vaulted Areas Make Home Appear Larger

Total Living Area:	1,378 sq. ft.
Blueprint Price Code:	A
Garage:	430 sq. ft.

FEATURES

- Double-door entry into secluded master suite

- Vaulted great room has fireplace centered between bookshelves

- Dining room is open and airy

- 3 bedrooms, 2 baths, 2-car garage

- Crawl space foundation

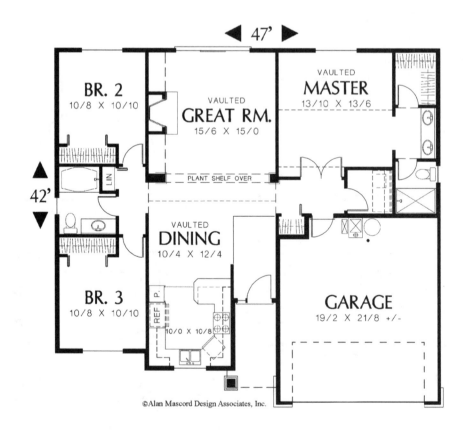

©Alan Mascord Design Associates, Inc.

Plan 574-AMD-1134

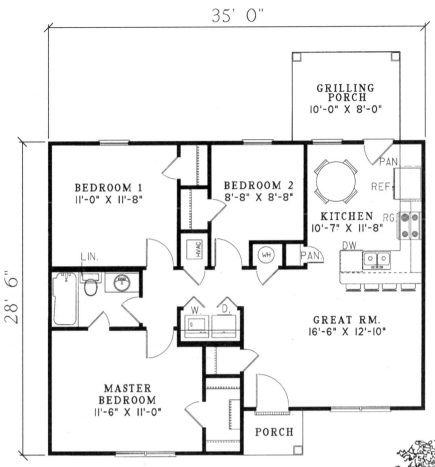

35' 0"

GRILLING
PORCH
10'-0" X 8'-0"

BEDROOM 1
11'-0" X 11'-8"

BEDROOM 2
8'-8" X 8'-8"

KITCHEN
10'-7" X 11'-8"

PAN
REF.
RG

28' 6"

LIN.

HVAC

WH

PAN

DW

GREAT RM.
16'-6" X 12'-10"

W.

D.

MASTER
BEDROOM
11'-6" X 11'-0"

PORCH

Convenient Grilling Porch

Total Living Area:	930 sq. ft.
Blueprint Price Code:	AA
Front porch:	102 sq. ft.

FEATURES

- Kitchen overlooks great room and includes space for counter dining
- Convenient laundry closet
- Master bedroom has walk-in closet and direct access to hall bath
- 3 bedrooms, 1 bath
- Slab or crawl space foundation, please specify when ordering

© Michael E. Nelson
NELSON DESIGN GROUP, LLC

Plan 574-NDG-106

Inviting
Victorian Details

Total Living Area:	**947 sq. ft.**
Blueprint Price Code:	**AA**
Front porch:	112 sq. ft.
Back porch:	40 sq. ft.

FEATURES

- Future expansion plans included which allow the home to become 392 square feet larger with 3 bedrooms and 2 baths

- Efficiently designed kitchen/ dining area accesses the outdoors onto a rear porch

- 2 bedrooms, 1 bath

- Crawl space or slab foundation, please specify when ordering

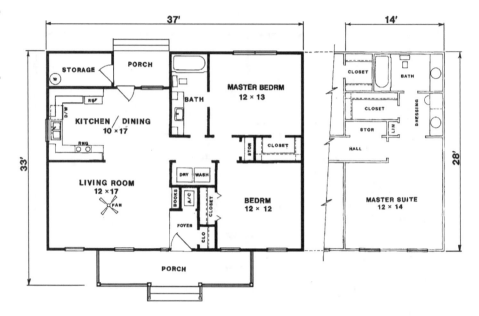

Plan 574-VL947

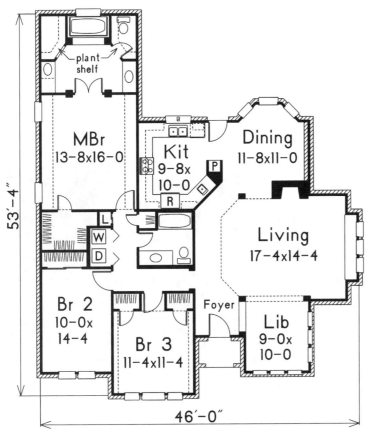

Corner Windows
Grace Library

Total Living Area: 1,824 sq. ft.
Blueprint Price Code: C
Detached garage: 576 sq. ft.

FEATURES

- Living room features 10' ceiling, fireplace and media center

- Dining room includes bay window and convenient kitchen access

- Master bedroom features large walk-in closet and double-doors leading into master bath

- Modified U-shaped kitchen features pantry and bar

- 3 bedrooms, 2 baths, 2-car detached garage

- Slab foundation

Plan 574-0316

Rustic Styling With All The Comforts

Total Living Area:	1,885 sq. ft.
Blueprint Price Code:	C
Side entry garage:	503 sq. ft.
Front porch:	219 sq. ft.

FEATURES

- Enormous covered patio

- Dining and great rooms combine to create one large and versatile living area

- Utility room directly off kitchen for convenience

- 3 bedrooms, 2 baths, 2-car side entry garage

- Basement foundation

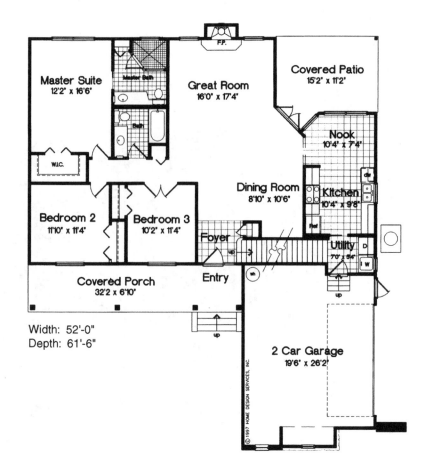

Width: 52'-0"
Depth: 61'-6"

Plan 574-HDS-1558-2

TO ORDER BLUEPRINTS USE THE FORM ON PAGE 256 OR CALL **TOLL-FREE 1-800-367-7667**

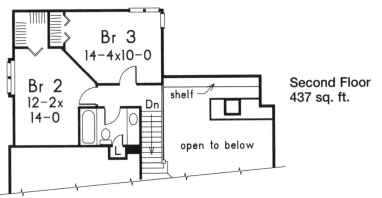

Br 3
14-4x10-0

Br 2
12-2x
14-0

shelf

Dn

L

Second Floor
437 sq. ft.

open to below

Gabled Front Porch Adds Charm And Value

Total Living Area:	**1,443 sq. ft.**
Blueprint Price Code:	**A**
Garage:	400 sq. ft.
Front porch:	103 sq. ft.

FEATURES

- Raised foyer and cathedral ceiling in living room

- Impressive tall-wall fireplace between living and dining rooms

- Open U-shaped kitchen with breakfast bay

- Angular side deck accentuates patio and garden

- First floor master bedroom suite has a walk-in closet and a corner window

- 3 bedrooms, 2 baths, 2-car garage

- Basement foundation

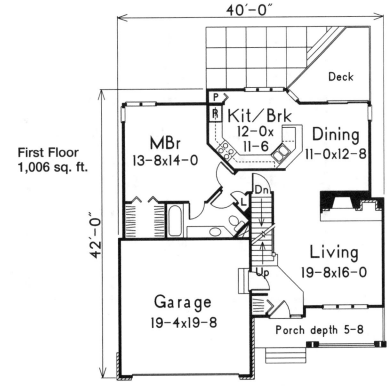

40'-0"

Deck

P
R

Kit/Brk
12-0x
11-6

Dining
11-0x12-8

First Floor
1,006 sq. ft.

42'-0"

MBr
13-8x14-0

Dn

L

Living
19-8x16-0

Up

Garage
19-4x19-8

Porch depth 5-8

Plan 574-0106

Quaint And Cozy

Total Living Area:	**1,191 sq. ft.**
Blueprint Price Code:	**AA**
Garage:	462 sq. ft.
Storage:	110 sq. ft.
Front porch:	214 sq. ft.

FEATURES

- Energy efficient home with 2" x 6" exterior walls

- Master bedroom located near living areas for maximum convenience

- Living room has cathedral ceiling and stone fireplace

- 3 bedrooms, 2 baths, 2-car side entry garage

- Slab or crawl space foundation, please specify when ordering

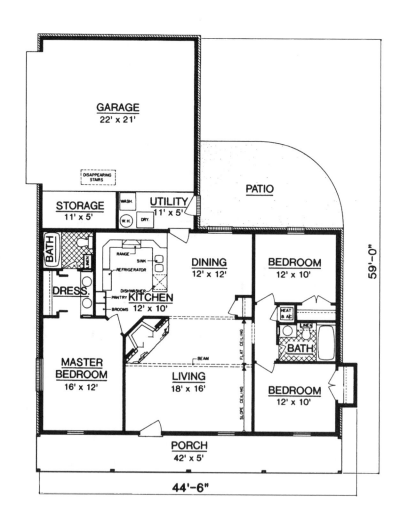

Plan 574-BF-DR1109

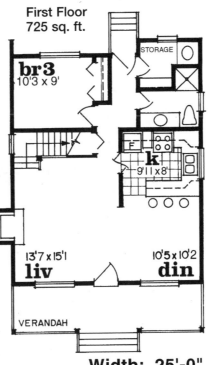

br2
13'4 x 10'6

STORAGE

STORAGE

13'4 x 12'
mbr

BALCONY

Second Floor
561 sq. ft.

First Floor
725 sq. ft.

STORAGE

br3
10'3 x 9'

k
9'11 x 8'

F

13'7 x 15'1
liv

10'5 x 10'2
din

VERANDAH

Width: 25'-0"
Depth: 36'-6"

Cozy Swiss Chalet Cottage

Total Living Area: 1,286 sq. ft.
Blueprint Price Code: A
Front porch: 150 sq. ft.

FEATURES

- Living room has warm fireplace and a dining room with a snack bar counter through to the kitchen

- U-shaped kitchen has a window sink

- The master bedroom has a private balcony and a full bath

- Lots of storage throughout this home

- 3 bedrooms, 2 baths

- Crawl space foundation

Plan 574-SH-SEA-013

Traditional Southern Style Home

Total Living Area: 1,785 sq. ft.
Blueprint Price Code: B
Detached garage: 528 sq. ft.
Front porch: 226 sq. ft.
Back porch: 107 sq. ft.

FEATURES

- 9' ceilings throughout home

- Luxurious master bath includes whirlpool tub and separate shower

- Cozy breakfast area is convenient to kitchen

- 3 bedrooms, 3 baths, 2-car detached garage

- Basement, crawl space or slab foundation, please specify when ordering

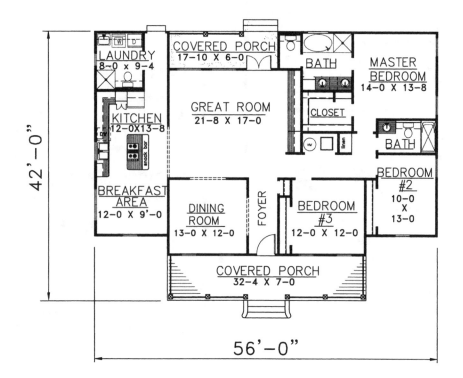

Plan 574-DH-1786

TO ORDER BLUEPRINTS USE THE FORM ON PAGE 256 OR CALL **TOLL-FREE 1-800-367-7667**

Built-In Media Center Focal Point In Living Room

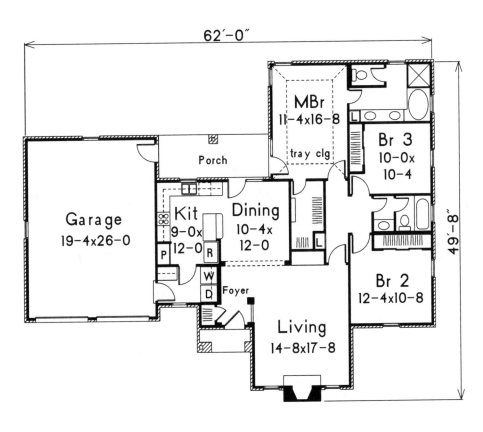

Total Living Area: 1,539 sq. ft.
Blueprint Price Code: B
Garage: 524 sq. ft.
Rear porch: 121 sq. ft.

FEATURES

- Standard 9' ceilings

- Master bedroom features 10' tray ceiling, access to porch, ample closet space and full bath

- Serving counter separates kitchen and dining room

- Foyer with handy coat closet opens to living area with fireplace

- Handy utility room near kitchen

- 3 bedrooms, 2 baths, 2-car garage

- Slab foundation

Plan 574-0246

Covered Porch
Adds Charm
To Entrance

Total Living Area:	**1,655 sq. ft.**
Blueprint Price Code:	**B**
Garage:	484 sq. ft.
Front porch:	256 sq. ft.

FEATURES

- Master bedroom features 9' ceiling, walk-in closet and bath with dressing area

- Oversized family room includes 10' ceiling and masonry see-through fireplace

- Island kitchen with convenient access to laundry room

- Handy covered walkway from garage to kitchen and dining area

- 3 bedrooms, 2 baths, 2-car garage

- Crawl space foundation

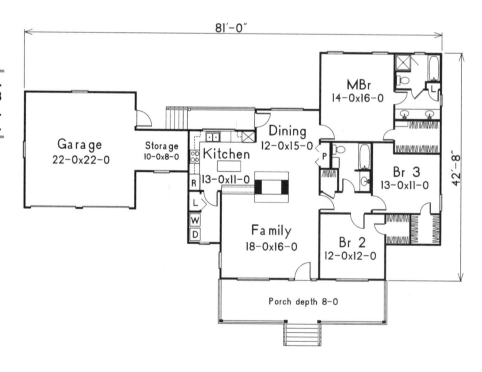

Plan 574-0294

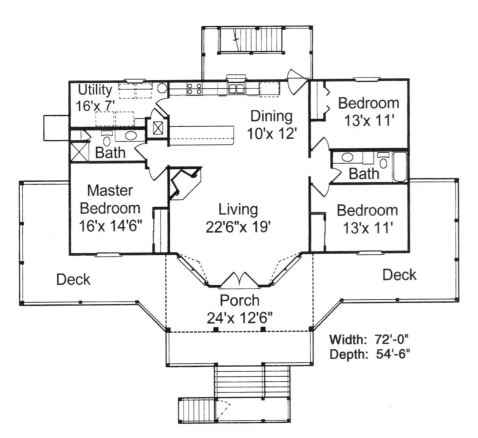

Utility
16'x 7'

Bath

Master
Bedroom
16'x 14'6"

Deck

Dining
10'x 12'

Bedroom
13'x 11'

Bath

Living
22'6"x 19'

Bedroom
13'x 11'

Deck

Porch
24'x 12'6"

Width: 72'-0"
Depth: 54'-6"

Sprawling Porch And Deck Allow For Terrific Views

Total Living Area:	1,649 sq. ft.
Blueprint Price Code:	B
Front porch:	390 sq. ft.
Deck:	719 sq. ft.

FEATURES

- Enormous two-story living room has lots of windows and a double-door access onto a spacious porch

- Master bedroom is separated from other bedrooms for privacy

- Well-organized kitchen has oversized counterspace for serving and dining

- 3 bedrooms, 2 baths

- Pier foundation

Plan 574-CHP-1632A

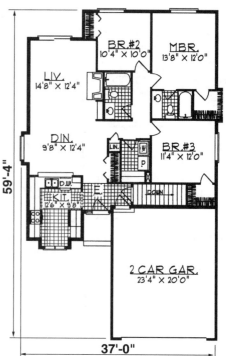

Attractive Gabled Front Window

Total Living Area: 1,342 sq. ft.
Blueprint Price Code: A
Garage: 466 sq. ft.

FEATURES

- Open living and dining rooms enjoy the warmth of a fireplace
- Compact yet efficient kitchen has everything within reach
- Centrally located laundry room
- 3 bedrooms, 2 baths, 2-car garage
- Basement foundation

Plan 567-JA-62995

Brick Accents Front Facade

Total Living Area: 1,430 sq. ft.
Blueprint Price Code: A
Garage: 595 sq. ft.

FEATURES

- Master suite features a private master bath and wall of windows
- U-shaped kitchen makes organization easy
- Great room has several windows making this a bright and cheerful place
- 2 bedrooms, 2 baths, 2-car garage
- Basement foundation

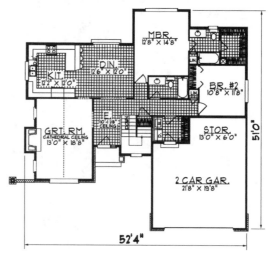

Plan 574-JA-50294

Ideal Home For A Narrow Lot

Total Living Area:	1,053 sq. ft.
Blueprint Price Code:	AA
Front porch:	61 sq. ft.

FEATURES

- Handy utility closet off breakfast room

- Sloped ceiling in great room adds a dramatic touch

- Organized kitchen has everything close by for easy preparation

- 3 bedrooms, 2 baths

- Slab or crawl space foundation, please specify when ordering

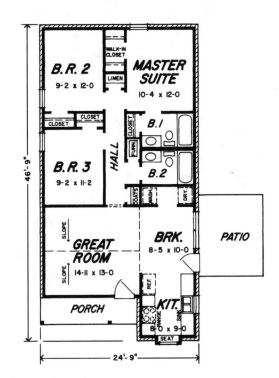

Plan 567-RJ-A1068V

Stone Accents Create A Tudor Feel

Total Living Area:	977 sq. ft.
Blueprint Price Code:	AA
Optional Garage:	288 sq. ft.
Front porch:	45 sq. ft.

FEATURES

- Large storage closet ideal for patio furniture storage or lawn equipment

- Large kitchen with enough room for dining looks into oversized living room

- Front covered porch adds charm

- 3 bedrooms, 2 baths, optional 1-car garage

- Slab or crawl space foundation, please specify when ordering

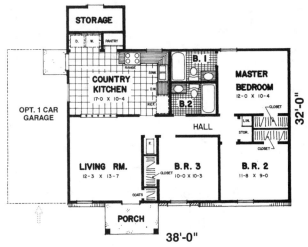

Plan 574-RJ-A921

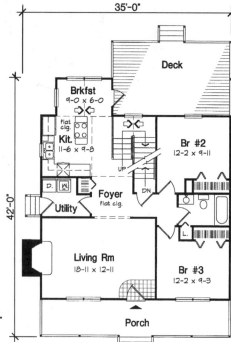

REAR VIEW

An Open Feel With Vaulted Ceilings

Total Living Area:	1,470 sq. ft.
Blueprint Price Code:	A
Front porch:	192 sq. ft.

FEATURES

- Vaulted breakfast room is cheerful and sunny

- Private second floor master bedroom with bath and walk-in closet

- Large utility room has access to the outdoors

- 3 bedrooms, 2 baths

- Basement, crawl space or slab foundation, please specify when ordering

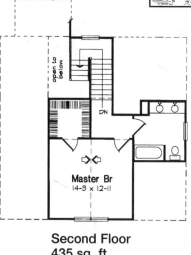

Second Floor
435 sq. ft.

First Floor
1,035 sq. ft.

Plan 574-GH-24706

Perfect Home For A Small Family

Total Living Area: 864 sq. ft.
Blueprint Price Code: AAA
Front porch: 72 sq. ft.

FEATURES

- L-shaped kitchen with convenient pantry is adjacent to dining area

- Easy access to laundry area, linen closet and storage closet

- Both bedrooms include ample closet space

- 2 bedrooms, 1 bath

- Crawl space foundation, drawings also include basement and slab foundations

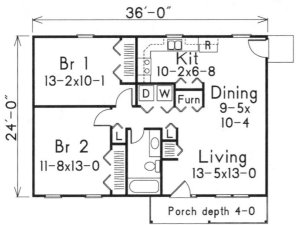

36'-0"

Br 1
13-2x10-1

Kit
10-2x6-8

Dining
9-5x 10-4

D W Furn

Br 2
11-8x13-0

Living
13-5x13-0

24'-0"

Porch depth 4-0

Plan 574-0502

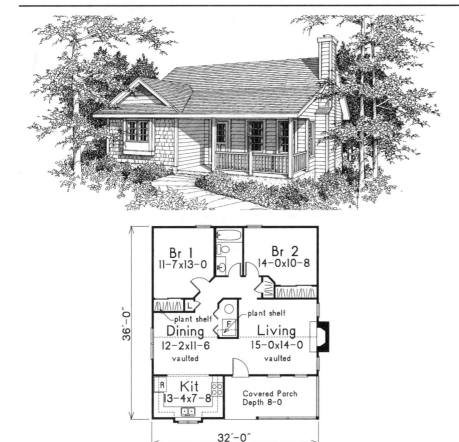

Quaint Cottage With Inviting Front Porch

Total Living Area: 1,020 sq. ft.
Blueprint Price Code: AA
Front porch: 144 sq. ft.

FEATURES

- Living room is warmed by a fireplace

- Dining and living rooms are enhanced by vaulted ceilings and plant shelves

- U-shaped kitchen with large window over the sink

- 2 bedrooms, 1 bath

- Slab foundation

Br 1
11-7x13-0

Br 2
14-0x10-8

L
plant shelf

plant shelf

F

Dining
12-2x11-6
vaulted

Living
15-0x14-0
vaulted

Kit
13-4x7-8

Covered Porch
Depth 8-0

36'-0"

32'-0"

Plan 574-0650

Efficient Floor Plan

Total Living Area:	**1,609 sq. ft.**
Blueprint Price Code:	**B**
Garage:	567 sq. ft.
Front porch:	180 sq. ft.

FEATURES

- Sunny bay window in breakfast room
- U-shaped kitchen with pantry
- Spacious utility room
- Bedrooms on second floor feature dormers
- Family room includes plenty of space for entertaining
- 3 bedrooms, 2 1/2 baths, 2-car garage
- Slab foundation

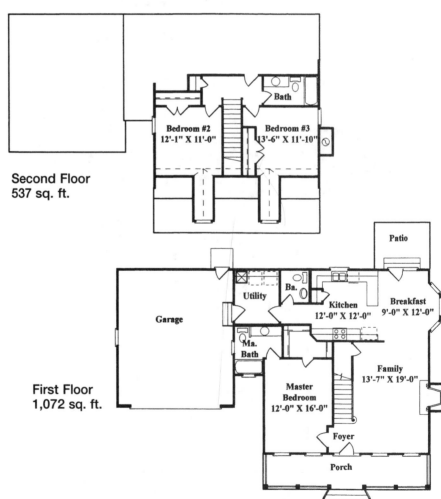

Second Floor
537 sq. ft.

First Floor
1,072 sq. ft.

Plan 574-CHP-1633-A-25

TO ORDER BLUEPRINTS USE THE FORM ON PAGE 256 OR CALL **TOLL-FREE 1-800-367-7667**

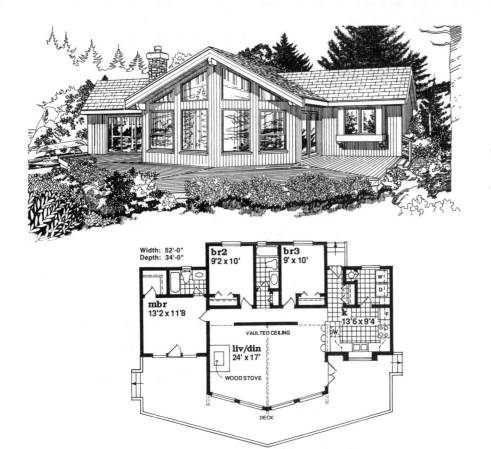

Bedrooms Separated From Living Areas

Total Living Area: 1,292 sq. ft.
Blueprint Price Code: A

FEATURES

- Master bedroom has access to the outdoors onto sundeck and a private bath
- Prominent woodstove enhances vaulted living/dining area
- Two secondary bedrooms share a bath
- Kitchen has a convenient snack counter
- 3 bedrooms, 2 baths
- Crawl space foundation

Plan 574-SH-SEA-232

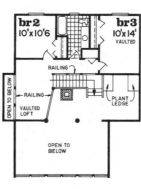

Expansive Deck Enhances Outdoor Living Areas

Total Living Area: 1,795 sq. ft.
Blueprint Price Code: B

FEATURES

- Window wall in living and dining areas brings the outdoors in
- Master bedroom has a full bath and walk-in closet
- Vaulted loft on second floor is a unique feature
- 3 bedrooms, 2 1/2 baths
- Basement or crawl space foundation, please specify when ordering

First Floor
1,157 sq. ft.

Second Floor
638 sq. ft.

Width: 36'-0"
Depth: 40'-0"

Plan 574-SH-SEA-285

Surrounding Porch For Country Views

Total Living Area:	**1,428 sq. ft.**
Blueprint Price Code:	**A**
Front porch:	**943 sq. ft.**

FEATURES

- Large vaulted family room opens to dining area and kitchen with breakfast bar and access to surrounding porch

- First floor master suite offers large bath, walk-in closet and nearby laundry facilities

- A spacious loft/bedroom #3 overlooking family room and an additional bedroom and bath conclude the second floor

- 3 bedrooms, 2 baths

- Basement foundation

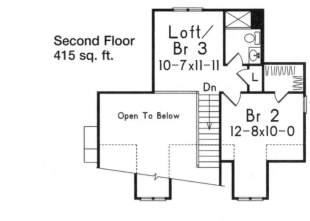

Second Floor
415 sq. ft.

Loft/ Br 3
10-7x11-11

Open To Below

Dn

Br 2
12-8x10-0

L

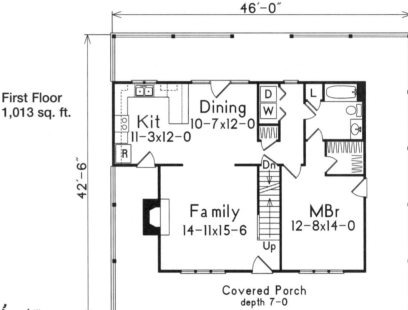

First Floor
1,013 sq. ft.

46'-0"

42'-6"

Kit
11-3x12-0

Dining
10-7x12-0

D W L

Family
14-11x15-6

MBr
12-8x14-0

Dn

Up

Covered Porch
depth 7-0

Plan 574-0726

 TO ORDER BLUEPRINTS USE THE FORM ON PAGE 256 OR CALL **TOLL-FREE 1-800-367-7667**

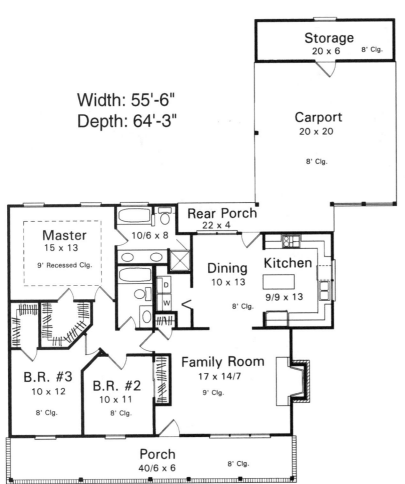

Width: 55'-6"
Depth: 64'-3"

Storage
20 x 6   8' Clg.

Carport
20 x 20

8' Clg.

Rear Porch
22 x 4

Master
15 x 13
9' Recessed Clg.

10/6 x 8

Dining
10 x 13
8' Clg.

Kitchen
9/9 x 13

D
W

Family Room
17 x 14/7
9' Clg.

B.R. #3
10 x 12
8' Clg.

B.R. #2
10 x 11
8' Clg.

Porch
40/6 x 6   8' Clg.

Plan 574-GM-1333

Carport
With Storage

Total Living Area:	**1,333 sq. ft.**
Blueprint Price Code:	**A**
Carport:	400 sq. ft.
Storage	120 sq. ft.
Front porch:	243 sq. ft.
Back porch:	85 sq. ft.

FEATURES

- Country charm with covered front porch

- Dining area looks into family room with fireplace

- Master suite has walk-in closet and private bath

- 3 bedrooms, 2 baths, 2-car attached carport

- Slab or crawl space foundation, please specify when ordering

Cottage-Style, Appealing And Cozy

Total Living Area:	**828 sq. ft.**
Blueprint Price Code:	**AAA**
Front porch:	84 sq. ft.

FEATURES

- Vaulted ceiling in living area enhances space
- Convenient laundry room
- Sloped ceiling creates unique style in bedroom #2
- Efficient storage space under the stairs
- Covered entry porch provides cozy sitting area and plenty of shade
- 2 bedrooms, 1 bath
- Crawl space foundation

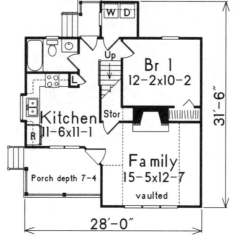

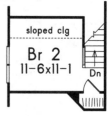

Second Floor
168 sq. ft.

First Floor
660 sq. ft.

Plan 574-0461

Convenient Center Entry

Total Living Area:	**1,134 sq. ft.**
Blueprint Price Code:	**AA**
Garage:	478 sq. ft.
Front porch:	36 sq. ft.

FEATURES

- Kitchen has plenty of counter space, island work top, large pantry and access to the garage
- Living room features vaulted ceiling, fireplace and access to an expansive patio
- Bedroom #1 has large walk-in closet
- Convenient linen closet in the hall
- 2 bedrooms, 1 bath, 2-car garage
- Basement foundation

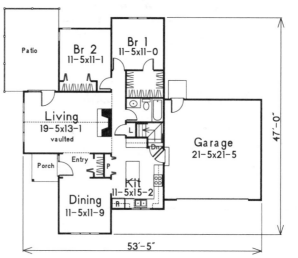

Plan 574-0500

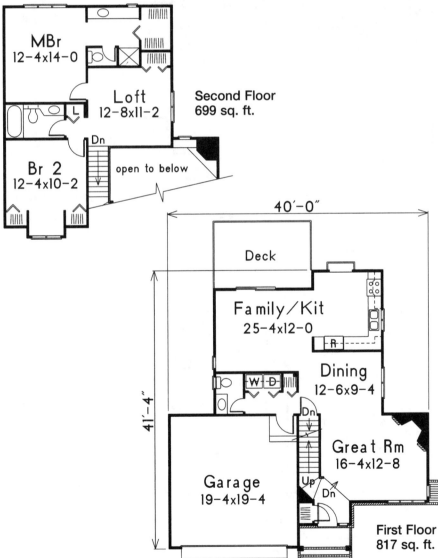

MBr
12-4x14-0

Loft
12-8x11-2

Second Floor
699 sq. ft.

Br 2
12-4x10-2

Dn

open to below

40'-0"

41'-4"

Deck

Family/Kit
25-4x12-0

R

W/D

Dining
12-6x9-4

Dn

Great Rm
16-4x12-8

Up

Dn

Garage
19-4x19-4

First Floor
817 sq. ft.

Contemporary Design For Open Family Living

Total Living Area: 1,516 sq. ft.
Blueprint Price Code: B
Garage: 393 sq. ft.

FEATURES

- All living and dining areas are interconnected for a spacious look and easy movement

- Covered entrance leads into sunken great room with a rugged corner fireplace

- Family kitchen combines practicality with access to other areas

- Second floor loft, opens to rooms below, converts to third bedroom

- Dormer in bedroom #2 adds interest

- 3 bedrooms, 2 1/2 baths, 2-car garage

- Basement foundation

Plan 574-0108

Two-Story Foyer Adds Spacious Feeling

Total Living Area:	1,814 sq. ft.
Blueprint Price Code:	**D**
Garage:	540 sq. ft.
Front porch:	316 sq. ft.

FEATURES

- Large master suite includes a spacious bath with garden tub, separate shower and large walk-in closet

- Spacious kitchen and dining area brightened by large windows and patio access

- Detached two-car garage with walkway leading to house adds charm to this country home

- Large front porch

- 3 bedrooms, 2 1/2 baths, 2-car detached garage

- Crawl space foundation, drawings also include slab foundation

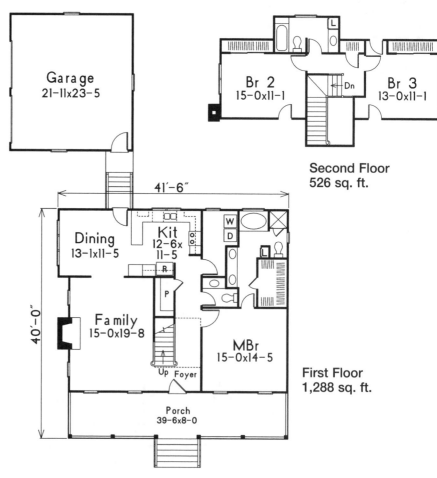

Garage
21-11x23-5

Br 2
15-0x11-1

Br 3
13-0x11-1

Dn

Second Floor
526 sq. ft.

41'-6"

40'-0"

Dining
13-1x11-5

Kit
12-6x
11-5

W
D

R

P

Family
15-0x19-8

MBr
15-0x14-5

Up   Foyer

First Floor
1,288 sq. ft.

Porch
39-6x8-0

Plan 574-0201

Breakfast Room With Arched Entry

Total Living Area:	1,087 sq. ft.
Blueprint Price Code:	AA
Front porch:	20 sq. ft.

FEATURES

- Compact and efficiently designed home
- Master bedroom separate from other bedrooms for privacy
- 10' ceiling in great room
- 3 bedrooms, 2 baths
- Slab or crawl space foundation, please specify when ordering

Plan 574-LBD-10-1B

Cozy Traditional

Total Living Area:	1,310 sq. ft.
Blueprint Price Code:	A
Garage:	449 sq. ft.
Front porch:	22 sq. ft.

FEATURES

- Family room features corner fireplace adding warmth
- Efficiently designed kitchen has a corner sink with windows
- Master bedroom includes large walk-in closet and private bath
- 3 bedrooms, 2 baths, 2-car garage
- Crawl space or slab foundation, please specify when ordering

Plan 574-LBD-13-1A

Central Living Room Great For Gathering

Total Living Area:	1,405 sq. ft.
Blueprint Price Code:	**A**
Front porch:	104 sq. ft.
Back porch:	91 sq. ft.

FEATURES

- Compact design has all the luxuries of a larger home

- Master bedroom has its privacy away from other bedrooms

- Living room has corner fireplace, access to the outdoors and easy access to the dining area and kitchen

- Large utility room with access outdoors

- 3 bedrooms, 2 baths

- Slab foundation

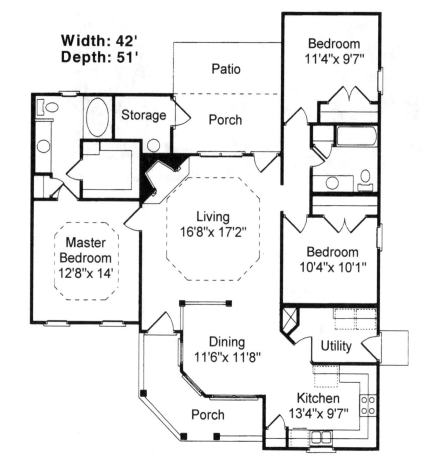

Width: 42'
Depth: 51'

Patio

Storage

Porch

Bedroom
11'4"x 9'7"

Master
Bedroom
12'8"x 14'

Living
16'8"x 17'2"

Bedroom
10'4"x 10'1"

Dining
11'6"x 11'8"

Utility

Porch

Kitchen
13'4"x 9'7"

Plan 574-CHP-1432-A-142

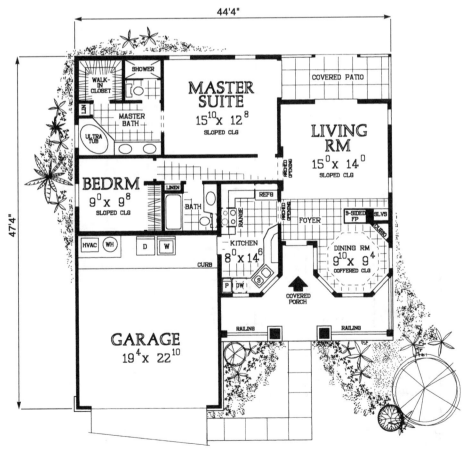

44'4"

47'4"

WALK-IN CLOSET

SHOWER

MASTER BATH

ULTRA TUB

MASTER SUITE
15¹⁰ x 12⁸
SLOPED CLG

COVERED PATIO

LIVING RM
15⁰ x 14⁰
SLOPED CLG

BEDRM
9⁰ x 9⁸
SLOPED CLG

LINEN

BATH

REFG

RANGE

KITCHEN
8⁰ x 14⁶

FOYER

9-SIDED FP

SLVS

DINING RM
9¹⁰ x 9⁴
COFFERED CLG

HVAC WH   D   W

CURB

P DW S

COVERED PORCH

RAILING   RAILING

GARAGE
19⁴ x 22¹⁰

Modern Rustic Design

Total Living Area:	**1,118 sq. ft.**
Blueprint Price Code:	**AA**
Garage:	445 sq. ft.
Front porch:	441 sq. ft.

FEATURES

- Upscale great room offers a sloped ceiling, fireplace with extended hearth and built-in shelves for an entertainment center

- Gourmet kitchen includes a cooktop island counter and a quaint morning room

- Master suite features a sloped ceiling, cozy sitting room, walk-in closet and a private bath with whirlpool tub

- 2 bedrooms, 2 baths, 2-car side entry garage

- Slab foundation

Plan 574-HP-C659

Screened Porch
Adds To This Plan

Total Living Area:	**1,496 sq. ft.**
Blueprint Price Code:	**A**
Garage:	282 sq. ft.
Storage:	84 sq. ft.

FEATURES

- Energy efficient home with 2" x 6" exterior walls

- Great room includes oversized stone fireplace for cozy gatherings

- Second floor includes den/studio making an ideal home office

- 3 bedrooms, 2 baths, 1-car rear entry garage

- Basement, crawl space or slab foundation, please specify when ordering

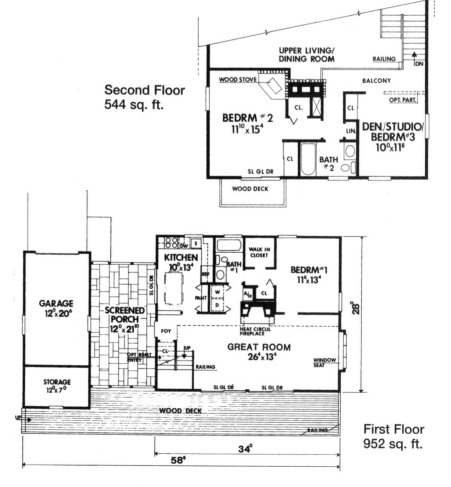

Second Floor
544 sq. ft.

First Floor
952 sq. ft.

Plan 574-AX-8162

Cozy And Functional Design

Total Living Area:	1,285 sq. ft.
Blueprint Price Code:	A
Front porch:	96 sq. ft.

FEATURES

- Dining nook creates warm feeling with sunny box bay window
- Second floor loft perfect for recreation space or office hideaway
- Bedrooms include walk-in closets allowing extra storage space
- Kitchen, dining and living areas combine making perfect gathering place
- 2 bedrooms, 1 bath
- Crawl space foundation

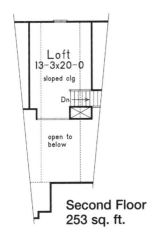

Loft
13-3x20-0
sloped clg

Dn

open to below

Second Floor
253 sq. ft.

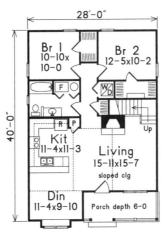

28'-0"

Br 1
10-10x
10-0

Br 2
12-5x10-2

F

W/D

Up

40'-0"

R P

Kit
11-4x11-3

Living
15-11x15-7
sloped clg

First Floor
1,032 sq. ft.

Din
11-4x9-10

Porch depth 6-0

Plan 574-0694

Large Front Porch Adds Welcoming Appeal

Total Living Area:	829 sq. ft.
Blueprint Price Code:	AAA
Front porch:	247 sq. ft.

FEATURES

- U-shaped kitchen opens into living area by a 42" high counter
- Oversized bay window and French door accent dining room
- Gathering space is created by the large living room
- Convenient utility room and linen closet
- 1 bedroom, 1 bath
- Slab foundation

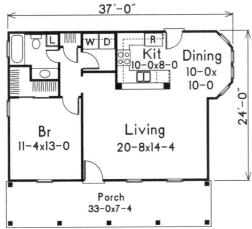

37'-0"

L

W D

R

Kit
10-0x8-0

Dining
10-0x
10-0

24'-0"

Br
11-4x13-0

Living
20-8x14-4

Porch
33-0x7-4

Plan 574-0241

Traditional
Ranch With Extras

Total Living Area:	**1,425 sq. ft.**
Blueprint Price Code:	**A**
Garage:	394 sq. ft.
Storage:	30 sq. ft.

FEATURES

- Kitchen and vaulted breakfast room are the center of activity

- Corner fireplace warms spacious family room

- Oversized serving bar extends seating in dining room

- 3 bedrooms, 2 baths, 2-car garage

- Crawl space, slab or walk-out basement foundation, please specify when ordering

Plan 574-FB-282

Sunny Bay
In Dining Area

Total Living Area:	**1,215 sq. ft.**
Blueprint Price Code:	**A**
Garage:	364 sq. ft.
Storage:	24 sq. ft.

FEATURES

- Serving bar counter extends kitchen into living area

- Convenient front hall bath

- Vaulted master bedroom has spacious walk-in closet and private bath

- Efficient galley-styled kitchen has everything within reach

- 3 bedrooms, 2 baths, 2-car garage

- Crawl space, slab or walk-out basement foundation, please specify when ordering

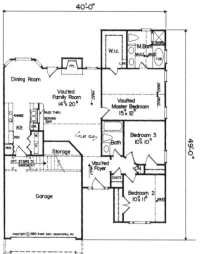

Plan 574-FB-489

Width: 47'-4"
Depth: 56'-6"

Second Floor
570 sq. ft.

First Floor
1,245 sq. ft.

Kitchen Overlooks Living Area

Total Living Area:	**1,815 sq. ft.**
Blueprint Price Code:	**C**
Garage:	573 sq. ft.
Front porch:	292 sq. ft.

FEATURES

- Well-designed kitchen opens to dining room and features raised breakfast bar

- First floor master suite has walk-in closet

- Front and back porches unite this home with the outdoors

- 3 bedrooms, 2 baths, 2-car side entry garage

- Basement, crawl space or slab foundation, please specify when ordering

Plan 574-RDD-1815-8

Year-Round Or Weekend Getaway Home

Total Living Area: 1,339 sq. ft.
Blueprint Price Code: A
Front porch: 224 sq. ft.

FEATURES

- Full-length covered porch enhances front facade
- Vaulted ceiling and stone fireplace add drama to family room
- Walk-in closets in bedrooms provide ample storage space
- Combined kitchen/dining area adjoins family room for perfect entertaining space
- 3 bedrooms, 2 1/2 baths
- Crawl space foundation

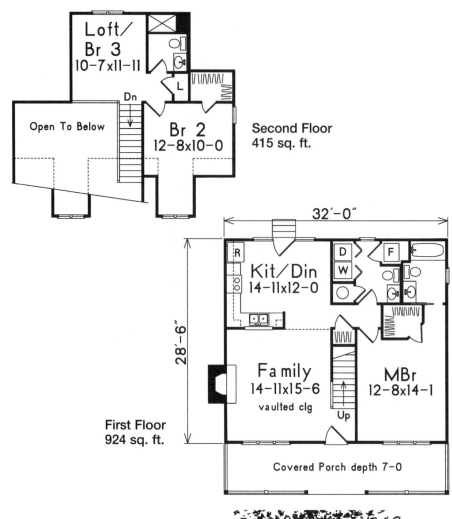

Loft/ Br 3
10-7x11-11

Open To Below

Dn

Br 2
12-8x10-0

Second Floor
415 sq. ft.

32'-0"

28'-6"

Kit/Din
14-11x12-0

R

D W F

Family
14-11x15-6
vaulted clg

Up

MBr
12-8x14-1

First Floor
924 sq. ft.

Covered Porch depth 7-0

Plan 574-0692

TO ORDER BLUEPRINTS USE THE FORM ON PAGE 256 OR CALL TOLL-FREE 1-800-367-7667

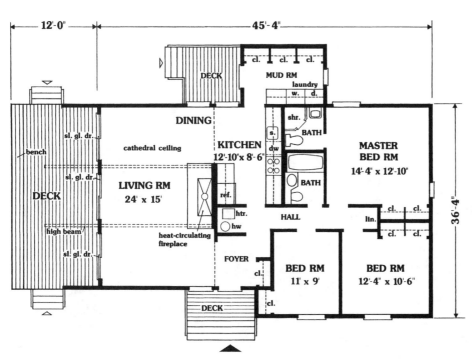

Multiple Decks Surround Home

Total Living Area: 1,207 sq. ft.
Blueprint Price Code: A

FEATURES

- Triple sets of sliding glass doors leading to sun deck brighten living room

- Oversized mud room has lots of extra closet space for convenience

- Centrally located heat circulating fireplace creates a focal point while warming the home

- 3 bedrooms, 2 baths

- Basement or crawl space foundation, please specify when ordering

Plan 574-AX-1140

Cozy Country Home

Total Living Area:	2,189 sq. ft.
Blueprint Price Code:	C
Detached garage:	528 sq. ft.
Front porch:	372 sq. ft.

FEATURES

- Study could easily be converted to a fourth bedroom

- Secluded master bedroom has all the luxuries for comfortable living

- All bedroom include spacious walk-in closets

- 3 bedrooms, 2 1/2 baths, 2-car detached garage

- Crawl space or slab foundation, please specify when ordering

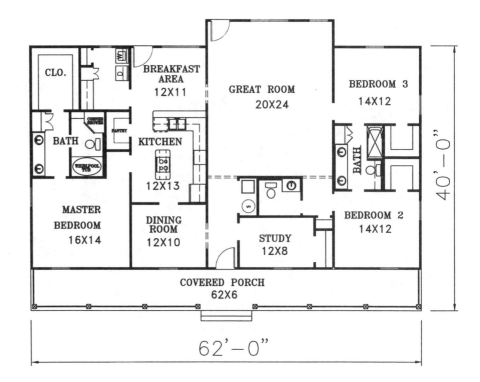

CLO.

BATH

MASTER BEDROOM 16X14

BREAKFAST AREA 12X11

PANTRY

KITCHEN 12X13

DINING ROOM 12X10

WHIRLPOOL TUB

CORNER SHOWER

GREAT ROOM 20X24

STUDY 12X8

BEDROOM 3 14X12

BATH

BEDROOM 2 14X12

COVERED PORCH 62X6

40'-0"

62'-0"

Plan 574-DH-2189

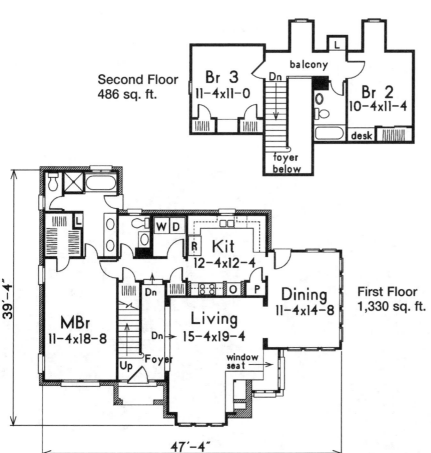

Second Floor
486 sq. ft.

Br 3
11-4x11-0

balcony

Dn

L

Br 2
10-4x11-4

desk

foyer
below

First Floor
1,330 sq. ft.

39'-4"

MBr
11-4x18-8

W D

R

Kit
12-4x12-4

Dn

Living
15-4x19-4

Dn

Up

Foyer

Dining
11-4x14-8

window
seat

47'-4"

Plan 574-0118

English Cottage With Modern Amenities

Total Living Area:	1,816 sq. ft.
Blueprint Price Code:	C
Detached garage:	506 sq. ft.

FEATURES

- Two-way living room fireplace with large nearby window seat

- Wrap-around dining room windows create sunroom appearance

- Master bedroom has abundant closet and storage space

- Rear dormers, closets and desk areas create interesting and functional second floor

- 3 bedrooms, 2 1/2 baths, 2-car detached garage

- Slab foundation, drawings also include crawl space foundation

Split-Level Has European Style

Total Living Area:	**1,224 sq. ft.**
Blueprint Price Code:	**A**
Front porch:	**120 sq. ft.**

FEATURES

- Energy efficient home with 2" x 6" exterior walls
- Charming window seats are featured in bedrooms #2 and #3
- Casual lower level includes secluded den ideal as an office as well as a family room, bedroom and a full bath
- 682 square feet of optional living area on the lower level
- 3 bedrooms, 2 baths
- Basement foundation

First Floor
1,224 sq. ft.

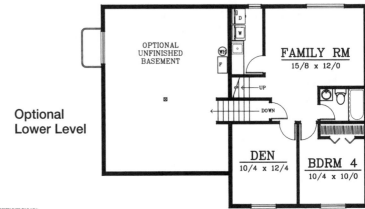

Optional
Lower Level

Plan 574-DDI-101-301

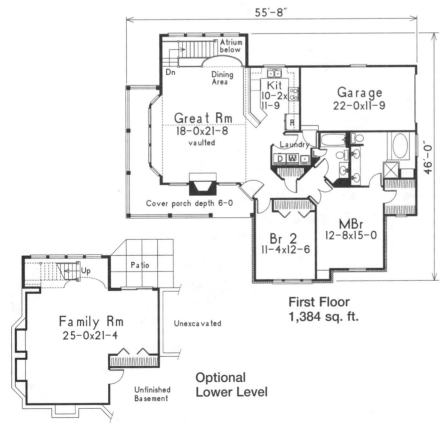

Rear View

55'–8"

Atrium below

Dn

Dining Area

Kit
10–2x
11–9

Garage
22–0x11–9

Great Rm
18–0x21–8
vaulted

Laundry

D W

Cover porch depth 6–0

46'–0"

Br 2
11–4x12–6

MBr
12–8x15–0

First Floor
1,384 sq. ft.

Up

Patio

Family Rm
25–0x21–4

Unexcavated

Unfinished Basement

Optional
Lower Level

Tranquility Of An Atrium Cottage

Total Living Area:	**1,384 sq. ft.**
Blueprint Price Code:	**A**
Garage:	267 sq. ft.
Front porch:	242 sq. ft.

FEATURES

- Wrap-around country porch for peaceful evenings

- Vaulted great room enjoys a large bay window, stone fireplace, pass-through kitchen and awesome rear views through atrium window wall

- Master suite features double entry doors, walk-in closet and a fabulous bath

- Atrium open to 611 square feet of optional living area below

- 2 bedrooms, 2 baths, 1-car side entry garage

- Walk-out basement foundation

Plan 567-0732

Screened Solarium
Adds Warmth

Total Living Area:	**1,627 sq. ft.**
Blueprint Price Code:	**B**
Front porch:	23 sq. ft.
Screened porch:	117 sq. ft.

FEATURES

- Energy efficient home with 2" x 6" exterior walls

- Family room has beautiful cathedral ceiling adding spaciousness and a fireplace creating a cozy feel

- Large kitchen had lots of room for dining

- 3 bedrooms, 2 baths

- Basement foundation

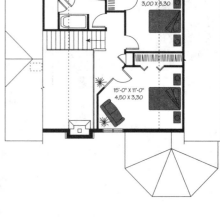

Second Floor
667 sq. ft.

First Floor
960 sq. ft.

29'-8"
8,9 m

35'-0"
10,5 m

Plan 574-DR-2945

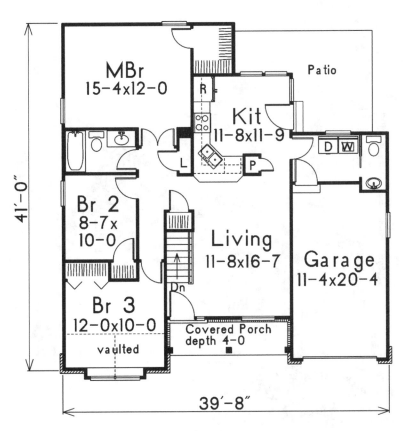

Innovative Ranch Has Cozy Corner Patio

Total Living Area:	**1,092 sq. ft.**
Blueprint Price Code:	**AA**
Garage:	241 sq. ft.
Front porch:	65 sq. ft.

FEATURES

- Box window and inviting porch with dormers create a charming facade

- Eat-in kitchen offers a pass-through breakfast bar, corner window wall to patio, pantry and convenient laundry with half bath

- Master bedroom features double entry doors and walk-in closet

- 3 bedrooms, 1 1/2 baths, 1-car garage

- Basement foundation

Plan 574-0478

Beautiful Country Victorian

Total Living Area:	**1,760 sq. ft.**
Blueprint Price Code:	**B**
Garage:	384 sq. ft.
Front porch:	193 sq. ft.

FEATURES

- Unfinished space above garage ideal for future expansion

- 9' ceilings on first floor

- Energy efficient home with 2" x 6" exterior walls

- 3 bedrooms, 2 1/2 baths, 1-car garage

- Basement foundation

Second Floor
880 sq. ft.

First Floor
880 sq. ft.

Plan 574-DR-2801

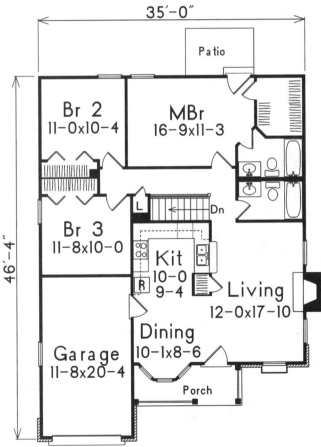

Patio

Br 2
11-0x10-4

MBr
16-9x11-3

35'-0"

46'-4"

Br 3
11-8x10-0

L

Dn

Kit
10-0
9-4

R

Living
12-0x17-10

Dining
10-1x8-6

Garage
11-8x20-4

Porch

Country Charm For A Small Lot

Total Living Area:	1,169 sq. ft.
Blueprint Price Code:	**AA**
Garage:	251 sq. ft.
Front porch:	65 sq. ft.

FEATURES

- Front facade features a distinctive country appeal

- Living room enjoys a wood-burning fireplace and pass-through to kitchen

- A stylish U-shaped kitchen offers an abundance of cabinet and counterspace with view to living room

- A large walk-in closet, access to rear patio and private bath are many features of the master bedroom

- 3 bedrooms, 2 baths, 1-car garage

- Basement foundation

Plan 574-0814

Four Seasons Cottage

Total Living Area:	1,484 sq. ft.
Blueprint Price Code:	A
Front porch:	18 sq. ft.
Rear porch:	44 sq. ft.
Screened porch:	161 sq. ft.

FEATURES

- Energy efficient home with 2" x 6" exterior walls
- Useful screened porch is ideal for dining and relaxing
- Corner fireplace warms living room
- Snack bar adds extra counter-space in kitchen
- 3 bedrooms, 2 baths
- Basement foundation

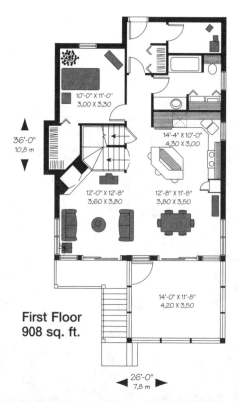

10'-0" X 11'-0"
3,00 X 3,30

14'-4" X 10'-0"
4,30 X 3,00

12'-0" X 12'-8"
3,60 X 3,80

12'-8" X 11'-8"
3,80 X 3,50

14'-0" X 11'-8"
4,20 X 3,50

36'-0"
10,8 m

26'-0"
7,8 m

First Floor
908 sq. ft.

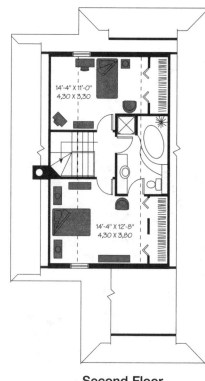

14'-4" X 11'-0"
4,30 X 3,30

14'-4" X 12'-8"
4,30 X 3,80

Second Floor
576 sq. ft.

Plan 574-DR-2916

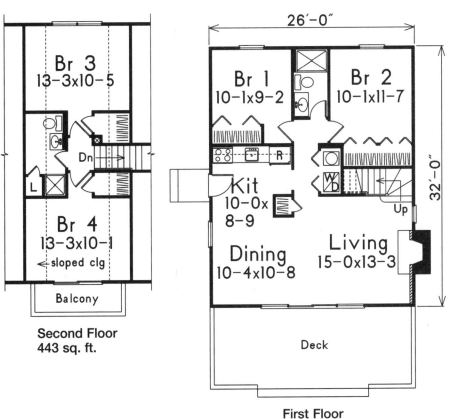

Second Floor
443 sq. ft.

Br 3
13-3x10-5

Dn

L

Br 4
13-3x10-1
← sloped clg

Balcony

26'-0"

Br 1
10-1x9-2

Br 2
10-1x11-7

R

Kit
10-0x
8-9

W
D

Up

Dining
10-4x10-8

Living
15-0x13-3

32'-0"

Deck

First Floor
832 sq. ft.

Rustic Haven

Total Living Area: **1,275 sq. ft.**
Blueprint Price Code: **A**

FEATURES

- Wall shingles and stone veneer fireplace all fashion an irresistible rustic appeal

- Living area features fireplace and opens to an efficient kitchen

- Two bedrooms on second floor

- 4 bedrooms, 2 baths

- Basement foundation, drawings also include crawl space and slab foundations

Plan 574-N015

Cozy Country Farmhouse

Total Living Area:	**920 sq. ft.**
Blueprint Price Code:	**AA**

FEATURES

- Bath has extra space for washer and dryer

- Plenty of seating for dining at kitchen counter

- Energy efficient home with 2" x 6" exterior walls

- 2 bedrooms, 1 bath

- Basement foundation

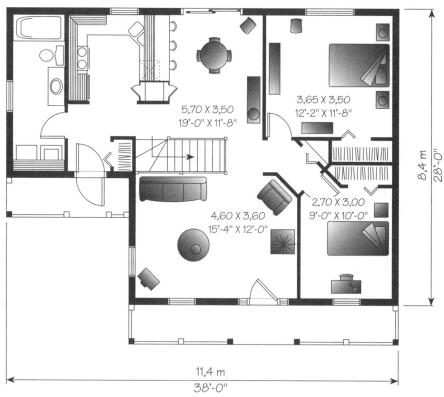

5,70 X 3,50
19'-0" X 11'-8"

3,65 X 3,50
12'-2" X 11'-8"

4,60 X 3,60
15'-4" X 12'-0"

2,70 X 3,00
9'-0" X 10'-0"

8,4 m
28'-0"

11,4 m
38'-0"

Plan 574-DR-1478

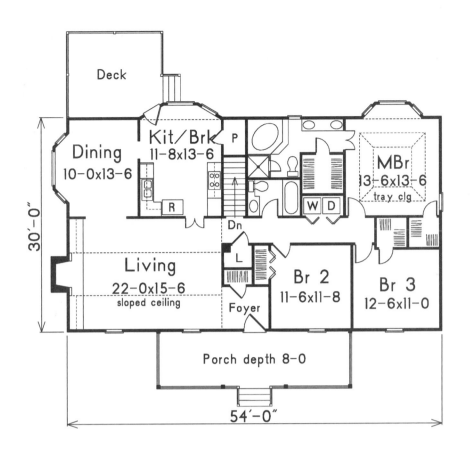

Bay Window
Graces Luxury
Master Bedroom

Total Living Area:	1,668 sq. ft.
Blueprint Price Code:	C
Drive under garage:	840 sq. ft.
Front porch:	224 sq. ft.

FEATURES

- Large bay windows in breakfast area, master bedroom and dining room

- Extensive walk-in closets and storage spaces throughout the home

- Handy entry covered porch

- Large living room has fireplace, built-in bookshelves and sloped ceiling

- 3 bedrooms, 2 baths, 2-car drive under garage

- Basement foundation

Plan 574-0112

Charming Country Cottage

Total Living Area: 991 sq. ft.
Blueprint Price Code: AA

FEATURES

- Energy efficient home with 2" x 6" exterior walls
- Master bedroom has large walk-in closet
- Large and open kitchen is well-organized
- 2 bedrooms, 2 baths
- Basement foundation

First Floor
596 sq. ft.

9'-4" X 10'-4"
2,80 X 3,10

8'-0" X 14'-4"
2,40 X 4,30

13'-0" X 12'-0"
3,90 X 3,60

10'-0" X 24'-0"
3,00 X 7,20

26'-8"
8,0 m

22'-8"
6,8 m

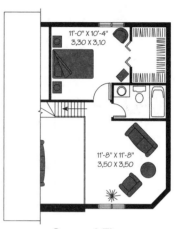

Second Floor
395 sq. ft.

11'-0" X 10'-4"
3,30 X 3,10

11'-8" X 11'-8"
3,50 X 3,50

Plan 574-DR-2919

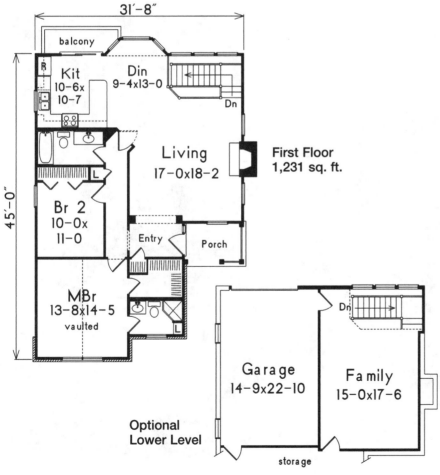

balcony

Kit
10-6x
10-7

Din
9-4x13-0

Dn

Living
17-0x18-2

First Floor
1,231 sq. ft.

Br 2
10-0x
11-0

Entry

Porch

MBr
13-8x14-5
vaulted

31'-8"

45'-0"

Optional
Lower Level

Garage
14-9x22-10

Dn

Family
15-0x17-6

storage

Atrium Living For Views On A Narrow Lot

Total Living Area:	**1,231 sq. ft.**
Blueprint Price Code:	**A**
Drive under garage:	**362 sq. ft.**
Front porch:	**59 sq. ft.**

FEATURES

- Dutch gables and stone accents provide an enchanting appearance for a small cottage

- The spacious living room offers a masonry fireplace, atrium with window wall and is open to a dining area with bay window

- A breakfast counter, lots of cabinet space and glass sliding doors to a walk-out balcony create a sensational kitchen

- 2 bedrooms, 2 baths, 1-car drive under garage

- Walk-out basement foundation

Plan 574-0807

Victorian Appeal With This Stone Cottage

Total Living Area: 1,231 sq. ft.
Blueprint Price Code: A
Garage: 306 sq. ft.

FEATURES

- Energy efficient home with 2" x 6" exterior walls
- Nice-sized bedrooms are appealing
- Enormous bath with oversized tub, double-vanity and separate shower
- Family room has cozy fireplace and spectacular bay window adding drama
- Plans include a two bedroom option
- 1 bedroom, 1 bath, 1-car garage
- Basement foundation

3,70 X 4,10
12'-4" X 13'-8"

4,20 X 3,90
14'-0" X 13'-0"

3,30 X 3,60
11'-0" X 12'-0"

4,10 X 4,80
13'-8" X 16'-0"

3,70 X 6,70
12'-4" X 22'-4"

41'-0"
12,3 m

Plan 574-DR-2268

Second Floor
847 sq. ft.

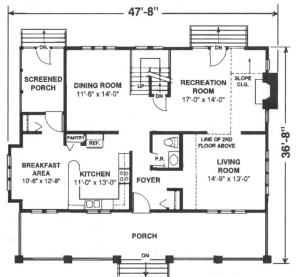

First Floor
1,162 sq. ft.

Extra Amenities Enhance Living

Total Living Area:	**2,009 sq. ft.**
Blueprint Price Code:	**C**
Front porch:	**396 sq. ft.**

FEATURES

- Spacious master bedroom has dramatic sloped ceiling and private bath with double sinks and walk-in closet

- Bedroom #3 has extra storage inside closet

- Versatile screened porch is ideal for entertaining year-round

- Sunny breakfast area located near kitchen and screened porch for convenience

- 3 bedrooms, 2 1/2 baths

- Basement foundation

Plan 574-1305

Beautiful Views Of Terrace From Dining Area

Total Living Area: 1,199 sq. ft.
Blueprint Price Code: AA
Side porch: 15 sq. ft.

FEATURES

- Energy efficient home with 2" x 6" exterior walls
- Open living is ideal for entertaining
- Spacious kitchen has lots of extra counterspace
- Nice-sized bedrooms are separated by bath
- 2 bedrooms, 1 bath
- Basement foundation

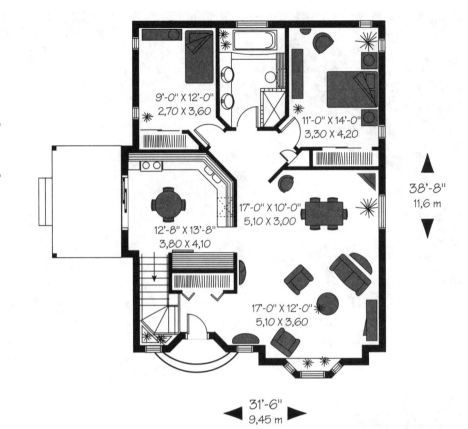

9'-0" X 12'-0"
2,70 X 3,60

11'-0" X 14'-0"
3,30 X 4,20

17'-0" X 10'-0"
5,10 X 3,00

12'-8" X 13'-8"
3,80 X 4,10

17'-0" X 12'-0"
5,10 X 3,60

38'-8"
11,6 m

31'-6"
9,45 m

Plan 574-DR-2160

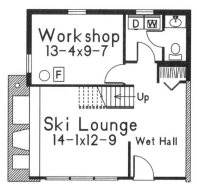

Second Floor
528 sq. ft.

Dorm
8-8x13-7

Dorm
8-8x13-7

sloped clg

sloped clg

Dn

Br 2
11-6x9-5

Br 3
11-6x9-5

Balcony

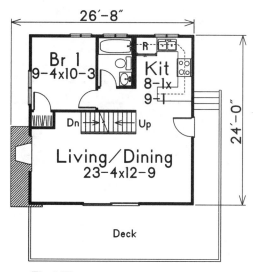

26'-8"

Br 1
9-4x10-3

Kit
8-1x
9-1

R

Dn

Up

Living/Dining
23-4x12-9

24'-0"

Deck

First Floor
576 sq. ft.

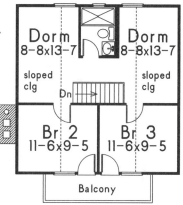

Workshop
13-4x9-7

D W

F

Up

Ski Lounge
14-1x12-9

Wet Hall

Lower Level
576 sq. ft.

Ski Chalet With Style

Total Living Area: **1,680 sq. ft.**
Blueprint Price Code: **B**

FEATURES

- Highly functional lower level includes wet hall with storage, laundry area, work shop and cozy ski lounge with enormous fireplace

- First floor warmed by large fireplace in living/dining area which features spacious wrap-around deck

- Lots of sleeping space for guests or a large family

- 5 bedrooms, 2 1/2 baths

- Basement foundation

Plan 574-N107

Traditional Farmhouse Appeal

Total Living Area: 1,245 sq. ft.
Blueprint Price Code: A
Front porch: 38 sq. ft.
Rear porch: 47 sq. ft.

FEATURES

- Energy efficient home with 2" x 6" walls

- Master bedroom has a reading area and private balcony

- Bay window brightens living area

- Combined laundry area and half bath

- 3 bedrooms, 1 1/2 baths

- Basement foundation

First Floor
626 sq. ft.

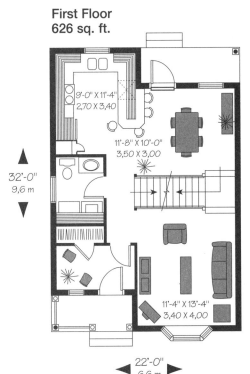

9'-0" X 11'-4"
2,70 X 3,40

11'-8" X 10'-0"
3,50 X 3,00

11'-4" X 13'-4"
3,40 X 4,00

32'-0"
9,6 m

◀ 22'-0" ▶
6,6 m

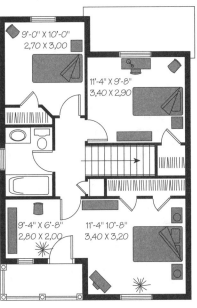

9'-0" X 10'-0"
2,70 X 3,00

11'-4" X 9'-8"
3,40 X 2,90

9'-4" X 6'-8"
2,80 X 2,00

11'-4" 10'-8"
3,40 X 3,20

Second Floor
619 sq. ft.

Plan 574-DR-1738

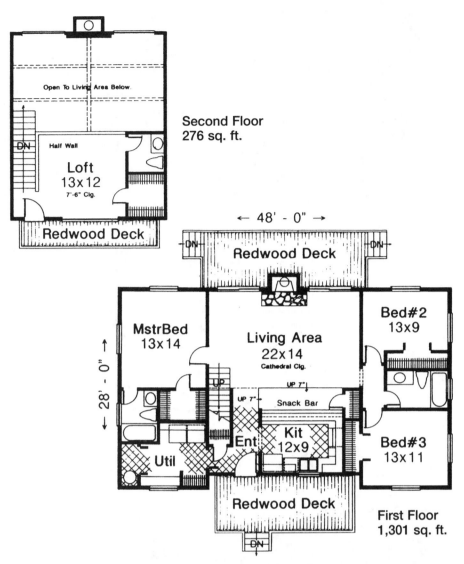

Second Floor
276 sq. ft.

Open To Living Area Below.

DN

Half Wall

Loft
13x12
7'-6" Clg.

Redwood Deck

← 48' - 0" →

DN   Redwood Deck   DN

MstrBed
13x14

Living Area
22x14
Cathedral Clg.

Bed#2
13x9

28' - 0"

UP

UP 7"

UP 7"

Snack Bar

Ent

Kit
12x9

Bed#3
13x11

Util

Redwood Deck

DN

First Floor
1,301 sq. ft.

Alpine Style Creates Cozy Cabin Feel

Total Living Area: 1,577 sq. ft.
Blueprint Price Code: B

FEATURES

- Large living area is a great gathering place with enormous stone fireplace, cathedral ceiling and kitchen with snack bar nearby

- Second floor loft has half wall creating an open atmosphere

- 3 bedrooms, 2 1/2 baths

- Crawl space foundation

Plan 574-FDG-4044

Ideal Home Or Retirement Retreat

Total Living Area: 1,013 sq. ft.
Blueprint Price Code: **AA**

FEATURES

- Vaulted ceiling in both family room and kitchen with dining area just beyond breakfast bar

- Plant shelf above kitchen is a special feature

- Oversized utility room has space for full-size washer and dryer

- Hall bath is centrally located with easy access from both bedrooms

- 2 bedrooms, 1 bath

- Slab foundation

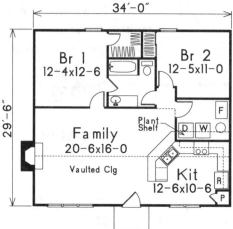

Plan 574-0693

Rustic Design With Modern Features

Total Living Area: 1,000 sq. ft.
Blueprint Price Code: **AA**
Front porch: 182 sq. ft.
Side porch: 53 sq. ft.

FEATURES

- Large mud room with separate covered porch entrance

- Full-length covered front porch

- Bedrooms on opposite sides of the home for privacy

- Vaulted ceiling creates an open and spacious feeling

- 2 bedrooms, 1 bath

- Crawl space foundation

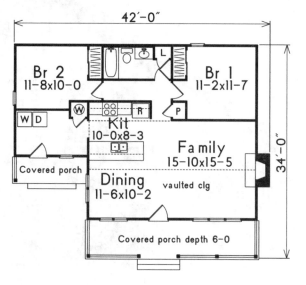

Plan 574-0765

Large Living And Dining Area

Total Living Area:	1,160 sq. ft.
Blueprint Price Code:	AA
Front porch:	72 sq. ft.

FEATURES

- U-shaped kitchen includes breakfast bar and convenient laundry area

- Master bedroom features private half bath and large closet

- Dining room has outdoor access

- Dining and great rooms combine to create an open living atmosphere

- 3 bedrooms, 1 1/2 baths

- Crawl space foundation, drawings also include basement and slab foundations

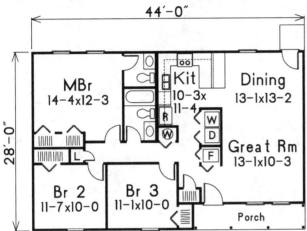

Plan 574-0543

Layout Creates Large Open Living Area

Total Living Area:	1,285 sq. ft.
Blueprint Price Code:	B
Front porch:	288 sq. ft.
Storage:	65 sq. ft.

FEATURES

- Accommodating home with ranch-style porch

- Large storage area on back of home

- Master bedroom includes dressing area, private bath and built-in bookcase

- Kitchen features pantry, breakfast bar and complete view to dining room

- 3 bedrooms, 2 baths

- Crawl space foundation, drawings also include basement and slab foundations

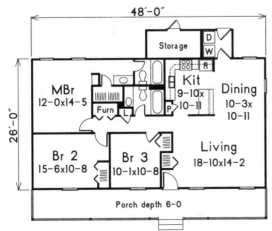

Plan 574-0529

A Vacation Oasis

Total Living Area: 1,106 sq. ft.
Blueprint Price Code: AA

FEATURES

- Delightful A-frame provides exciting vacation all year long

- Sundeck accesses large living room with open soaring ceiling

- Enormous sleeping area is provided on second floor with balcony overlook of living room below

- 2 bedrooms, 1 bath

- Pier foundation

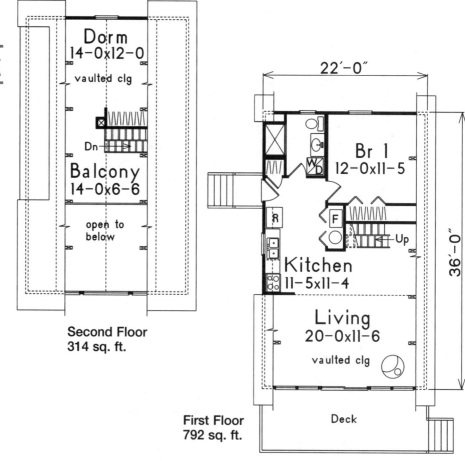

Dorm
14-0x12-0
vaulted clg

Dn

Balcony
14-0x6-6

open to below

Second Floor
314 sq. ft.

22'-0"

Br 1
12-0x11-5

Up

Kitchen
11-5x11-4

Living
20-0x11-6
vaulted clg

36'-0"

First Floor
792 sq. ft.

Deck

Plan 574-N026

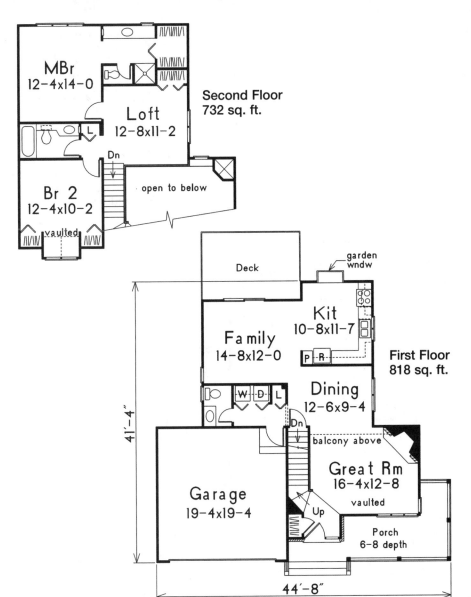

MBr
12-4x14-0

Loft
12-8x11-2

Second Floor
732 sq. ft.

Br 2
12-4x10-2

vaulted

Dn

open to below

garden wndw

Deck

Kit
10-8x11-7

Family
14-8x12-0

First Floor
818 sq. ft.

P R

Dining
12-6x9-4

W D L

Dn

balcony above

Great Rm
16-4x12-8

vaulted

Garage
19-4x19-4

Up

Porch
6-8 depth

41'-4"

44'-8"

Ornate Corner Porch Catches The Eye

Total Living Area:	**1,550 sq. ft.**
Blueprint Price Code:	**B**
Garage:	**394 sq. ft.**
Front porch:	**164 sq. ft.**

FEATURES

- Impressive front entrance with a wrap-around covered porch and raised foyer

- Corner fireplace provides a focal point in the vaulted great room

- Loft is easily converted to a third bedroom or activity center

- Large family/kitchen area includes greenhouse windows and access to the deck and utility area

- Secondary bedroom has a large dormer and window seat

- 2 bedrooms, 2 1/2 baths, 2-car garage

- Basement foundation

Plan 574-0207

Floor-To-Ceiling Window Expands Compact Two-Story

Total Living Area: 1,246 sq. ft.
Blueprint Price Code: A
Garage: 400 sq. ft.

FEATURES

- Corner living room window adds openness and light

- Out-of-the-way kitchen with dining area accesses the outdoors

- Private first floor master bedroom with corner window

- Large walk-in closet is located in bedroom #3

- Easily built perimeter allows economical construction

- 3 bedrooms, 2 baths, 2-car garage

- Basement foundation

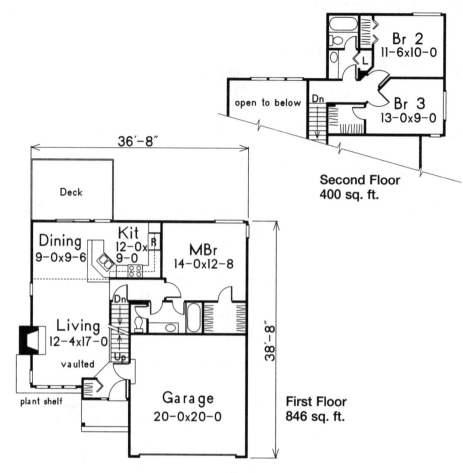

Second Floor
400 sq. ft.

First Floor
846 sq. ft.

Plan 574-0102

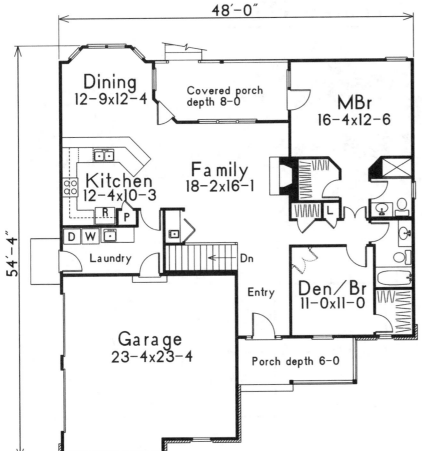

48'-0"

54'-4"

Dining
12-9x12-4

Covered porch
depth 8-0

MBr
16-4x12-6

Kitchen
12-4x10-3

Family
18-2x16-1

R   P

D W

Laundry

L

Dn

Entry

Den/Br
11-0x11-0

Garage
23-4x23-4

Porch depth 6-0

Flexible Design Is Popular

Total Living Area:	**1,440 sq. ft.**
Blueprint Price Code:	**A**
Garage:	552 sq. ft.
Front porch:	96 sq. ft.

FEATURES

- Open floor plan with access to covered porches in front and back
- Lots of linen, pantry and closet space throughout
- Laundry/mud room between kitchen and garage is a convenient feature
- 2 bedrooms, 2 baths
- Basement foundation

Plan 574-0769

Cozy Cottage Living

Total Living Area:	**1,332 sq. ft.**
Blueprint Price Code:	**A**

FEATURES

- A front porch deck, ornate porch roof, massive stone fireplace and Old English windows all generate inviting appeal

- Large living room accesses kitchen with spacious dining area

- Two spacious bedrooms with ample closet space comprise second floor

- 4 bedrooms, 2 baths

- Basement foundation, drawings also include slab and crawl space foundations

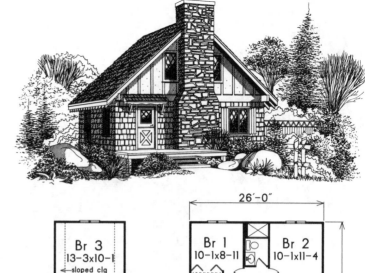

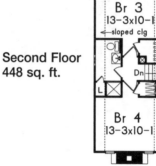

Second Floor
448 sq. ft.

Br 3
13-3x10-1
←sloped clg

Br 4
13-3x10-1

26'-0"

Br 1
10-1x8-11

Br 2
10-1x11-4

Kit
10-1x 8-11

Living
14-11x13-1

Up

Dining
10-4x10-9

Deck

32'-0"

First Floor
832 sq. ft.

Plan 574-N149

Classic Ranch, Pleasant Covered Front Porch

Total Living Area:	**1,416 sq. ft.**
Blueprint Price Code:	**A**
Garage:	**528 sq. ft.**
Front porch:	**172 sq. ft.**

FEATURES

- Excellent floor plan eases traffic

- Master bedroom features private bath

- Foyer opens to both formal living room and informal family room

- Great room has access to the outdoors through sliding doors

- 3 bedrooms, 2 baths, 2-car garage

- Crawl space foundation, drawings also include basement foundation

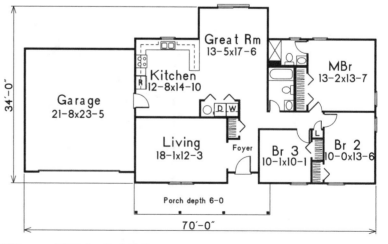

34'-0"

Garage
21-8x23-5

Great Rm
13-5x17-6

Kitchen
12-8x14-10

MBr
13-2x13-7

Living
18-1x12-3

Foyer

Br 3
10-1x10-1

Br 2
10-0x13-6

Porch depth 6-0

70'-0"

Plan 574-0198

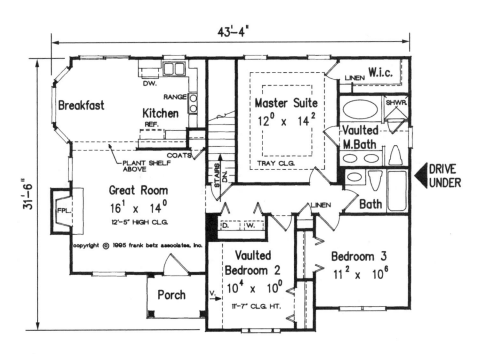

Handsome Stonework

Total Living Area: 1,124 sq. ft.
Blueprint Price Code: **AA**
Drive under garage: 458 sq. ft.
Front porch: 24 sq. ft.

FEATURES

- Varied ceiling heights throughout this home
- Enormous bayed breakfast room overlooks great room with fireplace
- Conveniently located washer and dryer closet
- 3 bedrooms, 2 baths, 2-car drive under garage
- Walk-out basement foundation

Plan 574-FB-894

Country-Style With Wrap-Around Porch

Total Living Area:	1,597 sq. ft.
Blueprint Price Code:	C
Garage:	548 sq. ft.
Front porch:	308 sq. ft.

FEATURES

- Spacious family room includes fireplace and coat closet

- Open kitchen/dining room provides breakfast bar and access to the outdoors

- Convenient laundry area located near kitchen

- Secluded master suite with walk-in closet and private bath

- 4 bedrooms, 2 1/2 baths, 2-car detached garage

- Basement foundation

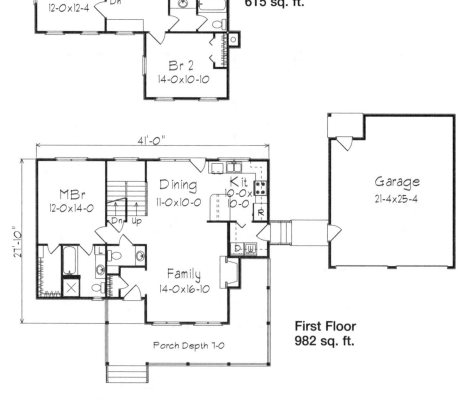

Second Floor
615 sq. ft.

First Floor
982 sq. ft.

Plan 574-0448

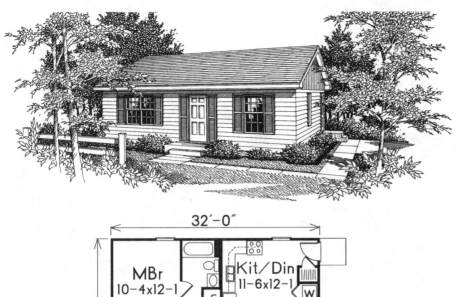

Ideal For
A Starter Home

Total Living Area:	**800 sq. ft.**
Blueprint Price Code:	**AAA**

FEATURES

- Master bedroom has walk-in closet and private access to bath

- Large living room features handy coat closet

- Kitchen includes side entrance, closet and convenient laundry area

- 2 bedrooms, 1 bath

- Crawl space foundation, drawings also include basement and slab foundations

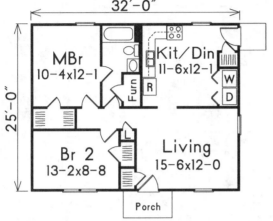

Plan 574-0582

Vaulted Ceiling
Adds Spaciousness

Total Living Area:	**990 sq. ft.**
Blueprint Price Code:	**AA**
Front porch:	378 sq. ft.

FEATURES

- Wrap-around porch on two sides of this home

- Private and efficiently designed

- Space for efficiency washer and dryer unit for convenience

- 2 bedrooms, 1 bath

- Crawl space foundation

Plan 574-0766

Attractive A-Frame

Total Living Area: 1,416 sq. ft.
Blueprint Price Code: A

FEATURES

- Wall of windows in dining/living area brightens interior

- Enormous wrap-around deck provides plenty of outdoor living area

- Second floor has a bedroom and a bath secluded for privacy

- Efficiently designed kitchen accesses deck through sliding glass doors

- 3 bedrooms, 2 baths

- Basement, crawl space or slab foundation, please specify when ordering

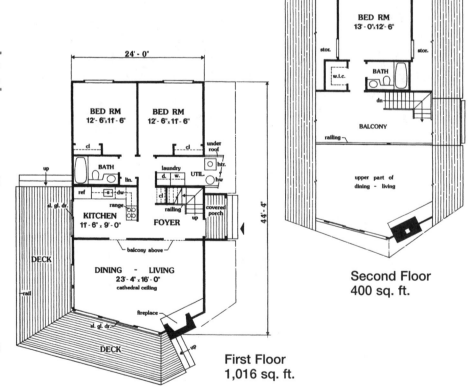

First Floor
1,016 sq. ft.

Second Floor
400 sq. ft.

Plan 574-AX-1160

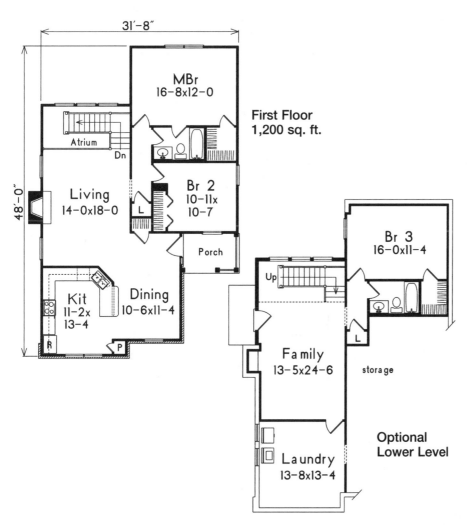

First Floor
1,200 sq. ft.

31'-8"

48'-0"

MBr
16-8x12-0

Atrium

Dn

Living
14-0x18-0

Br 2
10-11x
10-7

L

Porch

Kit
11-2x
13-4

Dining
10-6x11-4

R

P

Br 3
16-0x11-4

Up

L

Family
13-5x24-6

storage

Laundry
13-8x13-4

Optional
Lower Level

Exciting Living For A Narrow Sloping Lot

Total Living Area:	**1,200 sq. ft.**
Blueprint Price Code:	**A**
Front porch:	**59 sq. ft.**

FEATURES

- Entry leads to a large dining area which opens to kitchen and sun drenched living room

- An expansive window wall in the two-story atrium lends space and light to living room with fireplace

- The large kitchen features a breakfast bar, built-in pantry and storage galore

- 697 square feet of optional living area on the lower level includes a family room, bedroom #3 and a bath

- 2 bedrooms, 1 bath

- Walk-out basement foundation

Plan 574-0810

Trim Colonial
For Practical Living

Total Living Area:	1,582 sq. ft.
Blueprint Price Code:	**B**
Garage:	351 sq. ft.
Front porch:	155 sq. ft.

FEATURES

- Conservative layout gives privacy to living and dining areas

- Large fireplace and windows enhance the living area

- Rear door in garage is convenient to the garden and kitchen

- Full front porch adds charm

- Dormers add light to the foyer and bedrooms

- 3 bedrooms, 2 1/2 baths, 1-car garage

- Slab foundation, drawings also include crawl space foundation

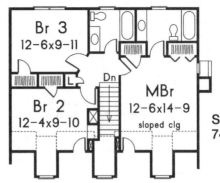

Second Floor
745 sq. ft.

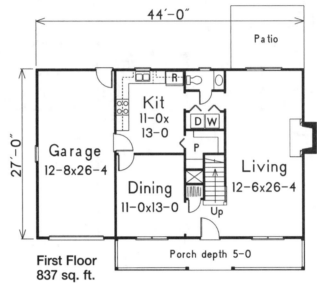

First Floor
837 sq. ft.

Plan 574-0111

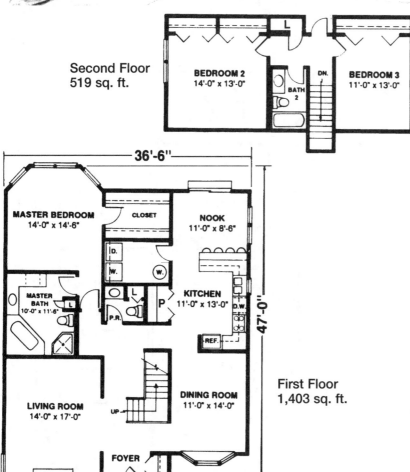

Second Floor
519 sq. ft.

BEDROOM 2
14'-0" x 13'-0"

BATH
2

DN.

BEDROOM 3
11'-0" x 13'-0"

36'-6"

MASTER BEDROOM
14'-0" x 14'-6"

CLOSET

NOOK
11'-0" x 8'-6"

D.
W.

W.

KITCHEN
11'-0" x 13'-0"

L

P

P.R.

D.W.

MASTER BATH
10'-0" x 11'-6"

L

REF.

47'-0"

LIVING ROOM
14'-0" x 17'-0"

UP

DINING ROOM
11'-0" x 14'-0"

First Floor
1,403 sq. ft.

FOYER

Terrific Cottage-Style Design

Total Living Area:	1,922 sq. ft.
Blueprint Price Code:	C
Front porch:	42 sq. ft.

FEATURES

- Master bedroom includes many luxuries such as an oversized private bath and large walk-in closet

- Kitchen area is spacious with a functional eat-in breakfast bar and is adjacent to nook ideal as a breakfast room

- Plenty of storage is featured in both bedrooms on the second floor and in the hall

- Enormous utility room is centrally located on the first floor

- 3 bedrooms, 2 1/2 baths

- Basement foundation

Plan 574-1297

Stylish
Master Bedroom
Off By Itself

Total Living Area:	1,565 sq. ft.
Blueprint Price Code:	B
Garage:	400 sq. ft.
Front porch:	55 sq. ft.

FEATURES

- Highly-detailed exterior adds value

- Large vaulted great room with a full wall of glass opens onto the corner deck

- Loft balcony opens to rooms below and adds to the spacious feeling

- Bay-windowed kitchen with a cozy morning room

- Master bath with platform tub, separate shower and a large walk-in closet

- 3 bedrooms, 2 1/2 baths, 2-car garage

- Basement foundation

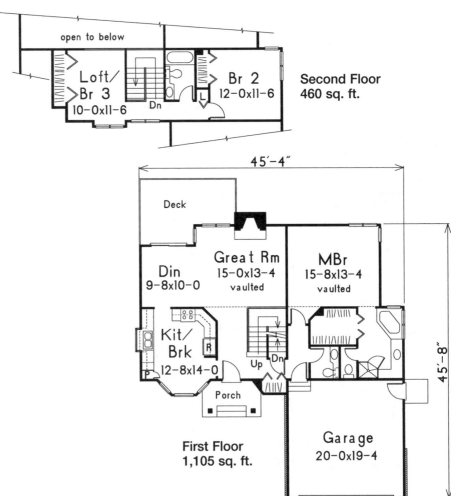

Second Floor
460 sq. ft.

First Floor
1,105 sq. ft.

Plan 574-0109

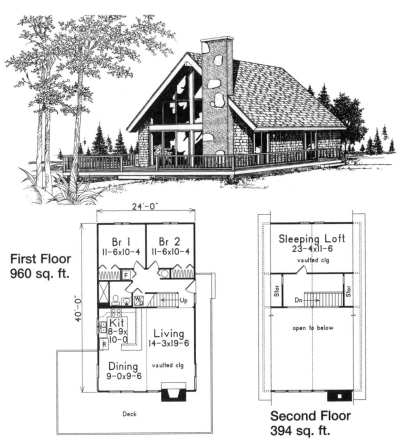

Leisure Living With Interior Surprise

Total Living Area: 1,354 sq. ft.
Blueprint Price Code: A

FEATURES

- Soaring ceilings highlight the kitchen, dining and living areas creating dramatic excitement

- A spectacular large deck surrounds the front and both sides of home

- An impressive kitchen is U-shaped with wrap-around breakfast bar and shares fantastic views with both upper and lower areas through an awesome wall of glass

- Two bedrooms with a bath, a loft for sleeping and second floor balcony overlooking living area, complete the home

- 3 bedrooms, 1 bath

- Crawl space foundation

First Floor 960 sq. ft.

24'-0"
40'-0"

Br 1
11-6x10-4

Br 2
11-6x10-4

Kit
8-9x10-0

Living
14-3x19-6

Dining
9-0x9-6
vaulted clg

Deck

Up

Sleeping Loft
23-4x11-6
vaulted clg

Stor
Stor
Dn

open to below

Second Floor 394 sq. ft.

Plan 574-N142

Efficient Ranch With Country Charm

Total Living Area: 1,364 sq. ft.
Blueprint Price Code: A
Front porch: 120 sq. ft.

FEATURES

- Master suite features spacious walk-in closet and private bath

- Great room highlighted with several windows

- Kitchen with snack bar adjacent to dining area

- Plenty of storage space throughout

- 3 bedrooms, 2 baths, optional 2-car garage

- Basement foundation, drawings also include crawl space foundation

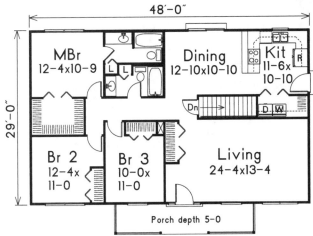

48'-0"
29'-0"

MBr
12-4x10-9

Dining
12-10x10-10

Kit
11-6x10-10

Br 2
12-4x11-0

Br 3
10-0x11-0

Living
24-4x13-4

Dn
D W

Porch depth 5-0

Plan 574-1336

Perfect Vacation Home

Total Living Area:	1,230 sq. ft.
Blueprint Price Code:	A

FEATURES

- Spacious living room accesses huge sun deck

- One of the second floor bedrooms features a balcony overlooking the deck

- Kitchen with dining area accesses outdoors

- Washer and dryer tucked under stairs

- 3 bedrooms, 1 bath

- Crawl space foundation, drawings also include slab foundation

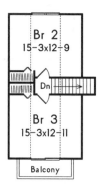

First Floor
780 sq. ft.

26'-0"

30'-0"

R

Kit

Br 1
9-2x
12-9

Dining
8-1x
16-6

D W W

Up

Living
25-5x12-11

Deck

Second Floor
450 sq. ft.

Br 2
15-3x12-9

Dn

Br 3
15-3x12-11

Balcony

Plan 574-0549

Country Cottage Offers Large Vaulted Living Space

Total Living Area:	962 sq. ft.
Blueprint Price Code:	AA
Front porch:	130 sq. ft.
Screened porch:	142 sq. ft.

FEATURES

- Both the kitchen and family room share warmth from the fireplace

- Charming facade features covered porch on one side, screened porch on the other and attractive planter boxes

- L-shaped kitchen boasts convenient pantry

- 2 bedrooms, 1 bath

- Crawl space foundation

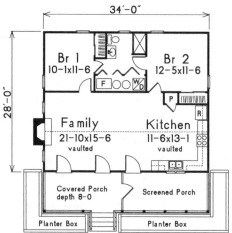

34'-0"

28'-0"

Br 1
10-1x11-6

Br 2
12-5x11-6

F

W
D

P

R

Family
21-10x15-6
vaulted

Kitchen
11-6x13-1
vaulted

Covered Porch
depth 8-0

Screened Porch

Planter Box

Planter Box

Plan 574-0651

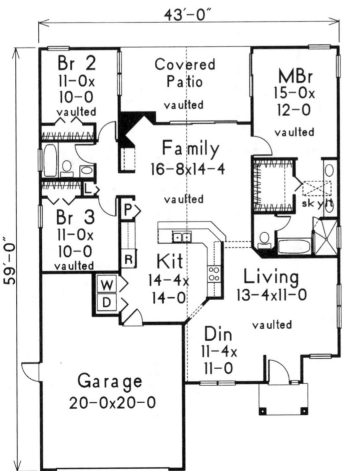

43'-0"

| Br 2 | Covered Patio | MBr |
| 11-0x 10-0 vaulted | vaulted | 15-0x 12-0 vaulted |

Family
16-8x14-4
vaulted

Br 3
11-0x
10-0
vaulted

P
R

Kit
14-4x
14-0

sky lt

Living
13-4x11-0

vaulted

W
D

Din
11-4x
11-0

Garage
20-0x20-0

59'-0"

Vaulted Ceilings
Add Dimension

Total Living Area:	1,550 sq. ft.
Blueprint Price Code:	**B**
Garage:	475 sq. ft.
Rear porch:	188 sq. ft.

FEATURES

- Cozy corner fireplace provides focal point in family room

- Master bedroom features large walk-in closet, skylight and separate tub and shower

- Convenient laundry closet

- Kitchen with pantry and breakfast bar connects to family room

- Family room and master bedroom access covered patio

- 3 bedrooms, 2 baths, 2-car garage

- Slab foundation

Plan 574-0357

Warm And Cozy Feeling

Total Living Area:	**2,202 sq. ft.**
Blueprint Price Code:	**D**
Drive under garage:	783 sq. ft.
Storage:	23 sq. ft.
Front porch:	271 sq. ft.

FEATURES

- 9' ceilings on first floor

- Guest bedroom located on the first floor for convenience could easily be converted to an office area

- Large kitchen with oversized island overlooks dining area

- 5 bedrooms, 4 full baths, 2 half baths, 2-car drive under garage

- Basement or walk-out basement foundation, please specify when ordering

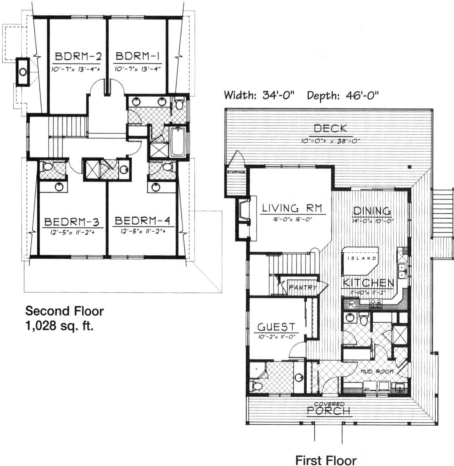

Second Floor
1,028 sq. ft.

Width: 34'-0"   Depth: 46'-0"

First Floor
1,174 sq. ft.

Plan 574-DDI-100213

Gable Facade Adds Appeal To This Ranch

Total Living Area: 1,304 sq. ft.
Blueprint Price Code: A
Garage: 443 sq. ft.

FEATURES

- Covered entrance leads into family room with 10' ceiling and fireplace

- 10' ceilings in kitchen, dining and family rooms

- Master bedroom features coffered ceiling, walk-in closet and private bath

- Efficient kitchen includes large window over the sink

- 3 bedrooms, 2 baths, 2-car garage

- Slab foundation

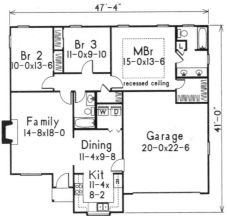

Plan 574-0292

Large Corner Deck Lends Way To Outdoor Living Area

Total Living Area: 1,283 sq. ft.
Blueprint Price Code: A
Garage: 390 sq. ft.

FEATURES

- Vaulted breakfast room with sliding doors that open onto deck

- Kitchen features convenient corner sink and pass-through to dining room

- Open living atmosphere in dining area and great room

- Vaulted great room features a fireplace

- 3 bedrooms, 2 baths, 2-car garage

- Basement foundation

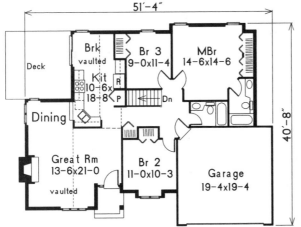

Plan 574-0272

Dramatic Look For Quiet Hideaway

Total Living Area: 1,750 sq. ft.
Blueprint Price Code: B

FEATURES

- Family room brightened by floor-to-ceiling windows and sliding doors providing access to large deck

- Second floor sitting area perfect for game room or entertaining

- Kitchen includes eat-in dining area plus outdoor dining patio as a bonus

- Plenty of closet and storage space throughout

- 3 bedrooms, 2 baths

- Basement foundation, drawings also include crawl space and slab foundations

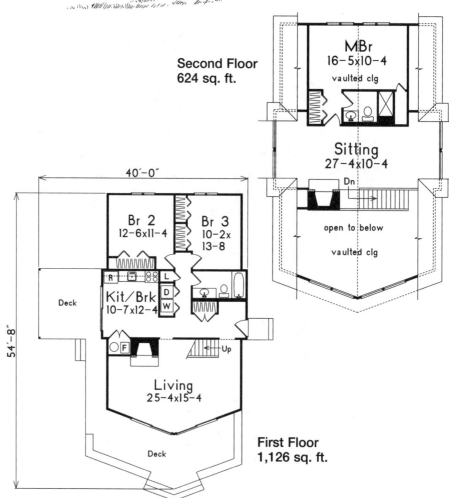

Second Floor
624 sq. ft.

MBr
16-5x10-4
vaulted clg

Sitting
27-4x10-4

Dn

open to below

vaulted clg

40'-0"

Br 2
12-6x11-4

Br 3
10-2x
13-8

Deck

Kit/Brk
10-7x12-4

54'-8"

Up

Living
25-4x15-4

Deck

First Floor
1,126 sq. ft.

Plan 574-N065

Charming Exterior And Cozy Interior

Total Living Area: 1,127 sq. ft.
Blueprint Price Code: AA
Garage: 387 sq. ft.

FEATURES

- Plant shelf joins kitchen and dining room
- Vaulted master suite has double walk-in closets, deck access and private bath
- Great room features vaulted ceiling, fireplace and sliding doors to covered deck
- Ideal home for a narrow lot
- 2 bedrooms, 2 baths, 2-car garage
- Basement foundation

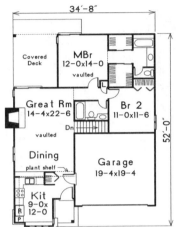

34'-8"

Covered Deck

MBr
12-0x14-0
vaulted

Great Rm
14-4x22-6
vaulted

Br 2
11-0x11-6

Dn

Dining
plant shelf

Garage
19-4x19-4

Kit
9-0x
12-0

52'-0"

Plan 574-0277

Gabled, Covered Front Porch

Total Living Area: 1,320 sq. ft.
Blueprint Price Code: A
Front porch: 122 sq. ft.

FEATURES

- Functional U-shaped kitchen features pantry
- Large living and dining areas join to create an open atmosphere
- Secluded master bedroom includes private full bath
- Covered front porch opens into large living area with convenient coat closet
- Utility/laundry room located near the kitchen
- 3 bedrooms, 2 baths
- Crawl space foundation

Porch

D W P

Kitchen
10-4x10-10

MBr
11-7x15-0

L

Dining
14-7x10-9

Br 3
11-0x10-0

Living
14-7x14-8

Br 2
11-0x10-0

Porch depth 6-0

44'-0"

30'-0"

Plan 574-0297

Brick And Siding Enhance This Traditional Home

Total Living Area: 1,170 sq. ft.
Blueprint Price Code: AA
Garage: 400 sq. ft.
Front porch: 19 sq. ft.

FEATURES

- Master bedroom enjoys privacy at the rear of this home

- Kitchen has angled bar that overlooks great room and breakfast area

- Living areas combine to create a greater sense of spaciousness

- Great room has a cozy fireplace

- 3 bedrooms, 2 baths, 2-car garage

- Slab foundation

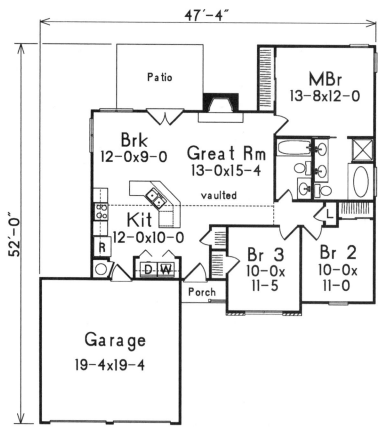

Plan 574-0670

Spacious Dining And Living Areas

Total Living Area: 1,104 sq. ft.
Blueprint Price Code: AA

FEATURES

- Master bedroom includes private bath
- Convenient side entrance to kitchen/dining area
- Laundry area located near kitchen
- Large living area creates comfortable atmosphere
- 3 bedrooms, 2 baths
- Crawl space foundation, drawings also include basement and slab foundations

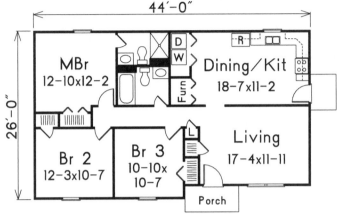

Plan 574-0505

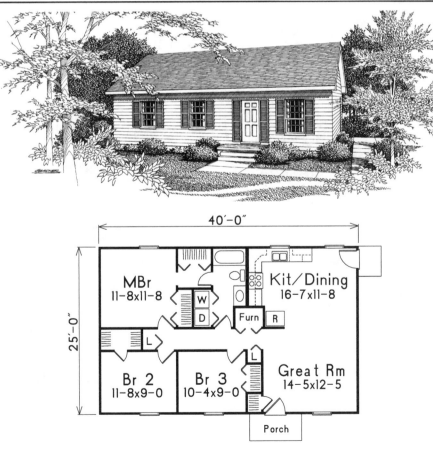

Open Living Space Creates Comfortable Atmosphere

Total Living Area: 1,000 sq. ft.
Blueprint Price Code: AA

FEATURES

- Bath includes convenient closeted laundry area
- Master bedroom includes double closets and private access to bath
- Foyer features handy coat closet
- L-shaped kitchen provides easy access outdoors
- 3 bedrooms, 1 bath
- Crawl space foundation, drawings also include basement and slab foundations

Plan 574-0503

Unique Yet Functional Design

Total Living Area: 1,316 sq. ft.
Blueprint Price Code: A

FEATURES

- Massive vaulted family/living room is accented with fireplace and views to outdoors through sliding glass doors

- Galley-style kitchen is centrally located

- Unique separate shower room near bath doubles as a convenient mud room

- 3 bedrooms, 1 bath

- Crawl space foundation

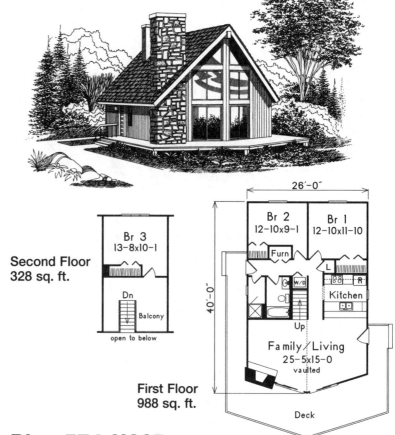

Br 3
13-8x10-1

Second Floor
328 sq. ft.

Dn

Balcony

open to below

26'-0"

Br 2
12-10x9-1

Br 1
12-10x11-10

Furn

W/D

Kitchen

40'-0"

Up

Family/Living
25-5x15-0
vaulted

First Floor
988 sq. ft.

Deck

Plan 574-N085

Master Suite Spacious And Private

Total Living Area: 1,160 sq. ft.
Blueprint Price Code: AA

FEATURES

- Kitchen/dining area combines with laundry area creating a functional organized area

- Spacious vaulted living area has large fireplace and is brightened by glass doors accessing large deck

- Ascend to second floor loft by spiral stairs and find a cozy hideaway

- Master suite brightened by many windows and includes private bath and double closets

- 1 bedroom, 1 bath

- Crawl space foundation

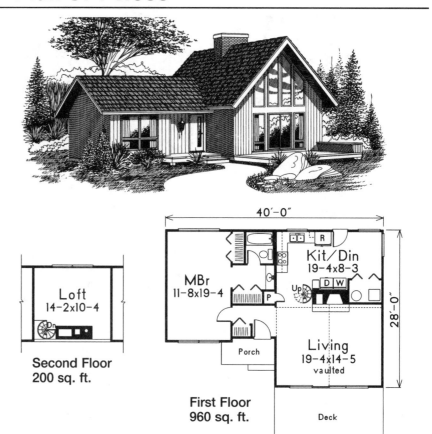

Loft
14-2x10-4

Dn

Second Floor
200 sq. ft.

40'-0"

Kit/Din
19-4x8-3

MBr
11-8x19-4

D W

Up

P

Porch

Living
19-4x14-5
vaulted

28'-0"

First Floor
960 sq. ft.

Deck

Plan 574-N089

REAR VIEW

Simple Roofline Makes Home Economical To Build

Total Living Area:	**1,792 sq. ft.**
Blueprint Price Code:	**B**
Drive under garage:	857 sq. ft.
Front porch:	336 sq. ft.

FEATURES

- Master bedroom has a private bath and large walk-in closet

- A central stone fireplace and windows on two walls are focal points in the living room

- Decorative beams and sloped ceiling add interest to the open living room, kitchen and dining room

- 3 bedrooms, 2 baths, 2-car drive under garage

- Basement foundation

56'-0"

32'-0"

Deck

Kitchen
12 x 11-4

Dining Rm
9 x 11-4

slope

DN

pantry

W
D

Ldry

MBr 1
14-2 x 14-4

slope

ov

slope

lin.

Living Rm
21-6 x 19-4

decor. beams

slope

Br 3
12 x 12-6

Br 2
12 x 12-6

Plan 574-GH-20198

Open Living Spaces

Total Living Area: 1,050 sq. ft.
Blueprint Price Code: AA
Garage: 266 sq. ft.
Front porch: 96 sq. ft.

FEATURES

- Master bedroom features a private bath and access outdoors onto a private patio

- A vaulted ceiling in the living and dining areas creates a feeling of spaciousness

- Laundry closet is convenient to all bedrooms

- Efficient U-shaped kitchen

- 3 bedrooms, 2 baths, 1-car garage

- Basement or slab foundation, please specify when ordering

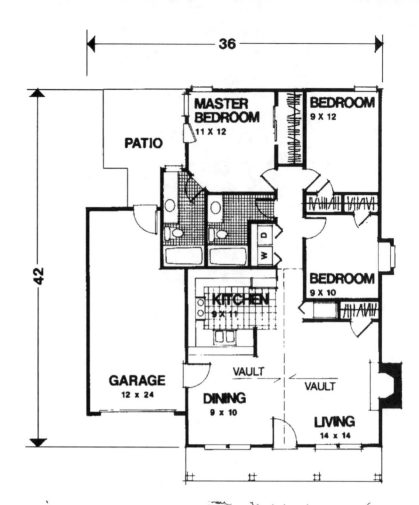

Plan 574-AP-1002

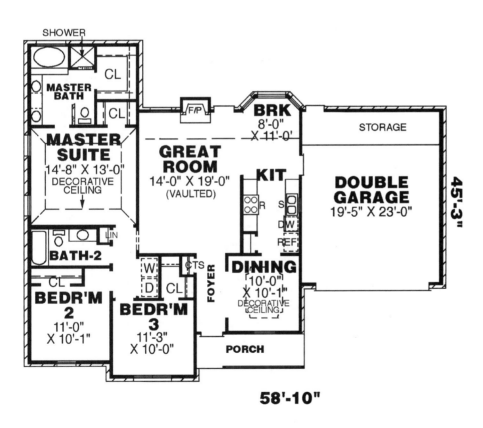

Perfect Ranch With All The Amenities

Total Living Area:	**1,429 sq. ft.**
Blueprint Price Code:	**A**
Garage:	479 sq. ft.
Front porch:	68 sq. ft.

FEATURES

- Master bedroom features a spacious private bath and double walk-in closets

- Formal dining room has convenient access to kitchen perfect when entertaining

- Additional storage can be found in the garage

- 3 bedrooms, 2 baths, 2-car garage

- Slab foundation

Plan 574-CHD-14-18

Trio Of Dormers
Adds Light

Total Living Area:	1,780 sq. ft.
Blueprint Price Code:	B
Garage:	569 sq. ft.
Front porch:	10 sq. ft.

FEATURES

- Traditional styling with the comforts of home

- First floor master bedroom has walk-in closet and bath

- Large kitchen and dining area open to deck

- 3 bedrooms, 2 1/2 baths, 2-car side entry garage

- Basement, crawl space or slab foundation, please specify when ordering

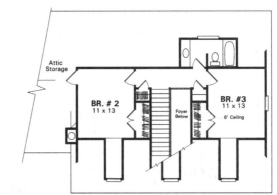

Second Floor
551 sq. ft.

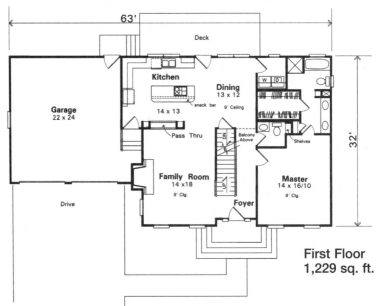

First Floor
1,229 sq. ft.

Plan 574-GM-1780

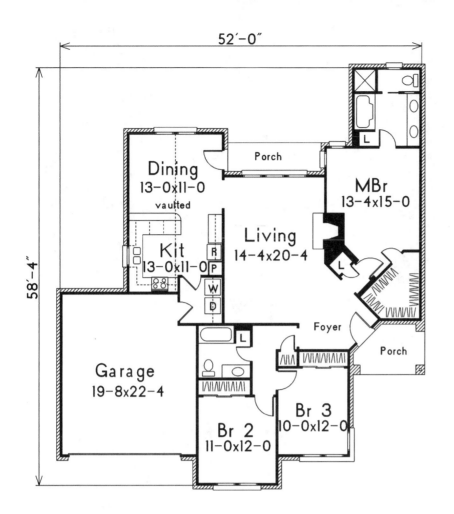

52'-0"

58'-4"

Dining
13-0x11-0
vaulted

Porch

MBr
13-4x15-0

Kit
13-0x11-0

Living
14-4x20-4

R
P
W
D

L

Garage
19-8x22-4

Foyer

Porch

L

Br 2
11-0x12-0

Br 3
10-0x12-0

Sheltered Entrance Opens To Stylish Features

Total Living Area:	1,661 sq. ft.
Blueprint Price Code:	B
Garage:	441 sq. ft.
Front porch:	53 sq. ft.

FEATURES

- Large open foyer with angled wall arrangement and high ceiling adds to spacious living room

- Kitchen and dining area has impressive cathedral ceiling and French door allowing access to the patio

- Utility room conveniently located near kitchen

- Secluded master bedroom has large walk-in closets, unique brick wall arrangement and 10' ceiling

- 3 bedrooms, 2 baths, 2-car garage

- Slab foundation

Plan 574-0216

Country Classic With Modern Floor Plan

Total Living Area: 1,921 sq. ft.
Blueprint Price Code: D
Garage: 576 sq. ft.
Front porch: 228 sq. ft.

FEATURES

- Energy efficient home with 2" x 6" exterior walls

- Sunken family room includes a built-in entertainment center and coffered ceiling

- Sunken formal living room features a coffered ceiling

- Dressing area has double sinks, spa tub, shower and French door to private deck

- Large front porch adds to home's appeal

- 3 bedrooms, 2 1/2 baths, 2-car garage

- Basement foundation

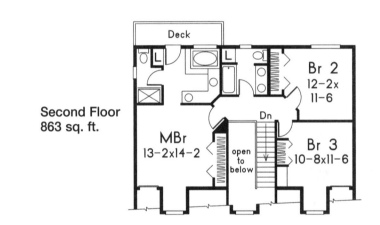

Second Floor 863 sq. ft.

Deck

Br 2
12-2x 11-6

MBr
13-2x14-2

Dn

open to below

Br 3
10-8x11-6

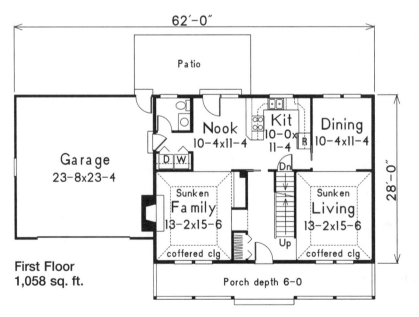

62'-0"

Patio

Garage
23-8x23-4

Nook
10-4x11-4

Kit
10-0x 11-4

Dining
10-4x11-4

D W

Dn

Sunken
Family
13-2x15-6

Up

Sunken
Living
13-2x15-6

coffered clg

coffered clg

28'-0"

First Floor
1,058 sq. ft.

Porch depth 6-0

Plan 574-0312

Irresistible Retreat

Total Living Area:	**448 sq. ft.**
Blueprint Price Code:	**AAA**

FEATURES

- Bedroom features large walk-in closet ideal for storage
- Combined dining/living area ideal for relaxing
- Galley style kitchen is compact and efficient
- Covered porch adds to front facade
- 1 bedroom, 1 bath
- Slab foundation

16'-0"

28'-0"

Br 1
9-10x9-0

Kit
6-5x8-2

R F

Din/Sitting
15-4x11-2

Porch

Plan 574-0695

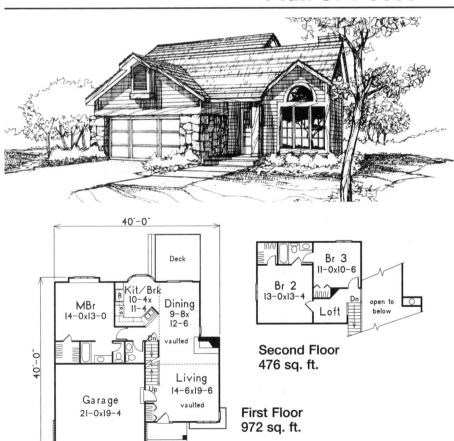

40'-0"

Deck

MBr
14-0x13-0

Kit/Brk
10-4x
11-4

Dining
9-8x
12-6

vaulted

Garage
21-0x19-4

Living
14-6x19-6

vaulted

Up

Dn

40'-0"

Br 3
11-0x10-6

Br 2
13-0x13-4

Loft

Dn

open to
below

**Second Floor
476 sq. ft.**

**First Floor
972 sq. ft.**

Vaulted
Living Area With
Corner Fireplace

Total Living Area:	**1,448 sq. ft.**
Blueprint Price Code:	**A**
Garage:	**433 sq. ft.**
Front porch:	**40 sq. ft.**

FEATURES

- Dining room conveniently adjoins kitchen and accesses rear deck
- Private first floor master bedroom
- Secondary bedrooms share a bath and cozy loft area
- 3 bedrooms, 2 1/2 baths, 2-car garage
- Basement foundation

Plan 574-0270

Open Living Area Plan Designed For Sloping Lot

Total Living Area:	1,835 sq. ft.
Blueprint Price Code:	D
Drive under garage:	504 sq. ft.
Front porch:	30 sq. ft.

FEATURES

- Family room opens onto balcony through double-doors

- Living room offers expansive living space with windows and cathedral ceiling

- Kitchen features angled breakfast bar and corner sink

- Master bedroom boasts vaulted ceiling, walk-in closet and deluxe bath

- 3 bedrooms, 2 1/2 baths, 2-car drive under garage

- Basement foundation

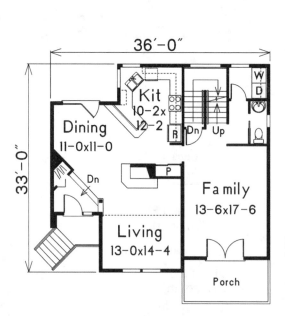

Br 2
10-2x13-0

Br 3
10-8x11-8

Dn

L

MBr
13-6x12-6
vaulted clg

open to below
vaulted clg

Second Floor
813 sq. ft.

36'-0"

33'-0"

Kit
10-2x
12-2

Dining
11-0x11-0

Dn

R

Dn   Up

W
D

Family
13-6x17-6

Living
13-0x14-4

Porch

First Floor
1,022 sq. ft.

Plan 574-0328

A Chalet For Lakeside Living

Total Living Area:	1,280 sq. ft.
Blueprint Price Code:	A

FEATURES

- Attention to architectural detail has created the look of an authentic Swiss cottage

- Spacious living room including adjacent kitchenette and dining area, enjoy views to front deck

- Hall bath shared by two sizable bedrooms is included on first and second floors

- 4 bedrooms, 2 baths

- Crawl space foundation, drawings also include basement and slab foundations

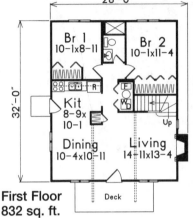

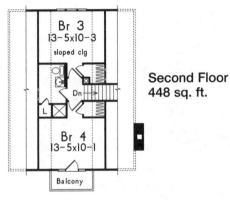

Second Floor
448 sq. ft.

First Floor
832 sq. ft.

Plan 574-N042

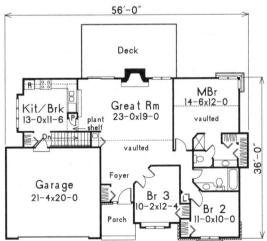

Distinctive Ranch Has A Larger Look

Total Living Area:	1,360 sq. ft.
Blueprint Price Code:	A
Garage:	447 sq. ft.
Front porch:	48 sq. ft.

FEATURES

- Double-gabled front facade frames large windows

- Entry area is open to vaulted great room, fireplace and rear deck creating an open feel

- Vaulted ceiling and large windows add openness to kitchen/breakfast room

- Bedroom #3 easily converts to a den

- Plan easily adapts to crawl space or slab construction, with the utilities replacing the stairs

- 3 bedrooms, 2 baths, 2-car garage

- Basement foundation

Plan 574-0105

Covered
Rear Porch

Total Living Area: 1,253 sq. ft.
Blueprint Price Code: A
Garage: 486 sq. ft.
Front porch: 208 sq. ft.

FEATURES

- Sloped ceiling and fireplace in family room adds drama

- U-shaped kitchen efficiently designed

- Large walk-in closets are found in all the bedrooms

- 3 bedrooms, 2 baths, 2-car garage

- Crawl space or slab foundation, please specify when ordering

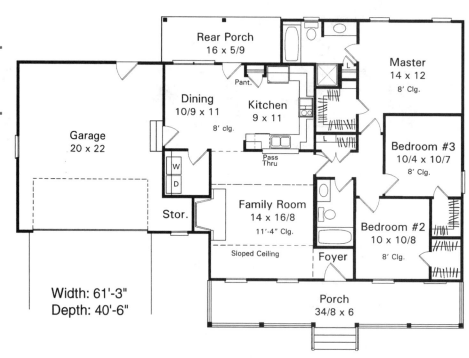

Width: 61'-3"
Depth: 40'-6"

Plan 574-GM-1253

Roughing It In Luxury

Total Living Area: 1,200 sq. ft.
Blueprint Price Code: A

FEATURES

- Ornate ranch-style railing enhances exterior while the stone fireplace provides a visual anchor

- Spectacular living room features inviting fireplace and adjoins a charming kitchen with dining area

- First floor bedroom, hall bath and two second floor bedrooms with half bath and exterior balcony complete the home

- 3 bedrooms, 1 1/2 baths

- Crawl space foundation, drawings also include slab foundation

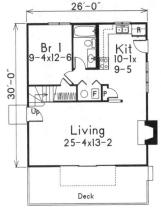

First Floor
780 sq. ft.

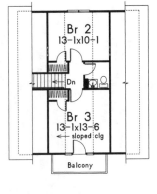

Second Floor
420 sq. ft.

Plan 574-N119

Open Layout Ensures Easy Living

Total Living Area: 976 sq. ft.
Blueprint Price Code: AA
Front porch: 32 sq. ft.

FEATURES

- Cozy front porch opens into large living room

- Convenient half bath is located on first floor

- All bedrooms are located on second floor for privacy

- Dining room has access to the outdoors

- 3 bedrooms, 1 1/2 baths

- Basement foundation

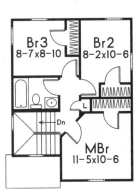

Second Floor
488 sq. ft.

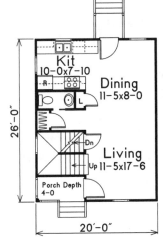

First Floor
488 sq. ft.

Plan 574-0493

Perfect Home
For Family Living

Total Living Area: 1,700 sq. ft.
Blueprint Price Code: B
Front porch: 179 sq. ft.

FEATURES

- Oversized laundry room has large pantry and storage area as well as access to the outdoors

- Master bedroom separated from other bedrooms for privacy

- Raised snack bar in kitchen allows extra seating for dining

- 3 bedrooms, 2 baths

- Crawl space foundation

50—0 WIDE X 42—0 DEPTH
(INCLUDING COVERED PORCH)

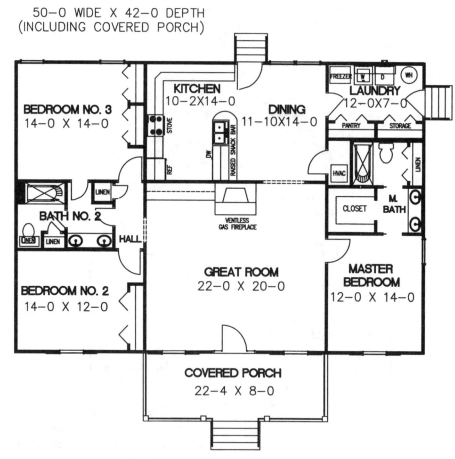

BEDROOM NO. 3
14—0 X 14—0

KITCHEN
10—2X14—0

DINING
11—10X14—0

LAUNDRY
12—0X7—0

FREEZER W D WH

PANTRY   STORAGE

REF STOVE DW RAISED SNACK BAR

HVAC

LINEN

BATH NO. 2

LINEN LINEN

HALL

VENTLESS
GAS FIREPLACE

CLOSET

M.
BATH

BEDROOM NO. 2
14—0 X 12—0

GREAT ROOM
22—0 X 20—0

MASTER
BEDROOM
12—0 X 14—0

COVERED PORCH
22—4 X 8—0

Plan 574-DH-2005

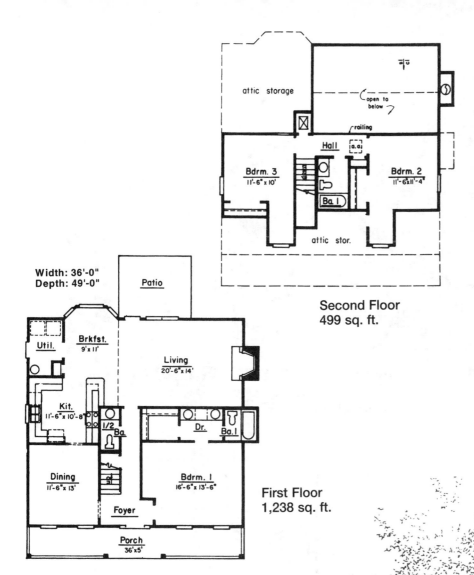

Width: 36'-0"
Depth: 49'-0"

Second Floor
499 sq. ft.

Bdrm. 3
11'-6" x 10'

Hall

Bdrm. 2
11'-6" x 11'-4"

Ba. 1

attic storage

open to below

railing

attic stor.

Patio

Util.

Brkfst.
9' x 11'

Living
20'-6" x 14'

Kit.
11'-6" x 10'-8"

1/2 Ba.

Dr.

Ba. 1

Dining
11'-6" x 13'

Bdrm. 1
16'-6" x 13'-6"

Foyer

Porch
36' x 5'

First Floor
1,238 sq. ft.

Quaint Country Home

Total Living Area:	1,737 sq. ft.
Blueprint Price Code:	B
Front porch:	180 sq. ft.

FEATURES

- U-shaped kitchen, sunny bayed breakfast room and living area become one large gathering area

- Living area has sloped ceilings and a balcony overlook from second floor

- Second floor includes lots of storage area

- 3 bedrooms, 2 1/2 baths

- Slab or crawl space foundation, please specify when ordering

Plan 574-CHP-1733-A-7

Dramatic Sloping Ceiling In Living Room

Total Living Area:	**1,432 sq. ft.**
Blueprint Price Code:	**A**
Garage:	**234 sq. ft.**
Front porch:	**41 sq. ft.**

FEATURES

- Enter into the two-story foyer from covered porch or garage

- Living room has square bay and window seat, glazed end wall with floor-to-ceiling windows and access to the deck

- Kitchen/dining room also opens to the deck for added convenience

- 3 bedrooms, 2 baths, 1-car garage

- Basement foundation, drawings also include slab foundation

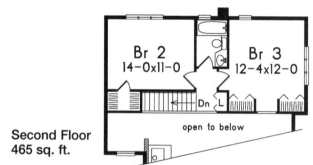

Second Floor
465 sq. ft.

Br 2
14-0x11-0

Br 3
12-4x12-0

Dn

open to below

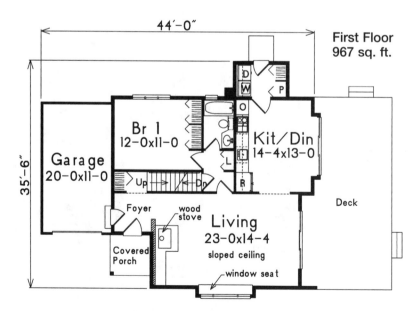

First Floor
967 sq. ft.

44'-0"

35'-6"

Garage
20-0x11-0

Br 1
12-0x11-0

Kit/Din
14-4x13-0

Up

Dn

Foyer

wood stove

Living
23-0x14-4
sloped ceiling

window seat

Deck

Covered Porch

Plan 574-0680

Elegance In A Starter Or Retirement Home

Total Living Area:	888 sq. ft.
Blueprint Price Code:	AAA
Garage:	275 sq. ft.
Front porch:	91 sq. ft.

FEATURES

- Home features an eye-catching exterior and includes a spacious porch
- The breakfast room with bay window is open to living room and adjoins kitchen with pass-through snack bar
- The bedrooms are quite roomy and feature walk-in closets and the master bedroom has double entry doors and access to rear patio
- The master bedroom has double entry doors and access to rear patio
- 2 bedrooms, 1 bath, 1-car garage
- Basement foundation

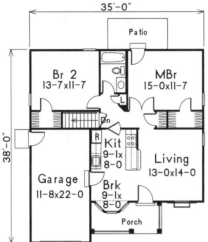

Plan 574-0813

Cleverly Angled Walls Add Interest To Home

Total Living Area:	1,400 sq. ft.
Blueprint Price Code:	A

FEATURES

- Inside and out, this home is pleasingly different
- Activity area showcases large free-standing fireplace and spacious dining room with views
- Laundry area is provided in a very functional kitchen
- Master suite with double-doors is a grand bedroom with nice amenities
- 2 bedrooms, 2 baths
- Crawl space foundation

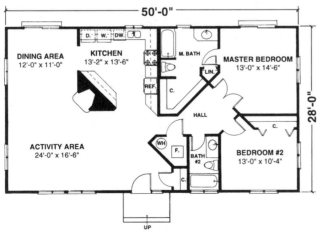

Plan 574-1413

Rustic Stone Exterior

Total Living Area:	**1,466 sq. ft.**
Blueprint Price Code:	**A**
Garage:	547 sq. ft.
Front porch:	137 sq. ft.

FEATURES

- Energy efficient home with 2" x 6" exterior walls

- Foyer separates the living room from the dining room and contains a generous coat closet

- Large living room with corner fireplace, bay window and pass-through to the kitchen

- Informal breakfast area opens to a large terrace through sliding glass doors which brightens area

- Master bedroom has a large walk-in closet and private bath

- 3 bedrooms, 2 baths, 2-car garage

- Basement foundation, drawings also include slab foundation

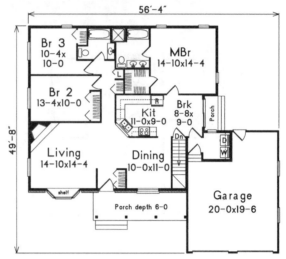

Plan 574-0679

Vaulted Ceilings Highlight This Home

Total Living Area:	**1,560 sq. ft.**
Blueprint Price Code:	**B**
Garage:	405 sq. ft.
Front porch:	45 sq. ft.

FEATURES

- Cozy breakfast room is tucked at the rear of this home and features plenty of windows for natural light

- Large entry has easy access to secondary bedrooms, laundry/utility, dining and living rooms

- Private master suite

- Kitchen overlooks living room with fireplace and patio access

- 3 bedrooms, 2 baths, 2-car garage

- Slab foundation

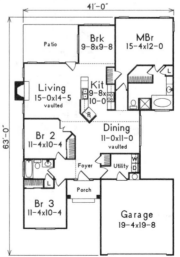

Plan 574-0667

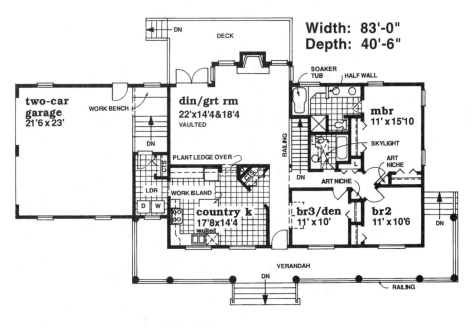

DN DECK

Width: 83'-0"
Depth: 40'-6"

SOAKER TUB   HALF WALL

two-car garage
21'6 x 23'

WORK BENCH

din/grt rm
22'x14'4 & 18'4
VAULTED

DN

PLANT LEDGE OVER

mbr
11' x 15'10

SKYLIGHT

ART NICHE

RAILING

DN

ART NICHE

LDR

WORK ISLAND

D   W

country k
17'8x14'4
vaulted

br3/den
11' x 10'

br2
11' x 10'6

DN

VERANDAH

DN

RAILING

Quaint Home Made For Country Living

Total Living Area:	1,578 sq. ft.
Blueprint Price Code:	B
Side entry garage:	606 sq. ft.
Front porch:	472 sq. ft.

FEATURES

- A fireplace warms the great room and is flanked by windows overlooking the rear deck

- Bedrooms are clustered on one side of the home for privacy from living areas

- Master bedroom has unique art niche at its entry and a private bath with separate tub and shower

- 3 bedrooms, 2 baths, 2-car side entry garage

- Basement or crawl space foundation, please specify when ordering

Plan 574-SH-SEA-245

Quaint
Alpine Style

Total Living Area: 1,563 sq. ft.
Blueprint Price Code: B
Front porch: 213 sq. ft.

FEATURES

- Master bedroom is located on second floor for privacy and includes amenities such as a private balcony, dressing area and bath with front balcony

- Centrally located utility room

- Double sliding glass doors add drama to living room

- Plenty of storage space throughout

- 3 bedrooms, 2 baths, 2-car garage

- Basement, crawl space or slab foundation, please specify when ordering

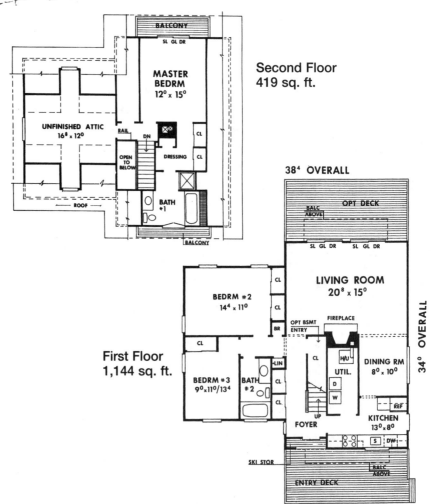

Second Floor
419 sq. ft.

First Floor
1,144 sq. ft.

Plan 574-AX-8382

Family Room With Fireplace Perfect For Central Gathering

Total Living Area: 1,631 sq. ft.
Blueprint Price Code: B
Drive under garage: 616 sq. ft.
Front porch: 115 sq. ft.

FEATURES

- 9' ceilings throughout this home
- Utility room conveniently located near kitchen
- Roomy kitchen and dining area boasts a breakfast bar and deck access
- Coffered ceiling accents master suite
- 3 bedrooms, 2 baths, 2-car drive under garage
- Basement foundation

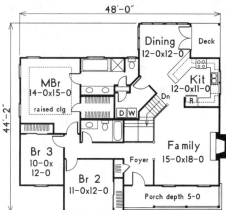

48'-0"

44'-2"

Dining 12-0x12-0

Deck

MBr 14-0x15-0 raised clg

Kit 12-0x11-0

Dn

R

Family 15-0x18-0

Foyer

Br 3 10-0x 12-0

Br 2 11-0x12-0

Porch depth 5-0

D W

Plan 574-0237

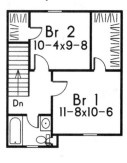

Two-Story Home Perfect Fit For Small Lot

Total Living Area: 858 sq. ft.
Blueprint Price Code: AAA
Front porch: 120 sq. ft.

FEATURES

- Stackable washer/dryer located in the kitchen
- Large covered porch graces this exterior
- Both bedrooms have walk-in closets
- 2 bedrooms, 1 bath
- Crawl space foundation

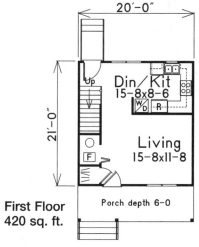

20'-0"

21'-0"

Up

Din/Kit 15-8x8-6

W D

R

Living 15-8x11-8

F

Porch depth 6-0

First Floor 420 sq. ft.

Second Floor 438 sq. ft.

Br 2 10-4x9-8

Br 1 11-8x10-6

Dn

Plan 574-0499

Large Loft Area Offers Endless Possibilities

Total Living Area: 1,426 sq. ft.
Blueprint Price Code: A

FEATURES

- Large front deck invites outdoor relaxation

- Expansive windows, skylights, vaulted ceiling and fireplace enhance the living/dining combination

- Nook, adjacent to the living room, has a cozy window seat

- Kitchen becomes a part of the living/dining area

- 1 bedroom, 1 bath

- Crawl space foundation

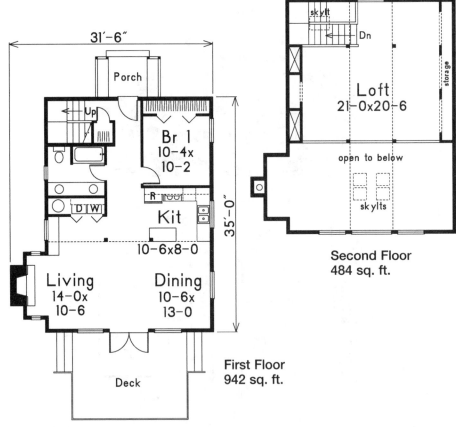

31'-6"

Porch

Up

Br 1
10-4x
10-2

Kit
10-6x8-0

Living
14-0x
10-6

Dining
10-6x
13-0

35'-0"

Deck

First Floor
942 sq. ft.

skylt

Dn

Loft
21-0x20-6

storage

open to below

skylts

Second Floor
484 sq. ft.

Plan 574-0683

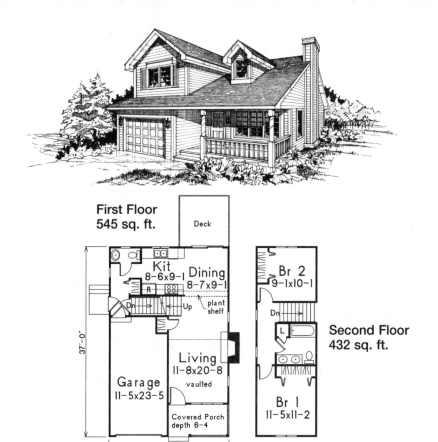

Special Planning In This Compact Home

Total Living Area:	**977 sq. ft.**
Blueprint Price Code:	**AA**
Garage:	271 sq. ft.
Front porch:	76 sq. ft.

FEATURES

- Comfortable living room features a vaulted ceiling, fireplace, plant shelf and coat closet

- Both bedrooms are located on second floor and share a bath with double-bowl vanity and linen closet

- Sliding glass doors in dining room provide access to the deck

- 2 bedrooms, 1 1/2 baths, 1-car garage

- Basement foundation

First Floor
545 sq. ft.

Second Floor
432 sq. ft.

Plan 574-0496

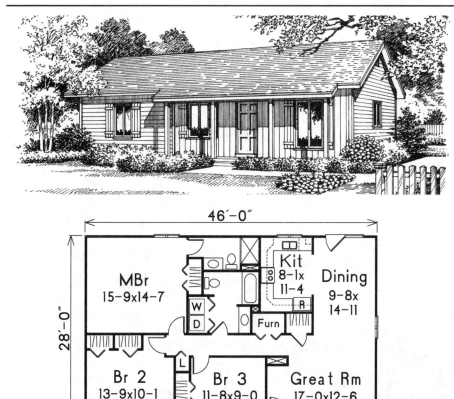

Peaceful Shaded Front Porch

Total Living Area:	**1,288 sq. ft.**
Blueprint Price Code:	**A**
Front porch:	384 sq. ft.

FEATURES

- Kitchen, dining area and great room join to create an open living space

- Master bedroom includes private bath

- Secondary bedrooms include ample closet space

- Hall bath features convenient laundry closet

- Dining room accesses the outdoors

- 3 bedrooms, 2 baths

- Crawl space foundation, drawings also include basement and slab foundations

Plan 574-0534

Private Bedroom Area

Total Living Area:	**1,550 sq. ft.**
Blueprint Price Code:	**B**
Detached garage:	548 sq. ft.
Front porch:	382 sq. ft.
Rear porch:	144 sq. ft.

FEATURES

- Wrap-around front porch is an ideal gathering place

- Handy snack bar is positioned so kitchen flows into family room

- Master bedroom has many amenities

- 3 bedrooms, 2 baths, 2-car detached garage

- Slab or crawl space foundation, please specify when ordering

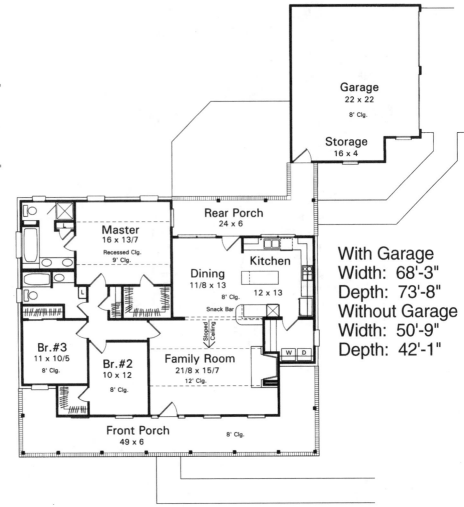

With Garage
Width: 68'-3"
Depth: 73'-8"
Without Garage
Width: 50'-9"
Depth: 42'-1"

Plan 574-GM-1550

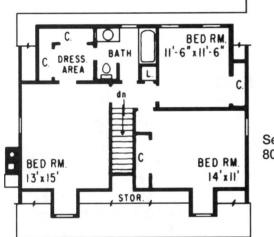

Second Floor
804 sq. ft.

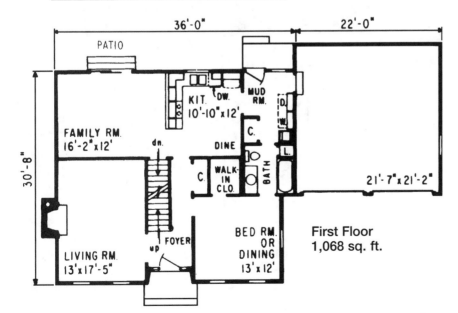

First Floor
1,068 sq. ft.

Design Has Traditional Elegance

Total Living Area:	**1,872 sq. ft.**
Blueprint Price Code:	**C**
Garage:	484 sq. ft.
Front porch:	26 sq. ft.

FEATURES

- Recessed porch has entry door with sidelights and roof dormers adding charm

- Foyer with handcrafted stair adjoins living room with fireplace

- First floor bedroom with access to bath and laundry room is perfect for master suite or live-in parent

- Largest of three second floor bedrooms enjoys his and hers closets and private access to hall bath

- 4 bedrooms, 2 baths, 2-car garage

- Basement foundation, drawings also include crawl space and slab foundations

Plan 574-T-109

Ranch-Style Home With Many Extras

Total Living Area:	1,295 sq. ft.
Blueprint Price Code:	A
Garage:	413 sq. ft.
Front porch:	191 sq. ft.

FEATURES

- Wrap-around porch is a lovely place for dining

- A fireplace gives a stunning focal point to the great room that is heightened with a sloped ceiling

- The master suite is full of luxurious touches such as a walk-in closet and a lush private bath

- 2 bedrooms, 2 baths, 2-car garage

- Basement foundation

Plan 574-HP-C689

Vaulted Rooms Brighten Interior

Total Living Area:	1,290 sq. ft.
Blueprint Price Code:	A
Side entry garage:	441 sq. ft.
Front porch:	55 sq. ft.

FEATURES

- Kitchen located conveniently between the dining room and breakfast area

- Master suite has private luxurious bath with walk-in closet

- Decorative plant shelves throughout this plan add style

- 3 bedrooms, 2 baths, 2-car side entry garage

- Slab or crawl space foundation, please specify when ordering

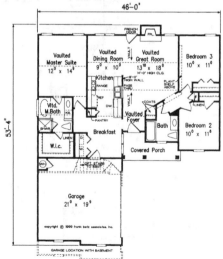

Plan 574-FB-3484

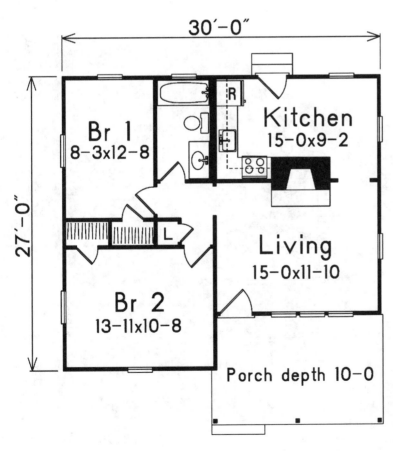

30′-0″

Br 1
8-3x12-8

Kitchen
15-0x9-2

R

27′-0″

L

Living
15-0x11-10

Br 2
13-11x10-8

Porch depth 10-0

Covered Porch Adds To Perfect Outdoor Getaway

Total Living Area:	733 sq. ft.
Blueprint Price Code:	AAA
Front porch:	155 sq. ft.

FEATURES

- Bedrooms separate from kitchen and living area for privacy

- Lots of closet space throughout this home

- Centrally located bath is easily accessible

- Kitchen features door to rear of home and a door separating it from the rest of the home

- 2 bedrooms, 1 bath

- Pier foundation

Plan 574-N131

Country Cottage Styling

Total Living Area:	**1,251 sq. ft.**
Blueprint Price Code:	**A**
Rear entry garage:	403 sq. ft.
Front porch:	114 sq. ft.

FEATURES

- Open living areas make this home feel larger
- Utility closet located on the second floor for convenience
- Lots of counterspace in kitchen
- 3 bedrooms, 2 baths, 2-car rear entry garage
- Crawl space foundation

Width: 27'-0"
Depth: 62'-0"

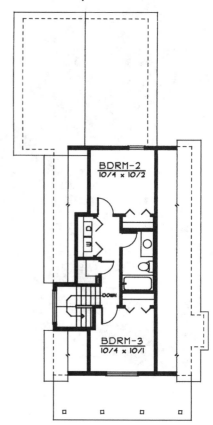

Second Floor
459 sq. ft.

First Floor
792 sq. ft.

Plan 574-DDI-95219

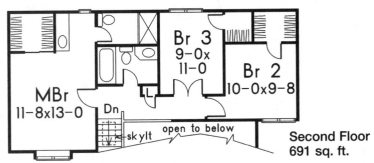

Br 3
9-0x
11-0

Br 2
10-0x9-8

MBr
11-8x13-0

Dn

skylt   open to below

Second Floor
691 sq. ft.

Exterior Accents Add Charm To This Compact Cottage

Total Living Area:	1,359 sq. ft.
Blueprint Price Code:	A
Garage:	480 sq. ft.
Front porch:	30 sq. ft.

FEATURES

- Lattice-trimmed porch, stone chimney and abundant windows lend outdoor appeal

- Spacious, bright breakfast area with pass-through to formal dining room

- Large walk-in closets in all bedrooms

- Extensive deck expands dining and entertaining areas

- 3 bedrooms, 2 1/2 baths, 2-car garage

- Basement foundation

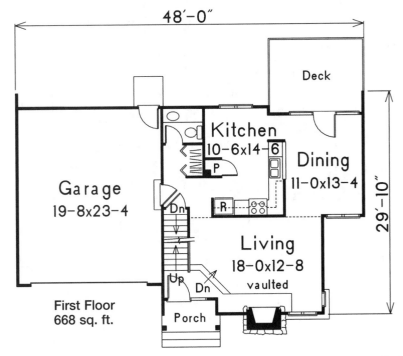

48'-0"

Deck

Kitchen
10-6x14-6

P

Dining
11-0x13-4

29'-10"

Garage
19-8x23-4

Dn

R

Up

Dn

Living
18-0x12-8
vaulted

First Floor
668 sq. ft.

Porch

Plan 574-0104

Covered Porch
Is Focal Point
Of Entry

Total Living Area:	**1,595 sq. ft.**
Blueprint Price Code:	**B**
Side entry garage:	470 sq. ft.
Front porch:	196 sq. ft.

FEATURES

- Dining room has convenient built-in desk and provides access to the outdoors

- L-shaped kitchen area features island cooktop

- Family room has high ceiling and a fireplace

- Private master suite includes large walk-in closet and bath with separate tub and shower units

- 3 bedrooms, 2 baths, 2-car side entry garage

- Slab foundation, drawings also include crawl space foundation

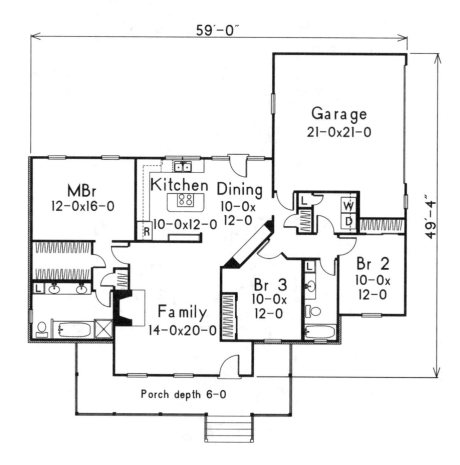

Plan 574-0293

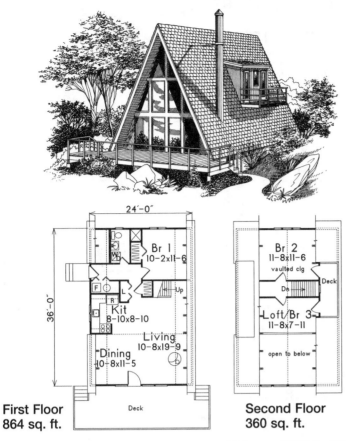

Fantastic A-Frame Get-Away

Total Living Area:	**1,224 sq. ft.**
Blueprint Price Code:	**A**

FEATURES

- Get away to this cozy A-frame featuring three bedrooms

- Living/dining room with free-standing fireplace walks out onto a large deck

- U-shaped kitchen has a unique built-in table at end of counter for intimate gatherings

- Both second floor bedrooms enjoy their own private balcony

- 3 bedrooms, 1 bath

- Crawl space foundation

First Floor
864 sq. ft.

Second Floor
360 sq. ft.

Plan 574-N061

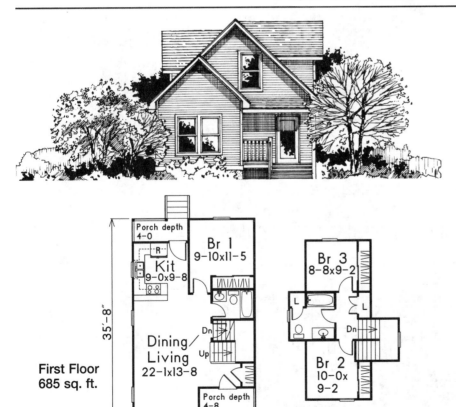

Compact Home, Perfect Fit For Narrow Lot

Total Living Area:	**1,085 sq. ft.**
Blueprint Price Code:	**AA**
Front porch:	**47 sq. ft.**

FEATURES

- Rear porch is a handy access through the kitchen

- Convenient hall linen closet located on the second floor

- Breakfast bar in kitchen offers additional counterspace

- Living and dining rooms combine for open living atmosphere

- 3 bedrooms, 2 baths

- Basement foundation

First Floor
685 sq. ft.

Second Floor
400 sq. ft.

Plan 574-0494

Southern Styling With Covered Porch

Total Living Area:	**1,491 sq. ft.**
Blueprint Price Code:	**A**
Drive under garage:	509 sq. ft.
Front porch:	209 sq. ft.

FEATURES

- Two-story family room has vaulted ceiling

- Well-organized kitchen has serving bar which overlooks family and dining rooms

- First floor master suite has tray ceiling, walk-in closet and master bath

- 3 bedrooms, 2 1/2 baths, 2-car drive under garage

- Walk-out basement foundation

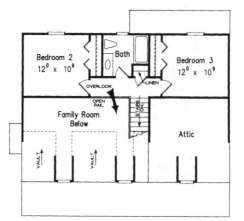

Second Floor
430 sq. ft.

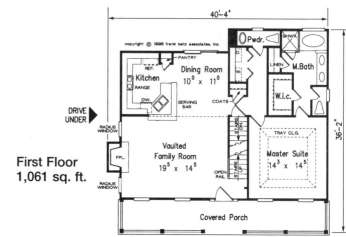

First Floor
1,061 sq. ft.

Plan 574-FB-1148

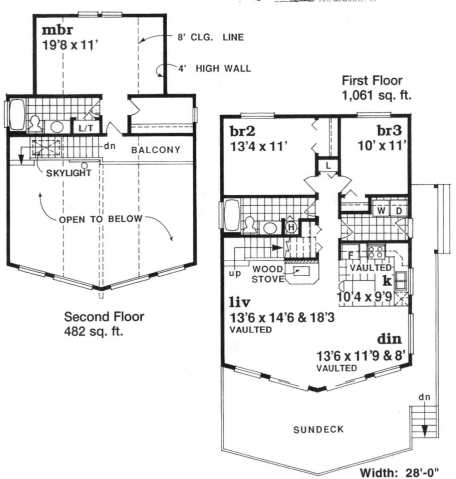

mbr
19'8 x 11'

8' CLG. LINE

4' HIGH WALL

L/T

dn   BALCONY

SKYLIGHT

OPEN TO BELOW

Second Floor
482 sq. ft.

First Floor
1,061 sq. ft.

br2
13'4 x 11'

br3
10' x 11'

L

W D

F

VAULTED

up WOOD
STOVE

k
10'4 x 9'9

liv
13'6 x 14'6 & 18'3
VAULTED

din
13'6 x 11'9 & 8'
VAULTED

dn

SUNDECK

Width: 28'-0"
Depth: 39'-9"

Expansive
Glass Wall

Total Living Area: 1,543 sq. ft.
Blueprint Price Code: B

FEATURES

- Enormous sundeck makes this a popular vacation style

- A woodstove warms the vaulted living and dining rooms

- A vaulted kitchen has a prep island and breakfast bar

- Second floor vaulted master bedroom has private bath and walk-in closet

- 3 bedrooms, 2 baths

- Crawl space foundation

Plan 574-SH-SEA-226

Flexible Layout For Various Uses

Total Living Area:	1,143 sq. ft.
Blueprint Price Code:	AA
Front porch:	160 sq. ft.

FEATURES

- Enormous stone fireplace in family room adds warmth and character
- Spacious kitchen with breakfast bar overlooks family room
- Separate dining area great for entertaining
- Vaulted family room and kitchen create an open atmosphere
- 2 bedrooms, 1 bath
- Crawl space foundation

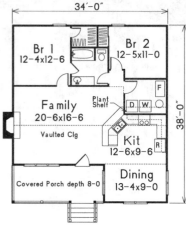

Plan 574-0698

Double Dormers Accent This Cozy Vacation Retreat

Total Living Area:	581 sq. ft.
Blueprint Price Code:	AAA

FEATURES

- Living/dining room features a convenient kitchenette and spiral steps leading to the loft area
- Large loft space easily converted to a bedroom or work area
- Entry space has a unique built-in display niche
- 1 bedroom, 1 bath
- Slab foundation

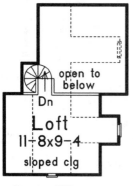

Second Floor
132 sq. ft.

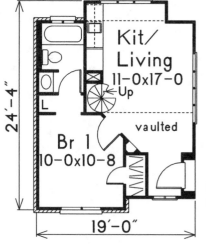

First Floor
449 sq. ft.

Plan 574-0243

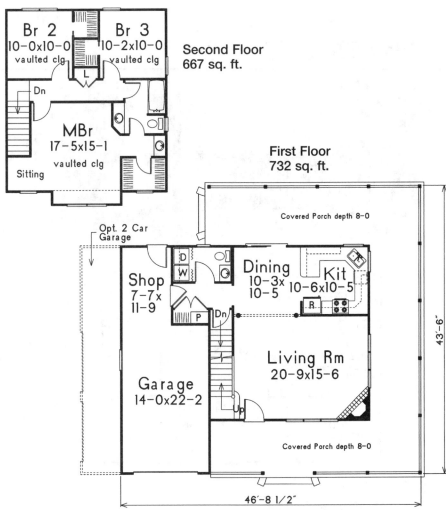

Br 2
10-0x10-0
vaulted clg

Br 3
10-2x10-0
vaulted clg

Second Floor
667 sq. ft.

Dn

MBr
17-5x15-1
vaulted clg

Sitting

First Floor
732 sq. ft.

Opt. 2 Car
Garage

Covered Porch depth 8-0

Shop
7-7x
11-9

D
W

Dining
10-3x
10-5

Kit
10-6x10-5

P

Dn

R

Living Rm
20-9x15-6

Garage
14-0x22-2

Up

43'-6"

Covered Porch depth 8-0

46'-8 1/2"

Covered Porch Surrounds Home

Total Living Area:	**1,399 sq. ft.**
Blueprint Price Code:	**A**
Garage:	406 sq. ft.
Front porch:	732 sq. ft.

FEATURES

• Living room overlooks dining area through arched columns

• Laundry room contains handy half bath

• Spacious master bedroom includes sitting area, walk-in closet and plenty of sunlight

• 3 bedrooms, 1 1/2 baths, 1-car garage

• Basement foundation, drawings also include crawl space and slab foundations

Plan 574-0795

Appealing Ranch Has Attractive Front Dormers

Total Living Area:	**1,642 sq. ft.**
Blueprint Price Code:	**B**
Garage:	528 sq. ft.
Front porch:	36 sq. ft.

FEATURES

- Walk-through kitchen boasts vaulted ceiling and corner sink overlooking family room

- Vaulted family room features cozy fireplace and access to rear patio

- Master bedroom includes sloped ceiling, walk-in closet and private bath

- 3 bedrooms, 2 baths, 2-car garage

- Basement foundation, drawings also include slab and crawl space foundations

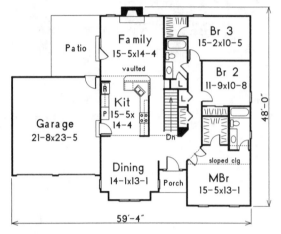

Plan 574-0282

Design Revolves Around Central Living Space

Total Living Area:	**1,364 sq. ft.**
Blueprint Price Code:	**A**
Drive under garage:	806 sq. ft.
Front porch:	100 sq. ft.

FEATURES

- Master bedroom includes full bath

- Pass-through kitchen opens into breakfast room with laundry closet and access to deck

- Adjoining dining and living rooms with vaulted ceilings and a fireplace create an open living area

- Dining room features large bay window

- 3 bedrooms, 2 baths, 2-car drive under garage

- Basement foundation

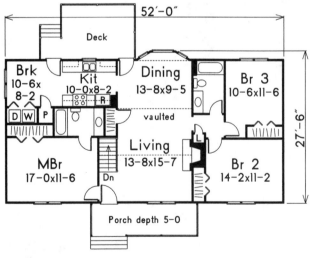

Plan 574-0252

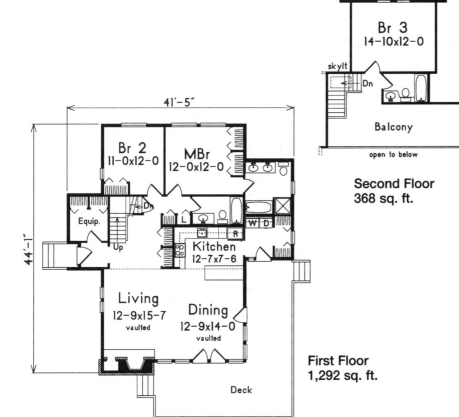

Br 3
14-10x12-0

skylt

Dn

Balcony

open to below

Second Floor
368 sq. ft.

41'-5"

Br 2
11-0x12-0

MBr
12-0x12-0

Equip.

Up

Dn

L

Kitchen
12-7x7-6

W D

R

44'-1"

Living
12-9x15-7
vaulted

Dining
12-9x14-0
vaulted

First Floor
1,292 sq. ft.

Deck

Dramatic Expanse Of Windows

Total Living Area: 1,660 sq. ft.
Blueprint Price Code: B

FEATURES

- Convenient gear and equipment room

- Spacious living and dining rooms look even larger with the openness of the foyer and kitchen

- Large wrap-around deck, a great plus for outdoor living

- Broad balcony overlooks living and dining rooms

- 3 bedrooms, 3 baths

- Partial basement/crawl space foundation, drawings also include slab foundation

Plan 574-0681

© COPYRIGHT 1990 RALPH JONES & ASSOC.

Decorative Accents Featured On Front Porch

Total Living Area:	1,455 sq. ft.
Blueprint Price Code:	**A**
Front porch:	322 sq. ft.
Rear porch:	261 sq. ft.

FEATURES

- Optional second floor bedroom and playroom have an additional 744 square feet of living area

- Spacious mud room has a large pantry, space for a freezer, sink/counter area and bath with shower

- Bedroom #2 can easily be converted to a study or office area

- 2 bedrooms, 2 baths

- Slab or crawl space foundation, please specify when ordering

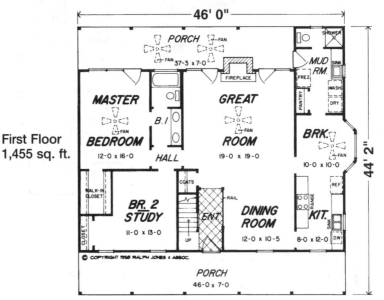

First Floor
1,455 sq. ft.

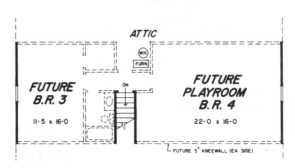

Optional
Second Floor

Plan 574-RJ-B1416

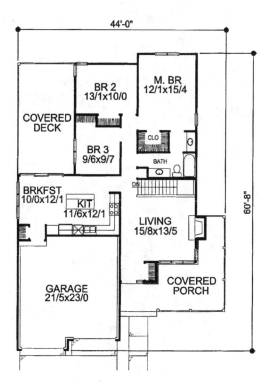

44'-0"

BR 2
13/1x10/0

M. BR
12/1x15/4

COVERED
DECK

CLO

BR 3
9/6x9/7

BATH

DN

BRKFST
10/0x12/1

KIT
11/6x12/1

LIVING
15/8x13/5

60'-8"

GARAGE
21/5x23/0

COVERED
PORCH

Covered Deck Off Breakfast Room

Total Living Area:	1,231 sq. ft.
Blueprint Price Code:	**A**
Garage:	447 sq. ft.
Front porch:	223 sq. ft.

FEATURES

- Covered front porch

- Master bedroom has separate sink area

- Large island in kitchen for eat-in dining or preparation area

- 3 bedrooms, 1 bath, 2-car garage

- Basement foundation

Plan 574-HDG-99004

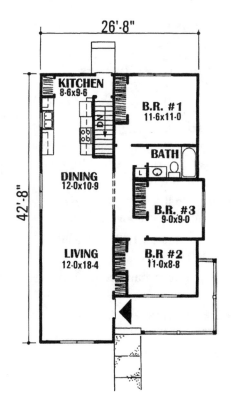

26'-8"

KITCHEN
8-6x9-6

B.R. #1
11-6x11-0

DN

BATH

DINING
12-0x10-9

B.R. #3
9-0x9-0

42'-8"

LIVING
12-0x18-4

B.R #2
11-0x8-8

Perfect For A Narrow Lot

Total Living Area:	1,042 sq. ft.
Blueprint Price Code:	**AA**
Front porch:	120 sq. ft.

FEATURES

- Dining and living areas combine for added space

- Cozy covered front porch

- Plenty of closet space throughout

- 3 bedrooms, 1 bath

- Basement foundation

Plan 574-HDG-97006

Split Foyer Plan Is Always A Favorite

Total Living Area:	**1,496 sq. ft.**
Blueprint Price Code:	**A**
Drive under garage:	709 sq. ft.
Front porch:	26 sq. ft.

FEATURES

- Vaulted living and dining rooms create a spacious feel to the main living areas

- Breakfast area and kitchen combine for convenience

- Large master bath has all the amenities

- Dining area has access onto deck

- 3 bedrooms, 2 baths, 2-car drive under garage

- Slab foundation

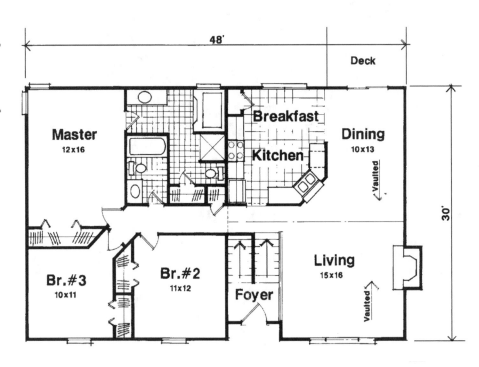

Plan 574-AP-1410

Cottage With Atrium

Total Living Area:	969 sq. ft.
Blueprint Price Code:	AA
Rear entry garage:	245 sq. ft.
Front porch:	94 sq. ft.

FEATURES

- Eye-pleasing facade enjoys stone accents with country porch for quiet evenings

- A bayed dining area, cozy fireplace and atrium with sunny two-story windows are the many features of the living room

- Step-saver kitchen includes a pass-through snack bar

- 325 square feet of optional living area on the lower level

- 2 bedrooms, 1 bath, 1-car rear entry drive under garage

- Walk-out basement foundation

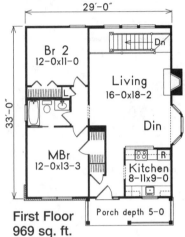

29'-0"

33'-0"

Br 2
12-0x11-0

Living
16-0x18-2

Din

MBr
12-0x13-3

Kitchen
8-11x9-0

First Floor
969 sq. ft.

Porch depth 5-0

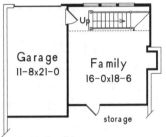

Garage
11-8x21-0

Family
16-0x18-6

storage

Optional Lower Level

Plan 574-0808

Clerestory Windows Enhance Home's Facade

Total Living Area:	1,176 sq. ft.
Blueprint Price Code:	AA

FEATURES

- Efficient kitchen offers plenty of storage, a dining area and a stylish eating bar

- A gathering space is created by the large central living room

- Closet and storage space throughout helps keep sporting equipment organized and easily accessible

- Each end of home is comprised of two bedrooms and full bath

- 4 bedrooms, 2 baths

- Crawl space foundation, drawings also include slab foundation

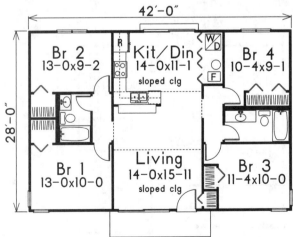

42'-0"

28'-0"

Br 2
13-0x9-2

Kit/Din
14-0x11-1
sloped clg

Br 4
10-4x9-1

Br 1
13-0x10-0

Living
14-0x15-11
sloped clg

Br 3
11-4x10-0

Plan 574-N064

Year-Round Hideaway

Total Living Area:	**416 sq. ft.**
Blueprint Price Code:	**AAA**
Front porch:	156 sq. ft.

FEATURES

- Open floor plan creates spacious feeling
- Covered porch has rustic appeal
- Plenty of cabinetry and work-space in kitchen
- Large linen closet centrally located and close to bath
- Sleeping area, 1 bath
- Slab foundation

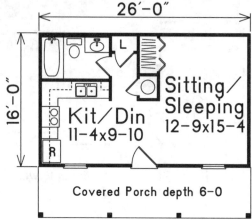

Plan 574-0700

Great Design For Vacation Home Or Year-Round Living

Total Living Area:	**990 sq. ft.**
Blueprint Price Code:	**AA**
Front porch:	161 sq. ft.

FEATURES

- Covered front porch adds charming feel
- Vaulted ceilings in kitchen, family and dining rooms creates a spacious feel
- Large linen, pantry and storage closets throughout
- 2 bedrooms, 1 bath
- Crawl space foundation

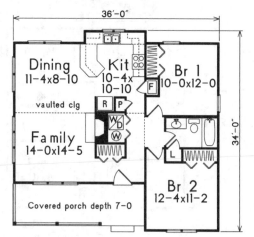

Plan 574-0767

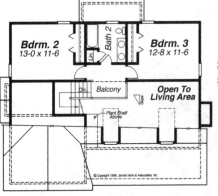

Second Floor
555 sq. ft.

Bdrm. 2
13-0 x 11-6

Bath 2

Bdrm. 3
12-8 x 11-6

Balcony

Open To
Living Area

Plant Shelf
Above

© Copyright 1996, Jannie Vann & Associates, Inc.

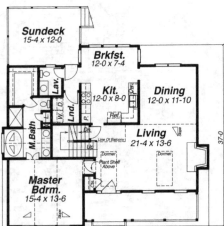

Sundeck
15-4 x 12-0

Brkfst.
12-0 x 7-4

Lav.

Kit.
12-0 x 8-0

Dining
12-0 x 11-10

W.D. Lnd.

Ref.

M.Bath

Line Of Balcony

Living
21-4 x 13-6

Dormer

Plant Shelf
Above

Dormer

Master
Bdrm.
15-4 x 13-6

37-0

43-4

First Floor
1,210 sq. ft.

Country Cottage

Total Living Area:	**1,765 sq. ft.**
Blueprint Price Code:	**B**
Drive under garage:	606 sq. ft.
Front porch:	144 sq. ft.

FEATURES

- Palladian window accenting stone gable adds new look to a popular cottage design

- Dormers open into vaulted area inside

- Kitchen extends to breakfast room with access to sun deck

- 3 bedrooms, 2 1/2 baths, 2-car drive under garage

- Basement foundation

Plan 574-JV-1765-A-SJ

Covered Porches
All Around

Total Living Area:	1,725 sq. ft.
Blueprint Price Code:	B
Side entry garage:	496 sq. ft.
Front porch:	135 sq. ft.

FEATURES

- Spectacular arches when entering foyer

- Dining room has double-doors leading to kitchen

- Unique desk area off kitchen ideal for computer work station

- 3 bedrooms, 2 baths, 2-car side entry garage

- Slab or crawl space foundation, please specify when ordering

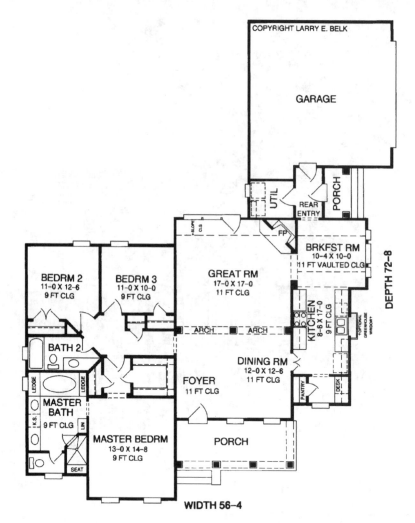

COPYRIGHT LARRY E. BELK

GARAGE

PORCH

UTIL

REAR ENTRY

FP

BRKFST RM
10-4 X 10-0
11 FT VAULTED CLG

DEPTH 72-8

BEDRM 2
11-0 X 12-6
9 FT CLG

BEDRM 3
11-0 X 10-0
9 FT CLG

GREAT RM
17-0 X 17-0
11 FT CLG

KITCHEN
8-6 X 17-0
9 FT CLG

OPTIONAL GREENHOUSE WINDOW

BATH 2

ARCH   ARCH

DINING RM
12-0 X 12-6
11 FT CLG

PANTRY

DESK

LEDGE   LEDGE

MASTER BATH
9 FT CLG

W.K.S.

LIN

FOYER
11 FT CLG

MASTER BEDRM
13-0 X 14-8
9 FT CLG

PORCH

SEAT

WIDTH 56-4

Plan 574-LBD-17-14A

TO ORDER BLUEPRINTS USE THE FORM ON PAGE 256 OR CALL **TOLL-FREE** 1-800-367-7667

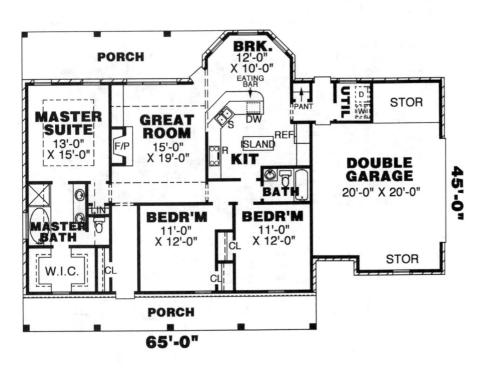

Cozy Home
For Family Living

Total Living Area:	**1,612 sq. ft.**
Blueprint Price Code:	**B**
Side entry garage:	535 sq. ft.
Front porch:	244 sq. ft.

FEATURES

- Covered porch in rear of home creates an outdoor living area

- Master suite is separated from other bedrooms for privacy

- Eating bar in kitchen extends into breakfast area for additional seating

- 3 bedrooms, 2 baths, 2-car side entry garage

- Slab foundation

Plan 574-CHD-15-54

Corner Window Wall Dominates Design

Total Living Area:	**784 sq. ft.**
Blueprint Price Code:	**AAA**

FEATURES

- Outdoor relaxation will be enjoyed with this home's huge wrap-around wood deck

- Upon entering the spacious living area, a cozy free-standing fireplace, sloped ceiling and corner window wall catch the eye

- Charming pullman-style kitchen features pass-through peninsula to dining area

- 3 bedrooms, 1 bath

- Pier foundation

Plan 574-N087

Large Windows Brighten Home Inside And Out

Total Living Area:	**1,260 sq. ft.**
Blueprint Price Code:	**A**

FEATURES

- Living area features enormous stone fireplace and sliding glass doors for accessing deck

- Kitchen/dining area is organized with lots of cabinet and counter space

- Second bedroom is vaulted and has closet space along one entire wall

- 3 bedrooms, 1 bath

- Crawl space foundation

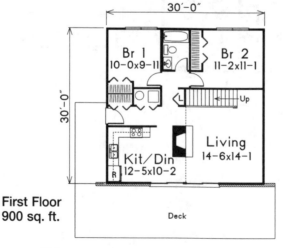

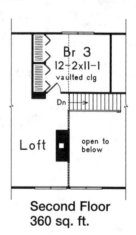

First Floor
900 sq. ft.

Second Floor
360 sq. ft.

Plan 574-N113

Ideal Vacation Style For Views

Total Living Area:	**1,650 sq. ft.**
Blueprint Price Code:	**B**
Front porch:	103 sq. ft.
Back porch:	113 sq. ft.

FEATURES

- Master suite located on second floor for privacy

- Open living space connects to dining area

- Two-story living area features lots of windows for views to the outdoors and a large fireplace

- Efficiently designed kitchen

- 4 bedrooms, 2 baths

- Pier foundation

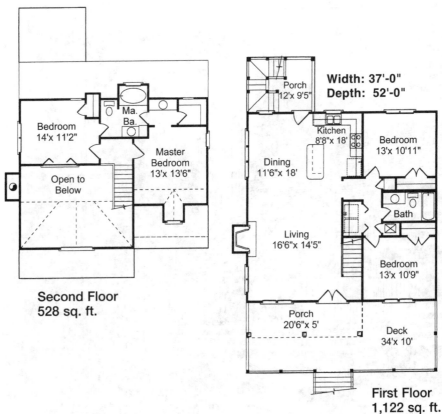

Width: 37'-0"
Depth: 52'-0"

Porch
12'x 9'5"

Kitchen
8'8"x 18'

Dining
11'6"x 18'

Bedroom
13'x 10'11"

Bath

Living
16'6"x 14'5"

Bedroom
13'x 10'9"

Porch
20'6"x 5'

Deck
34'x 10'

First Floor
1,122 sq. ft.

Bedroom
14'x 11'2"

Ma. Ba.

Master Bedroom
13'x 13'6"

Open to Below

Second Floor
528 sq. ft.

Plan 574-CHP-1642-A-10

Skylights Brighten Living Area

Total Living Area: 1,487 sq. ft.
Blueprint Price Code: AA

FEATURES

- Kitchen has pass-through counter with space for dining
- First floor bedroom can easily be converted to a den with spacious walk-in closet and access to deck outdoors
- Second floor bedroom also has a private deck
- 3 bedroom, 1 1/2 baths
- Basement foundation

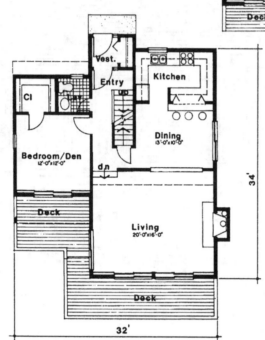

Second Floor
576 sq. ft.

First Floor
911 sq. ft.

Plan 574-GH-26112

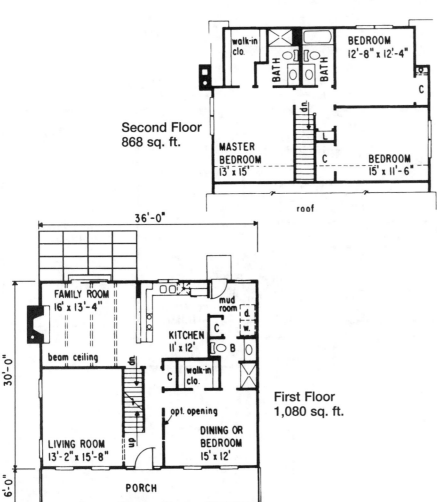

Second Floor
868 sq. ft.

First Floor
1,080 sq. ft.

Well-Designed Home Makes Great Use Of Space

Total Living Area:	**1,948 sq. ft.**
Blueprint Price Code:	**C**
Front porch:	216 sq. ft.

FEATURES

- Family room offers warmth with oversized fireplace and rustic beamed ceiling

- Fully appointed kitchen extends into family room

- Practical mud room adjacent to kitchen

- 3 bedrooms, 2 1/2 baths

- Basement foundation, drawings also include crawl space and slab foundations

Plan 574-1233

Rustic Styling Enhances This Ranch

Total Living Area:	**1,398 sq. ft.**
Blueprint Price Code:	**A**
Garage:	573 sq. ft.
Front porch:	65 sq. ft.

FEATURES

- Country kitchen has vaulted ceiling, spacious eating bar and lots of extra space for dining

- Enormous vaulted great room has cozy fireplace flanked by windows and ceiling beams for an added rustic appeal

- Master suite bath has shower and step-up tub with stained glass ledge and plant niche accents

- 3 bedrooms, 2 baths, 2-car garage

- Slab or crawl space foundation, please specify when ordering

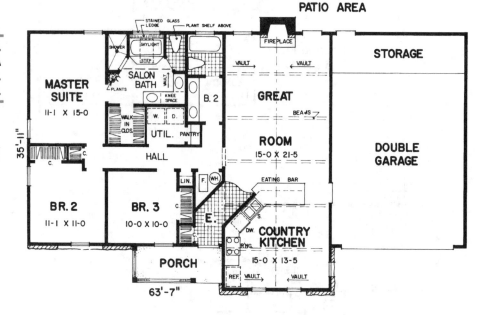

Plan 574-RJ-A1369A

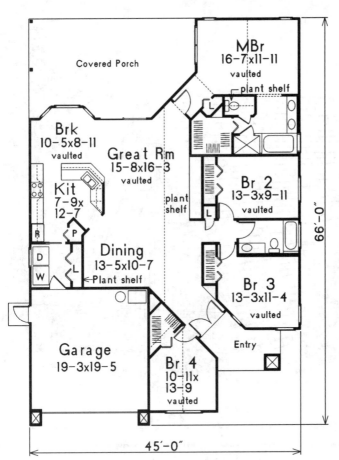

Covered Porch

MBr
16-7x11-11
vaulted

plant shelf

Brk
10-5x8-11
vaulted

Great Rm
15-8x16-3
vaulted

Kit
7-9x
12-7

plant shelf

Br 2
13-3x9-11
vaulted

Dining
13-5x10-7

Plant shelf

Br 3
13-3x11-4
vaulted

Garage
19-3x19-5

Br 4
10-11x
13-9
vaulted

Entry

66'-0"

45'-0"

Wonderful Great Room

Total Living Area:	**1,865 sq. ft.**
Blueprint Price Code:	**D**
Garage:	400 sq. ft.
Rear porch:	400 sq. ft.

FEATURES

- Large foyer opens into expansive dining/great room area

- Home features vaulted ceilings throughout

- Master suite features bath with double-bowl vanity, shower, tub and toilet in separate room for privacy

- 4 bedrooms, 2 baths, 2-car garage

- Slab foundation, drawings also include crawl space foundation

Plan 574-0335

Vacation Retreat With Attractive A-Frame Styling

Total Living Area:	1,312 sq. ft.
Blueprint Price Code:	A
Front porch:	88 sq. ft.

FEATURES

- Expansive deck extends directly off living area
- L-shaped kitchen is organized and efficient
- Bedroom to the left of the kitchen makes a great quiet retreat or office
- Living area flanked with windows for light
- 3 bedrooms, 1 1/2 baths
- Pier foundation

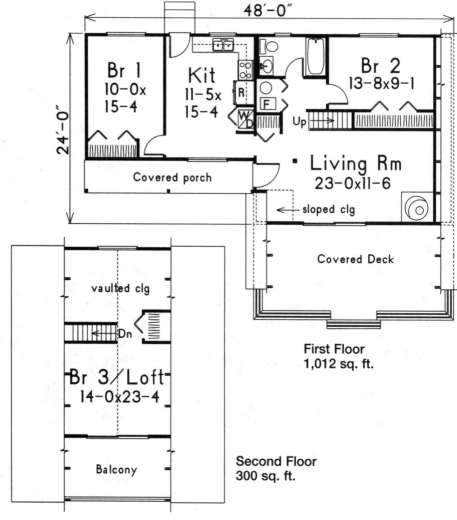

48'-0"

24'-0"

Br 1
10-0x 15-4

Kit
11-5x 15-4

R
W D
F

Br 2
13-8x9-1

Up

Covered porch

Living Rm
23-0x11-6

sloped clg

Covered Deck

First Floor
1,012 sq. ft.

vaulted clg

Dn

Br 3/Loft
14-0x23-4

Balcony

Second Floor
300 sq. ft.

Plan 574-N027

Compact Ranch An Ideal Starter Home

Total Living Area:	**988 sq. ft.**
Blueprint Price Code:	**AA**
Garage:	400 sq. ft.

FEATURES

- Great room features corner fireplace

- Vaulted ceiling and corner windows add space and light in great room

- Eat-in kitchen with vaulted ceiling accesses deck for outdoor living

- Master bedroom features separate vanity and private access to the bath

- 2 bedrooms, 1 bath, 2-car garage

- Basement foundation

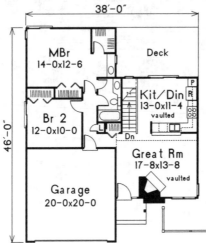

Plan 574-0273

Compact Home With Functional Design

Total Living Area:	**1,396 sq. ft.**
Blueprint Price Code:	**A**
Carport:	264 sq. ft.
Front porch:	56 sq. ft.

FEATURES

- Gabled front adds interest to facade

- Living and dining rooms share a vaulted ceiling

- Master bedroom features a walk-in closet and private bath

- Functional kitchen with a center work island and convenient pantry

- 3 bedrooms, 2 baths, 1-car carport

- Basement foundation, drawings also include crawl space foundation

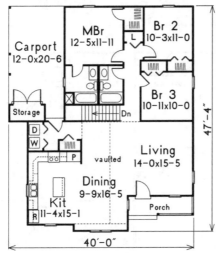

Plan 574-0296

Screened Area Makes A Great Place To Relax

Total Living Area:	1,434 sq. ft.
Blueprint Price Code:	**A**
Garage:	624 sq. ft.
Front porch:	288 sq. ft.

FEATURES

- Private second floor master bedroom features a private bath and a roomy walk-in closet

- A country kitchen with peninsula counter adjoins the living room creating a larger living area

- The living room has a warm fireplace and a volume ceiling

- 3 bedrooms, 2 baths, 2-car garage

- Basement, crawl space or slab foundation, please specify when ordering

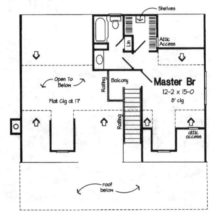

Second Floor
416 sq. ft.

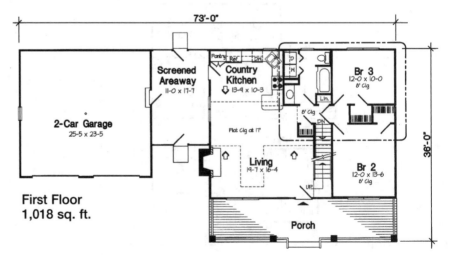

First Floor
1,018 sq. ft.

Plan 574-GH-24711

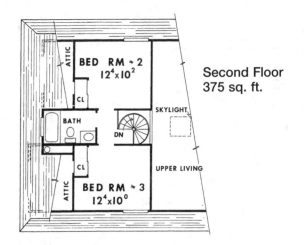

BED RM #2
12⁴ x 10²

ATTIC

CL

BATH

DN

SKYLIGHT

CL

UPPER LIVING

ATTIC

BED RM #3
12⁴ x 10⁰

Second Floor
375 sq. ft.

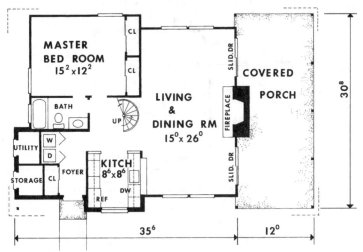

MASTER
BED ROOM
15² x 12²

CL

CL

SLID. DR

COVERED
PORCH

BATH

UP

FIREPLACE

LIVING
&
DINING RM
15⁰ x 26⁰

UTILITY

W

D

KITCH
8⁶ x 8⁶

SLID. DR

STORAGE

CL

FOYER

DW

REF

35⁶

12⁰

30⁸

First Floor
928 sq. ft.

Log Cabin Styling

Total Living Area: 1,303 sq. ft.
Blueprint Price Code: A
Covered porch: 353 sq. ft.

FEATURES

- Huge fireplace surrounded by sliding glass doors provides easy access to covered porch
- Two-story living and dining rooms brightened by skylight and large windows
- 3 bedrooms, 2 baths
- Basement, crawl space or slab foundation, please specify when ordering

Plan 574-AX-7836

Cottage-Style Adds Charm

Total Living Area:	**1,496 sq. ft.**
Blueprint Price Code:	**A**
Side entry garage:	477 sq. ft.
Front porch:	124 sq. ft.

FEATURES

- Large utility room with sink and extra counterspace

- Covered patio off breakfast nook extends dining to the outdoors

- Eating counter in kitchen overlooks vaulted family room

- 3 bedrooms, 2 baths, 2-car side entry garage

- Crawl space foundation

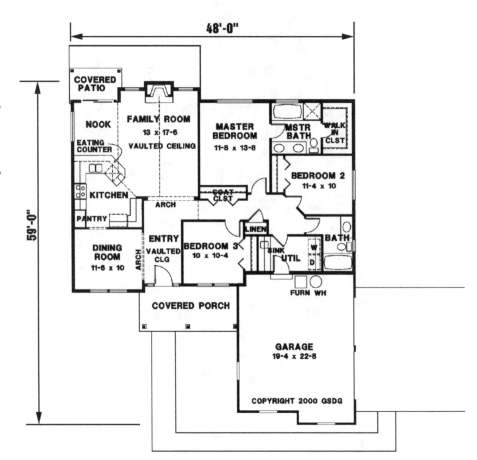

Plan 574-GSD-1748

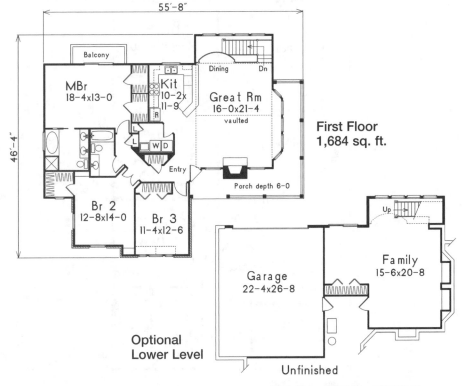

Rear View

55'-8"

46'-4"

Balcony

MBr
18-4x13-0

Kit
10-2x
11-9

Dining

Dn

Great Rm
16-0x21-4
vaulted

First Floor
1,684 sq. ft.

R

L

W D

L

Entry

Porch depth 6-0

Br 2
12-8x14-0

Br 3
11-4x12-6

Optional
Lower Level

Up

Garage
22-4x26-8

Family
15-6x20-8

Unfinished

Plan 574-0739

A Special
Home For Views

Total Living Area:	**1,684 sq. ft.**
Blueprint Price Code:	**B**
Garage:	**596 sq. ft.**
Front porch:	**236 sq. ft.**

FEATURES

- Delightful wrap-around porch anchored by full masonry fireplace

- The vaulted great room includes a large bay window, fireplace, dining balcony and atrium window wall

- His and hers walk-in closets, large luxury bath and sliding doors to exterior balcony are a few fantastic features of the master bedroom

- Atrium open to 611 square feet of optional living area on the lower level

- 3 bedrooms, 2 baths, 2-car drive under garage

- Walk-out basement foundation

Four Bedroom Living For A Narrow Lot

Total Living Area:	**1,452 sq. ft.**
Blueprint Price Code:	**A**
Front porch:	55 sq. ft.

FEATURES

- Large living room features cozy corner fireplace, bayed dining area and access from entry with guest closet

- Forward master bedroom suite enjoys having its own bath and linen closet

- Three additional bedrooms share a bath with double-bowl vanity

- 4 bedrooms, 2 baths

- Basement foundation

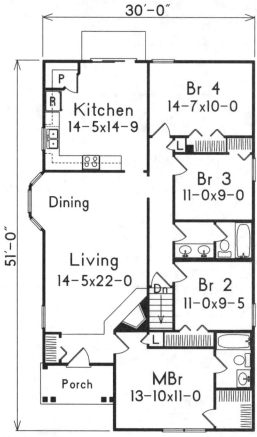

Plan 574-0806

Second Floor
587 sq. ft.

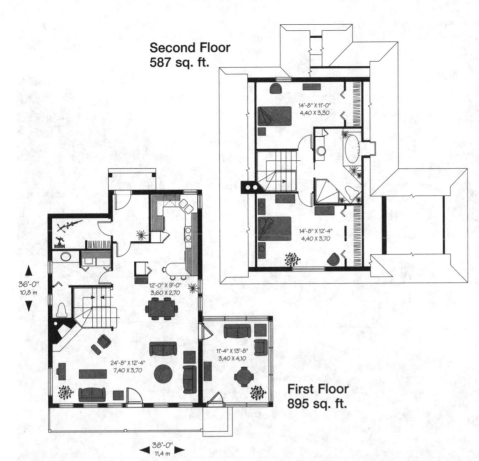

14'-8" X 11'-0"
4,40 X 3,30

14'-8" X 12'-4"
4,40 X 3,70

36'-0"
10,8 m

12'-0" X 9'-0"
3,60 X 2,70

24'-8" X 12'-4"
7,40 X 3,70

11'-4" X 13'-8"
3,40 X 4,10

First Floor
895 sq. ft.

38'-0"
11,4 m

Comfortable Home Has Character

Total Living Area:	**1,482 sq. ft.**
Blueprint Price Code:	**A**
Side porch:	104 sq. ft.
Storage:	48 sq. ft.
Screened porch:	180 sq. ft.

FEATURES

- Energy efficient home with 2" x 6" exterior walls

- Corner fireplace warms living area

- Screened is spacious and connects to other living areas in the home

- Two bedrooms on second floor share a spacious bath

- 2 bedrooms, 1 1/2 baths

- Basement foundation

Plan 574-DR-2940

Terrific Design
Loaded With Extras

Total Living Area: 865 sq. ft.
Blueprint Price Code: AAA

FEATURES

- Central living area provides an enormous amount of space for gathering around the fireplace

- Outdoor ladder on wrap-around deck connects top deck with main deck

- Kitchen is bright and cheerful with lots of windows and access to deck

- 2 bedrooms, 1 bath

- Pier foundation

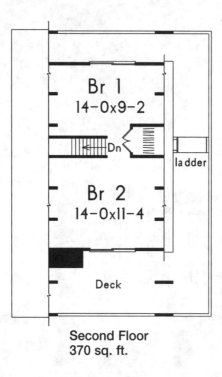

Second Floor
370 sq. ft.

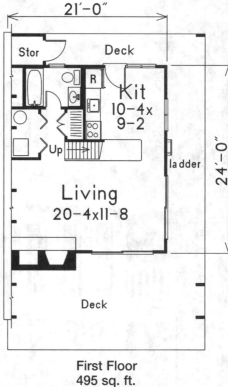

First Floor
495 sq. ft.

Plan 574-N147

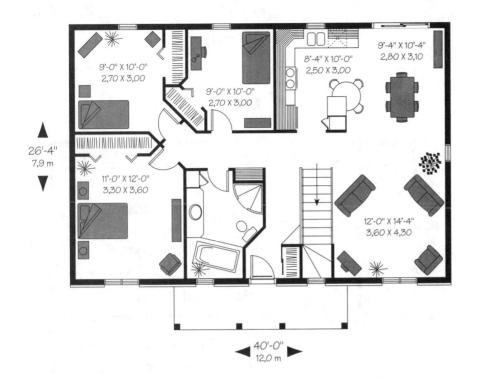

9'-0" X 10'-0"
2,70 X 3,00

9'-0" X 10'-0"
2,70 X 3,00

8'-4" X 10'-0"
2,50 X 3,00

9'-4" X 10'-4"
2,80 X 3,10

26'-4"
7,9 m

11'-0" X 12'-0"
3,30 X 3,60

12'-0" X 14'-4"
3,60 X 4,30

40'-0"
12,0 m

Home Has Cozy Country Feeling

Total Living Area: 1,053 sq. ft.
Blueprint Price Code: AA
Front porch: 78 sq. ft.

FEATURES

- Spacious kitchen and dining room
- Roomy bath includes an over-sized tub
- Entry has a handy coat closet
- 3 bedrooms, 1 bath
- Basement foundation

Plan 574-DR-2115

Sensational Cottage Retreat

Total Living Area:	647 sq. ft.
Blueprint Price Code:	AAA
Front porch:	110 sq. ft.

FEATURES

- Large vaulted room for living/sleeping with plant shelves on each end, stone fireplace and wide glass doors for views

- Roomy kitchen is vaulted and has a bayed dining area and fireplace

- Step down into a sunken and vaulted bath featuring a 6'-0" whirlpool tub-in-a-bay with shelves at each end for storage

- A large palladian window adorns each end of the cottage giving a cheery atmosphere throughout

- 1 living/sleeping room, 1 bath

- Crawl space foundation

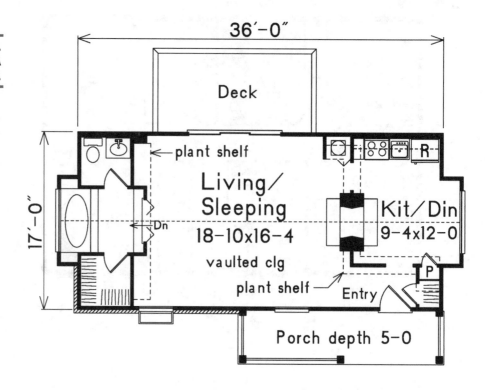

Plan 574-0658

Gables Add
Charm To Facade

Total Living Area: 1,258 sq. ft.
Blueprint Price Code: A

FEATURES

- Energy efficient 2" x 6" exterior walls

- Family and dining rooms share a fireplace for warmth

- Powder room has laundry facilities for convenience

- 2 bedrooms, 2 baths

- Basement foundation

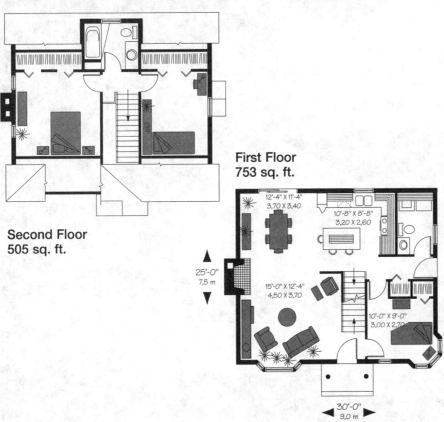

Second Floor
505 sq. ft.

First Floor
753 sq. ft.

12'-4" X 11'-4"
3,70 X 3,40

10'-8" X 8'-8"
3,20 X 2,60

15'-0" X 12'-4"
4,50 X 3,70

10'-0" X 9'-0"
3,00 X 2,70

25'-0"
7,5 m

30'-0"
9,0 m

Plan 574-DR-2540

Functional Layout For Comfortable Living

Total Living Area:	**1,360 sq. ft.**
Blueprint Price Code:	**A**
Garage:	544 sq. ft.
Front porch:	184 sq. ft.

FEATURES

- Kitchen/dining room features island work space and plenty of dining area

- Master bedroom with large walk-in closet and private bath

- Laundry room adjacent to the kitchen for easy access

- Convenient workshop in garage

- Large closets in secondary bedrooms

- 3 bedrooms, 2 baths, 2-car side entry garage

- Basement foundation, drawings also include crawl space and slab foundations

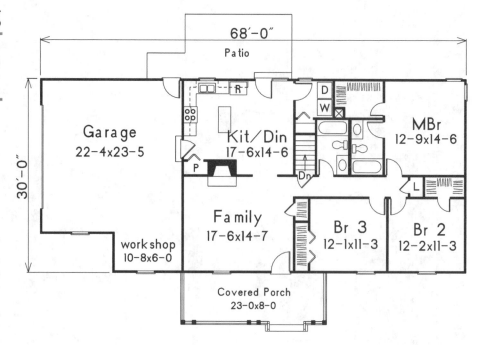

Plan 574-0217

Special Details Makes This Home Unique

Total Living Area: 1,066 sq. ft.
Blueprint Price Code: AA
Front porch: 106 sq. ft.

FEATURES

- Energy efficient home with 2" x 6" exterior walls

- Separate front hall with closet makes an interesting entrance

- Family room has see-through fireplace which it shares with master bedroom

- Dining area has access to out-door balcony/patio

- 2 bedrooms, 1 bath

- Basement foundation

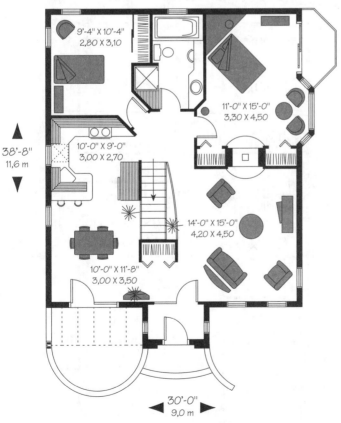

9'-4" X 10'-4"
2,80 X 3,10

11'-0" X 15'-0"
3,30 X 4,50

10'-0" X 9'-0"
3,00 X 2,70

14'-0" X 15'-0"
4,20 X 4,50

10'-0" X 11'-8"
3,00 X 3,50

38'-8"
11,6 m

30'-0"
9,0 m

Plan 574-DR-2162

Three Bedroom Luxury In A Small Home

Total Living Area: 1,161 sq. ft.
Blueprint Price Code: AA
Front porch: 57 sq. ft.

FEATURES

- Brickwork and feature window add elegance to home for a narrow lot

- Living room enjoys a vaulted ceiling, fireplace and opens to kitchen area

- U-shaped kitchen offers a breakfast area with bay window, snack bar and built-in pantry

- 3 bedrooms, 2 baths

- Basement foundation

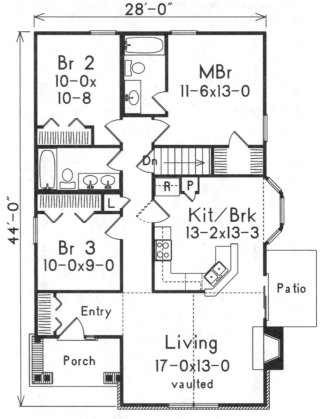

28'-0"

44'-0"

Br 2
10-0x
10-8

MBr
11-6x13-0

Dn

R P

Kit/Brk
13-2x13-3

Br 3
10-0x9-0

Patio

Entry

Living
17-0x13-0
vaulted

Porch

Plan 574-0811

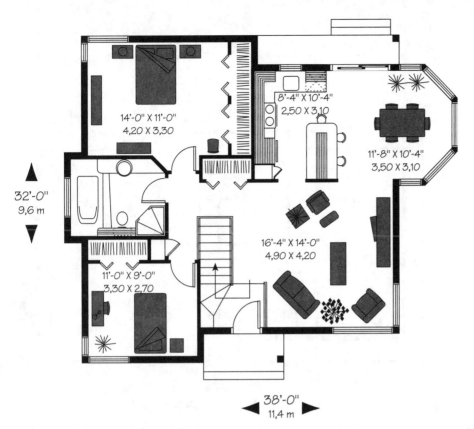

Contemporary Style Is Open And Airy

Total Living Area: 994 sq. ft.
Blueprint Price Code: AA

FEATURES

- Energy efficient home with 2" x 6" exterior walls

- Beautiful and sunny dining area

- Kitchen has center island ideal for food preparation as well as additional dining

- Plenty of closets and storage throughout

- 2 bedrooms, 1 bath

- Basement foundation

14'-0" X 11'-0"
4,20 X 3,30

8'-4" X 10'-4"
2,50 X 3,10

11'-8" X 10'-4"
3,50 X 3,10

32'-0"
9,6 m

16'-4" X 14'-0"
4,90 X 4,20

11'-0" X 9'-0"
3,30 X 2,70

38'-0"
11,4 m

Plan 574-DR-2106

Enchanting Country Cottage

Total Living Area: 1,140 sq. ft.
Blueprint Price Code: AA
Drive under garage: 492 sq. ft.
Front porch: 151 sq. ft.

FEATURES

- Open and spacious living and dining areas for family gatherings
- Well-organized kitchen with an abundance of cabinetry and a built-in pantry
- Roomy master bath features double-bowl vanity
- 3 bedrooms, 2 baths, 2-car drive under garage
- Basement foundation

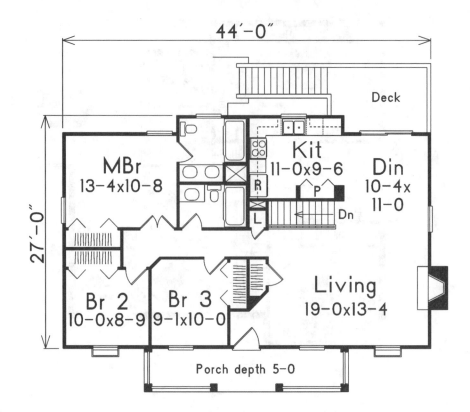

Plan 574-0477

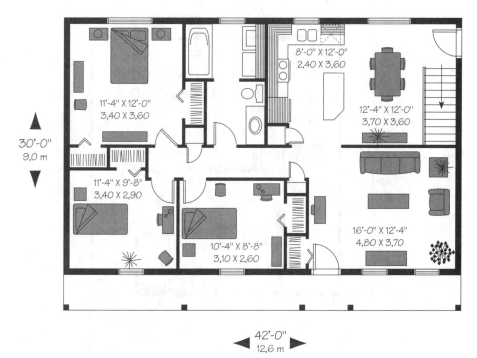

Combined Kitchen
And Dining Room

Total Living Area:	**1,092 sq. ft.**
Blueprint Price Code:	**AA**
Front porch:	168 sq. ft.

FEATURES

- Sunken family room adds interest

- Nice-sized bedrooms all are convenient to bath

- Handy work island in kitchen

- 3 bedrooms, 1 bath

- Basement foundation

Plan 574-DR-1051

A Cottage With Class

Total Living Area:	**576 sq. ft.**
Blueprint Price Code:	**AAA**
Front porch:	**41 sq. ft.**

FEATURES

- Perfect country retreat features vaulted living room and entry with skylights and plant shelf above

- Double-doors enter a vaulted bedroom with bath access

- Kitchen offers generous storage and pass-through breakfast bar

- 1 bedroom, 1 bath

- Crawl space foundation

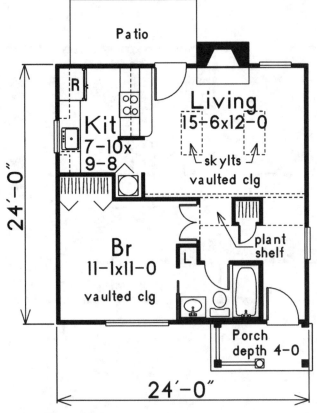

Patio

Kit
7-10x
9-8

Living
15-6x12-0
skylts
vaulted clg

plant
shelf

Br
11-1x11-0

vaulted clg

L

Porch
depth 4-0

24'-0"

24'-0"

Plan 574-0476

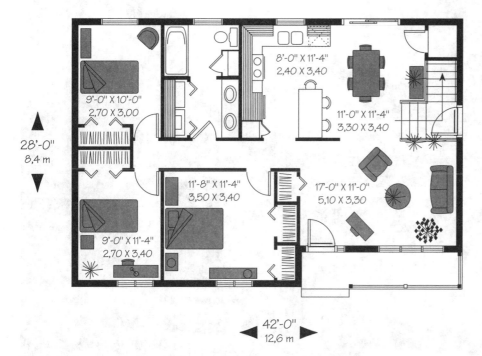

Plenty Of Space
For Family Living

Total Living Area:	**1,106 sq. ft.**
Blueprint Price Code:	**AA**
Front porch:	70 sq. ft.

FEATURES

- Energy efficient home with 2" x 6" exterior walls

- Kitchen has additional counter for dining

- Well-organized bath includes laundry closet

- Dining area has access outdoors through sliding glass doors

- 3 bedrooms, 1 bath

- Basement foundation

Plan 574-DR-2126

Stylish Retreat
For A Narrow Lot

Total Living Area:	**1,084 sq. ft.**
Blueprint Price Code:	**AA**
Front porch:	149 sq. ft.

FEATURES

- Delightful country porch for quiet evenings

- The living room offers a front feature window which invites the sun and includes a fireplace and dining area with private patio

- The U-shaped kitchen features lots of cabinets and bayed breakfast room with built-in pantry

- Both bedrooms have walk-in closets and access to their own bath

- 2 bedrooms, 2 baths

- Basement foundation

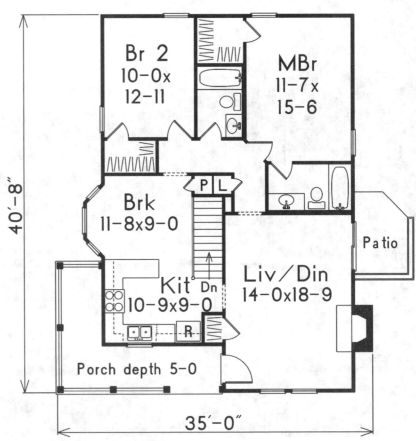

Plan 574-0809

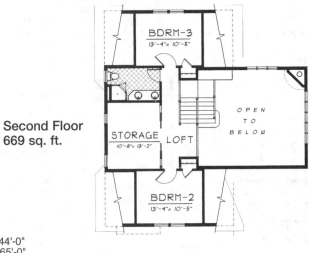

Second Floor
669 sq. ft.

BDRM-3
13'-4"x 10'-5"

STORAGE
10'-8"x 13'-2"

LOFT

OPEN TO BELOW

BDRM-2
13'-4"x 10'-5"

Width: 44'-0"
Depth: 65'-0"

65'-4"

43'-2"

GARAGE
23'-6"x 24'-0"

WALK-IN

MASTER
15'-0"x 12'-11"

BATH

UTILITY MUD ROOM

LIVING RM
18'-2"x 19'-0"

DECK
160 sq. ft.

DINING
12'-6"x 13'-0"

KITCHEN
12'-1"x 10'-0"

PORCH
COVERED

First Floor
1,435 sq. ft.

Truly Unique Design

Total Living Area:	**2,104 sq. ft.**
Blueprint Price Code:	**C**
Garage:	600 sq. ft.
Front porch/Deck:	783 sq. ft.

FEATURES

- 9' ceilings on the first floor

- Living room opens onto deck through double French doors

- Second floor includes large storage room

- 3 bedrooms, 2 baths, 2-car garage

- Crawl space foundation

Plan 574-DDI-100214

Open Ranch Design Gives Expansive Look

Total Living Area:	1,630 sq. ft.
Blueprint Price Code:	B
Garage:	457 sq. ft.
Front porch:	31 sq. ft.

FEATURES

- Crisp facade and full windows front and back offer open viewing

- Wrap-around rear deck is accessible from breakfast room, dining room and master bedroom

- Vaulted ceiling in living room and master bedroom

- Sitting area and large walk-in closet complement master bedroom

- Master bedroom has a private sitting area

- 3 bedrooms, 2 baths, 2-car garage

- Basement foundation

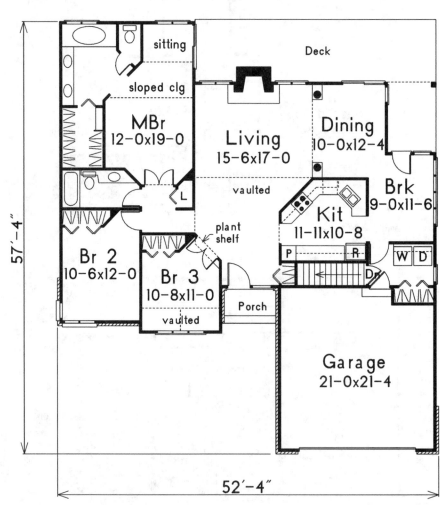

Plan 574-0161

Comfortable One-Story Country Home

Total Living Area:	1,367 sq. ft.
Blueprint Price Code:	A
Garage:	430 sq. ft.
Front porch:	156 sq. ft.

FEATURES

- Neat front porch shelters the entrance

- Dining room has full wall of windows and convenient storage area

- Breakfast area leads to the rear terrace through sliding doors

- Large living room with high ceiling, skylight and fireplace

- 3 bedrooms, 2 baths, 2-car garage

- Basement foundation, drawings also include slab foundation

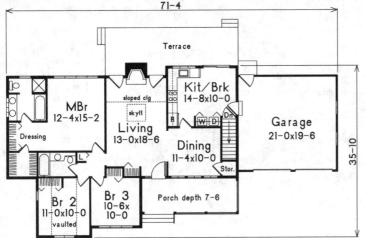

Plan 574-0676

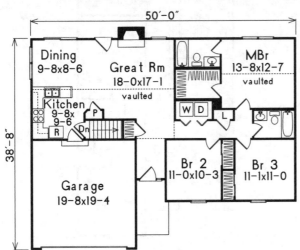

Open Floor Plan Makes Home Feel Larger

Total Living Area:	1,277 sq. ft.
Blueprint Price Code:	A
Garage:	400 sq. ft.

FEATURES

- Vaulted ceilings in master bedroom, great room, kitchen and dining room

- Laundry closet located near bedrooms for convenience

- Compact but efficient kitchen

- 3 bedrooms, 2 baths, 2-car garage

- Basement foundation

Plan 574-0779

Ideal Design
For A Narrow Lot

Total Living Area:	985 sq. ft.
Blueprint Price Code:	AA
Rear entry garage:	367 sq. ft.
Front porch:	181 sq. ft.

FEATURES

- Breakfast room combines with kitchen for a cozy eating space

- Large laundry area tucked at the back of this home near the kitchen for convenience

- Charming covered front entry

- 2 bedrooms, 1 bath, 2-car rear entry garage

- Crawl space or slab foundation, please specify when ordering

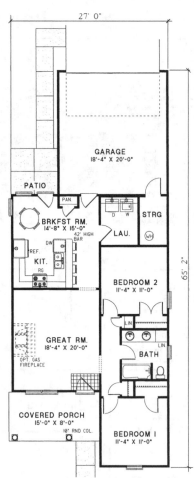

Plan 574-NDG-130

Excellent For Weekend Entertaining

Total Living Area:	924 sq. ft.
Blueprint Price Code:	AA
Front porch:	133 sq. ft.

FEATURES

- Box bay window seats brighten interior while enhancing front facade

- Spacious kitchen with lots of cabinet space and large pantry

- T-shaped covered porch is screened in for added enjoyment

- Plenty of closet space throughout with linen closets in both bedrooms

- 2 bedrooms, 1 bath

- Slab foundation

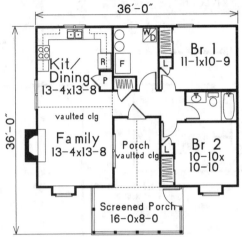

Plan 574-0697

Recessed Stone Entry Provides A Unique Accent

Total Living Area:	717 sq. ft.
Blueprint Price Code:	AAA

FEATURES

- Incline ladder leads up to cozy loft area

- Living room features plenty of windows and vaulted ceiling

- U-shaped kitchen includes a small bay window at the sink

- 1 bedroom, 1 bath

- Slab foundation

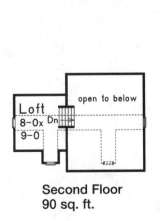

First Floor 627 sq. ft.

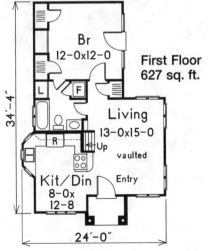

Second Floor 90 sq. ft.

Plan 574-0242

Built-In Computer Desk

Total Living Area:	1,525 sq. ft.
Blueprint Price Code:	B
Garage:	415 sq. ft.
Front porch:	180 sq. ft.

FEATURES

- Corner fireplace highlighted in great room

- Unique glass block window over whirlpool tub in master bath

- Open bar overlooks both the kitchen and great room

- Breakfast room leads to outdoor grilling and covered porch

- 3 bedrooms, 2 baths, 2-car garage

- Crawl space, basement, walk-out basement or slab foundation, please specify when ordering

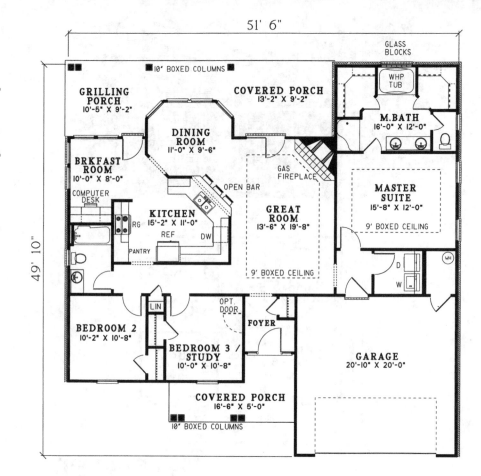

Plan 574-NDG-113-1

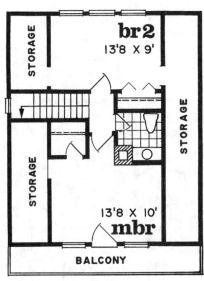

br2
13'8 X 9'

STORAGE

STORAGE

STORAGE

mbr
13'8 X 10'

BALCONY

Second Floor
401 sq. ft.

Width: 24'-0"
Depth: 36'-0"

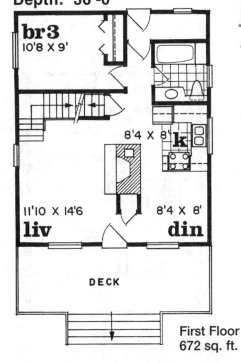

br3
10'8 X 9'

8'4 X 8' **k**

11'10 X 14'6

liv

8'4 X 8'

din

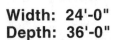

DECK

First Floor
672 sq. ft.

Chalet Cottage

Total Living Area:	1,073 sq. ft.
Blueprint Price Code:	AA
Front porch:	192 sq. ft.

FEATURES

- The front-facing deck and covered balcony add to outdoor living areas

- The fireplace is the main focus in the living room, separating the living room from the dining room

- Three large storage areas are found on the second floor

- 3 bedrooms, 1 1/2 baths

- Basement or crawl space foundation, please specify when ordering

Plan 574-SH-SEA-008

Width: 30'-0"
Depth: 52'-0"

Craftsman Cottage

Total Living Area:	1,649 sq. ft.
Blueprint Price Code:	B
Side entry garage:	401 sq. ft.
Front porch:	210 sq. ft.

FEATURES

- Energy efficient home with 2" x 6" exterior walls

- Ideal design for a narrow lot

- Country kitchen includes an island and eating bar

- Master bedroom has 12' vaulted ceiling and a charming arched window

- 4 bedrooms, 2 1/2 baths, 2-car side entry garage

- Basement or crawl space foundation, please specify when ordering

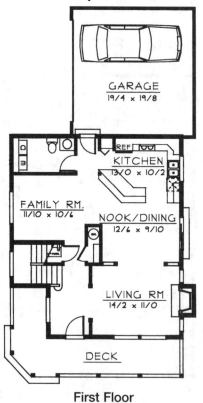

First Floor
858 sq. ft.

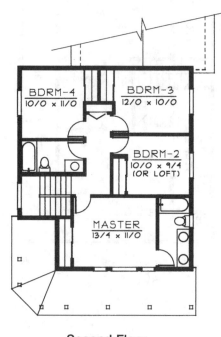

Second Floor
791 sq. ft.

Plan 574-DDI-95-234

TO ORDER BLUEPRINTS USE THE FORM ON PAGE 256 OR CALL **TOLL-FREE 1-800-367-7667**

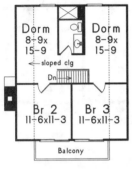

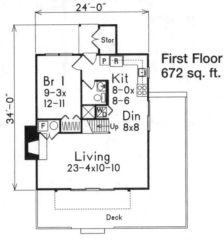

First Floor
672 sq. ft.

Second Floor
672 sq. ft.

Plan 574-N127

Irresistible Cottage Adorns Any Setting

Total Living Area:	**1,344 sq. ft.**
Blueprint Price Code:	**A**

FEATURES

- Beautiful stone fireplace, bracketed balcony and surrounding deck create appealing atmosphere

- Enormous living room, open to dining area, enjoys views to deck through two large sliding doors

- Second floor delivers lots of sleeping area and views from exterior balcony

- 5 bedrooms, 2 baths

- Crawl space foundation, drawings also include slab foundation

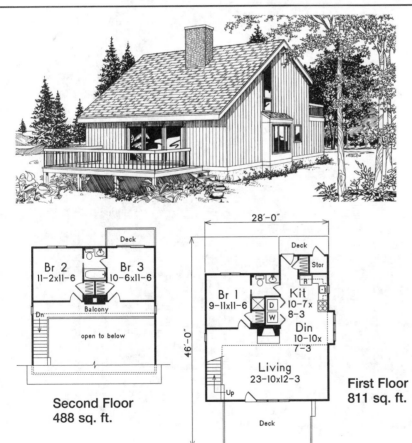

Second Floor
488 sq. ft.

First Floor
811 sq. ft.

Plan 574-N063

Breathtaking Balcony Overlook

Total Living Area:	**1,299 sq. ft.**
Blueprint Price Code:	**A**

FEATURES

- Convenient storage for skis, etc. located outside front entrance

- Kitchen and dining room receive light from box bay window

- Large vaulted living room features cozy fireplace and overlook from second floor balcony

- Two second floor bedrooms share jack and jill bath

- Second floor balcony extends over entire length of living room below

- 3 bedrooms, 2 baths

- Crawl space foundation, drawings also include slab foundation

Formal Country Charm

Total Living Area:	**1,325 sq. ft.**
Blueprint Price Code:	**A**
Drive under garage:	724 sq. ft.
Front porch:	145 sq. ft.

FEATURES

- Sloped ceiling and a fireplace in living area creates a cozy feeling

- Formal dining and breakfast areas have an efficiently designed kitchen between them

- Master bedroom has walk-in closet with luxurious private bath

- 3 bedrooms, 2 baths, 2-car drive under garage

- Basement foundation

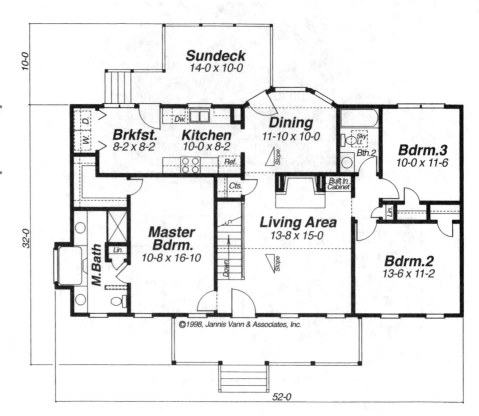

© 1998, Jannis Vann & Associates, Inc.

Plan 574-JV-1325-B

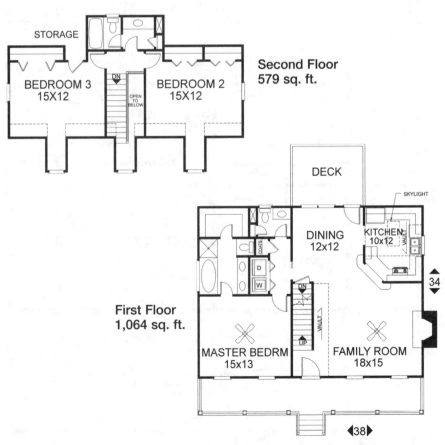

STORAGE

Second Floor
579 sq. ft.

BEDROOM 3
15X12

DN

OPEN TO BELOW

BEDROOM 2
15X12

DECK

SKYLIGHT

DINING
12x12

KITCHEN
10x12

VAULT

First Floor
1,064 sq. ft.

COATS

D

W

DN

VAULT

34

MASTER BEDRM
15x13

UP

VAULT

FAMILY ROOM
18x15

◀38▶

Plan 574-AP-1612

Appealing
Charming Porch

Total Living Area:	1,643 sq. ft.
Blueprint Price Code:	**B**
Drive under garage:	567 sq. ft.
Front porch:	228 sq. ft.

FEATURES

- First floor master bedroom has private bath, walk-in closet and easy access to laundry closet

- Comfortable family room features a vaulted ceiling and a cozy fireplace

- Two bedrooms on the second floor share a bath

- 3 bedrooms, 2 1/2 baths, 2-car drive under garage

- Basement or crawl space foundation, please specify when ordering

Charming Country Cottage

Total Living Area:	**864 sq. ft.**
Blueprint Price Code:	**AAA**
Front porch:	198 sq. ft.

FEATURES

- Large laundry area accesses the outdoors as well as the kitchen

- Front covered porch creates an ideal outdoor living area

- Snack bar in kitchen creates a quick and easy dining area

- 2 bedrooms, 1 bath

- Crawl space or slab foundation, please specify when ordering

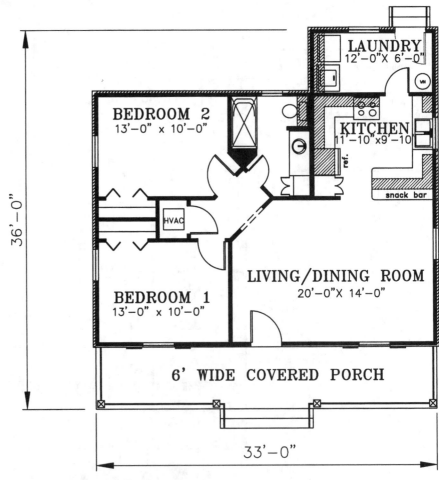

Plan 574-DH-864G

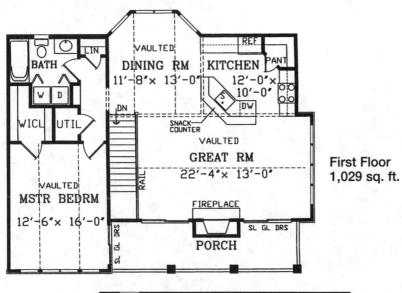

39'-2" OVERALL

30'-0" OVERALL

BATH   LIN

W   D

WICL   UTIL

VAULTED
MSTR BEDRM
12'-6" x 16'-0"

VAULTED
DINING RM
11'-8" x 13'-0"

REF
KITCHEN
12'-0" x
10'-0"

PANT
S
DW

DN

SNACK
COUNTER

VAULTED
GREAT RM
22'-4" x 13'-0"

RAIL

SL GL DRS

FIREPLACE

SL GL DRS

PORCH

First Floor
1,029 sq. ft.

WORK SHOP
16'-2" x 9'-0"

CL

TWO CAR GARAGE
22'-0" x 23'-0"

GARAGE
12'-6" x 20'-0"

UP

COVERED PORCH

Lower Level
159 sq. ft.

Luxurious And Spacious One Bedroom

Total Living Area:	1,029 sq. ft.
Blueprint Price Code:	**AA**
Garage:	781 sq. ft.
Front porch:	145 sq. ft.
Workshop:	159 sq. ft.

FEATURES

- Luxurious amenities provided throughout home including walk-in closet large pantry and spacious work shop
- Vaulted ceilings throughout and spaciousness
- Bath includes utility closet for convenience
- Snack counter in kitchen over-looks into vaulted great room
- 1 bedroom, 1 bath, 3-car garage
- Basement, crawl space or slab foundation, please specify when ordering

Plan 574-AX-98366

Ideal For Entertaining

Total Living Area:	1,870 sq. ft.
Blueprint Price Code:	C
Drive under garage:	649 sq. ft.
Front porch:	240 sq. ft.

FEATURES

• Kitchen is open to the living and dining areas

• Breakfast area has cathedral ceiling creating a sunroom effect

• Master suite is spacious with all the amenities

• Second floor bedrooms share hall bath

• 3 bedrooms, 2 1/2 baths, 2-car drive under garage

• Basement foundation

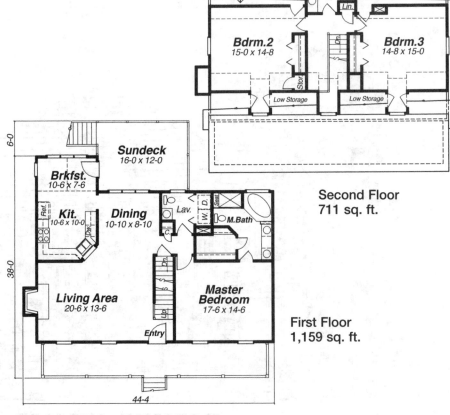

Second Floor
711 sq. ft.

First Floor
1,159 sq. ft.

Plan 574-JV-1870-A

Quaint Victorian Home

Total Living Area:	972 sq. ft.
Blueprint Price Code:	AA

FEATURES

- Energy efficient home with 2" x 6" exterior walls

- Spacious dining area overlooks into kitchen

- Two bedrooms separated by a large shared bath

- Convenient laundry closet

- Cheerful bay window in living area

- 2 bedrooms, 1 bath

- Basement foundation

10'-8" X 9'-0"
3,20 X 2,70

9'-0" X 10'-0"
2,70 X 3,00

9'-0" X 13'-8"
2,70 X 4,10

35'-0"
10,5 m

11'-0" X 13'-0"
3,30 X 3,90

12'-0" X 20'-0"
3,60 X 6,00

30'-0"
9,0 m

Plan 574-DR-2109

Country Feel With All The Comforts

Total Living Area:	1,103 sq. ft.
Blueprint Price Code:	AA
Garage:	244 sq. ft.

FEATURES

- Energy efficient home with 2" x 6" exterior walls

- All bedrooms in one area of the house for privacy

- Bay window enhances dining area

- Living and dining areas combine for a spacious feeling

- Lots of storage throughout

- 2 bedrooms, 1 bath, 1-car garage

- Basement foundation

10'-0" X 12'-8"
3,00 X 3,80

12'-4" X 13'-0"
2,70 X 3,90

12'-0" X 10'-0"
3,60 X 3,00

11'-4" X 10'-0"
3,40 X 3,00

48'-0"
14,4 m

12'-0" X 20'-4"
3,60 X 6,10

13'-0" X 14'-4"
3,90 X 4,30

30'-8"
9,2 m

Plan 574-DR-2250

Cottage Retreat

Total Living Area:	**960 sq. ft.**
Blueprint Price Code:	**AA**

FEATURES

- Cozy, yet open floor plan is perfect for a vacation getaway or a guest house

- Spacious kitchen features peninsula cooktop with breakfast bar that overlooks the large living room

- Bath is complete with laundry facilities

- Front deck is ideal for enjoying views or outdoor entertaining

- 2 bedrooms, 1 bath

- Crawl space foundation

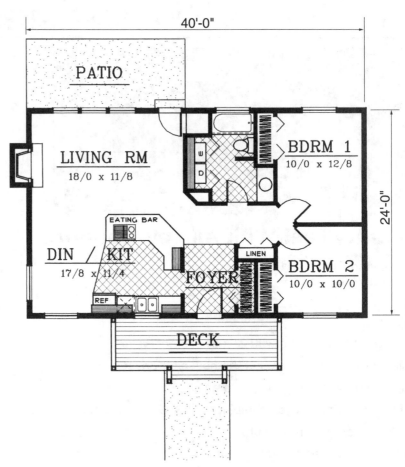

Plan 574-DDI-92103

Quaint Country Home Is Ideal

Total Living Area:	**1,028 sq. ft.**
Blueprint Price Code:	**AA**
Front porch:	105 sq. ft.
Rear porch:	25 sq. ft.

FEATURES

- Master bedroom conveniently located on first floor

- Well-designed bath contains laundry facilities

- L-shaped kitchen has a handy pantry

- Tall windows flank family room fireplace

- Cozy covered porch provides unique angled entry into home

- 3 bedrooms, 1 bath

- Crawl space foundation

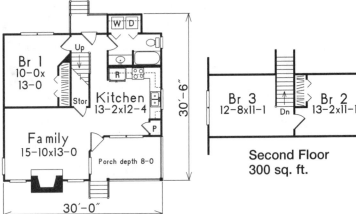

First Floor
728 sq. ft.

Br 1
10-0x13-0

Kitchen
13-2x12-4

Family
15-10x13-0

Porch depth 8-0

30'-6"

30'-0"

Second Floor
300 sq. ft.

Br 3
12-8x11-1

Br 2
13-2x11-1

Plan 574-0462

Designed For Comfort And Utility

Total Living Area:	**720 sq. ft.**
Blueprint Price Code:	**AAA**
Front porch:	288 sq. ft.

FEATURES

- Abundant windows in living and dining rooms provide generous sunlight

- Secluded laundry area with handy storage closet

- U-shaped kitchen with large breakfast bar opens into living area

- Large covered deck offers plenty of outdoor living space

- 2 bedrooms, 1 bath

- Crawl space foundation, drawings also include slab foundation

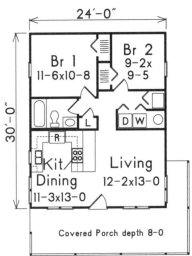

24'-0"

30'-0"

Br 1
11-6x10-8

Br 2
9-2x9-5

Kit
Dining
11-3x13-0

Living
12-2x13-0

Covered Porch depth 8-0

Plan 574-0547

Wrap-Around Country Porch

Total Living Area:	1,875 sq. ft.
Blueprint Price Code:	C
Side entry garage:	576 sq. ft.
Front porch:	408 sq. ft.

FEATURES

- Country-style exterior with wrap-around porch and dormers

- Large second floor bedrooms share a dressing area and bath

- Master bedroom suite includes bay window, walk-in closet, dressing area and bath

- 3 bedrooms, 2 baths, 2-car side entry garage

- Crawl space foundation, drawings also include basement and slab foundations

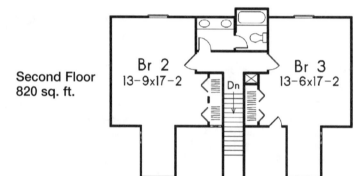

Second Floor
820 sq. ft.

Br 2
13-9x17-2

Dn

Br 3
13-6x17-2

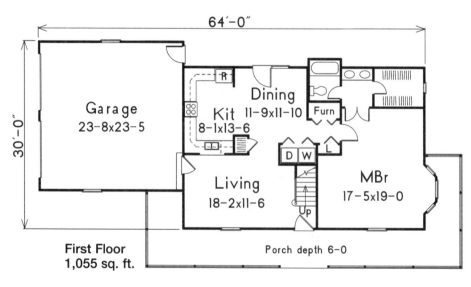

64'-0"

30'-0"

Garage
23-8x23-5

Dining
11-9x11-10

Kit
8-1x13-6

Furn

Living
18-2x11-6

D W L

Up

MBr
17-5x19-0

First Floor
1,055 sq. ft.

Porch depth 6-0

Plan 574-0523

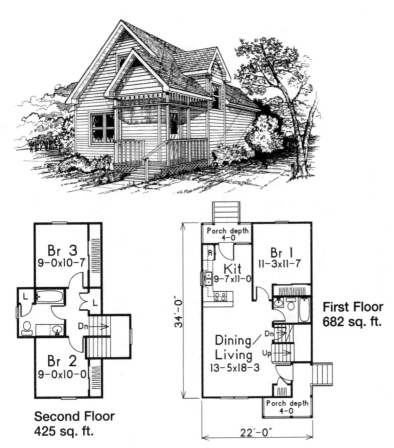

Charming Home With Cozy Porches

Total Living Area:	1,107 sq. ft.
Blueprint Price Code:	AA
Front porch:	67 sq. ft.

FEATURES

- L-shaped kitchen has serving bar overlooking the dining/living room
- Second floor bedrooms share a bath with linen closet
- Front porch opens into foyer with convenient coat closet
- 3 bedrooms, 2 baths
- Basement foundation

Br 3
9-0x10-7

Br 2
9-0x10-0

Second Floor
425 sq. ft.

Porch depth 4-0

Kit
9-7x11-0

Br 1
11-3x11-7

34'-0"

First Floor
682 sq. ft.

Dining / Living
13-5x18-3

Porch depth 4-0

22'-0"

Plan 574-0497

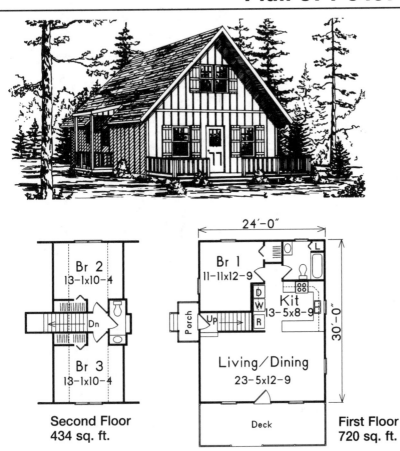

Open Living Area

Total Living Area:	1,154 sq. ft.
Blueprint Price Code:	AA

FEATURES

- U-shaped kitchen with large breakfast bar and handy laundry area
- Private second floor bedrooms share half bath
- Large living/dining area opens to deck
- 3 bedrooms, 1 1/2 baths
- Crawl space foundation, drawings also include slab foundation

Br 2
13-1x10-4

Br 3
13-1x10-4

Second Floor
434 sq. ft.

24'-0"

Br 1
11-11x12-9

Kit
13-5x8-9

Porch

30'-0"

Living/Dining
23-5x12-9

Deck

First Floor
720 sq. ft.

Plan 574-0548

Breezeway Joins Living Space With Garage

Total Living Area:	1,874 sq. ft.
Blueprint Price Code:	C
Garage:	528 sq. ft.
Front porch:	331 sq. ft.

FEATURES

- 9' ceilings throughout first floor

- Two-story foyer opens into large family room with fireplace

- First floor master suite includes private bath with tub and shower

- 4 bedrooms, 2 1/2 baths, 2-car garage

- Basement foundation, drawings also include slab foundation

Second Floor
633 sq. ft.

Br 2
11-0x10-7

Br 3
11-4x11-0

Br 4
11-4x11-0

Dn

open to foyer

plant shelf

73'-4"

38'-6"

Garage
21-4x23-4

Dining
13-4x10-0

Kitchen
13-4x10-0

Family
13-4x18-2

MBr
13-4x15-0

Dn

Up

Foyer

plant shelf

Porch
41-4x8-0

First Floor
1,241 sq. ft.

Plan 574-0362

High Ceilings Create A Feeling Of Luxury

Total Living Area:	1,707 sq. ft.
Blueprint Price Code:	C
Garage:	572 sq. ft.
Front porch:	29 sq. ft.

FEATURES

- The formal living room off the entry hall has a high sloping ceiling and prominent fireplace

- Kitchen and breakfast area allow access to garage and rear porch

- Oversized garage provides direct access to the kitchen

- Master bedroom has impressive vaulted ceiling, luxurious master bath, large walk-in closet and separate tub and shower

- Utility room conveniently located near bedrooms

- 3 bedrooms, 2 baths, 2-car garage

- Slab foundation

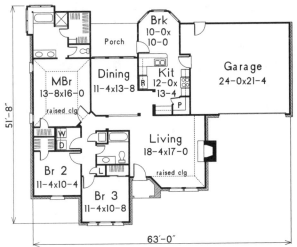

Plan 574-0212

Economical Ranch For Easy Living

Total Living Area:	1,314 sq. ft.
Blueprint Price Code:	A
Garage:	462 sq. ft.
Front porch:	126 sq. ft.

FEATURES

- Energy efficient home with 2" x 6" exterior walls

- Covered porch adds immediate appeal and welcoming charm

- Open floor plan combined with vaulted ceiling offers spacious living

- Functional kitchen complete with pantry and eating bar

- Cozy fireplace in the living room

- Private master bedroom features a large walk-in closet and bath

- 3 bedrooms, 2 baths, 2-car garage

- Basement foundation

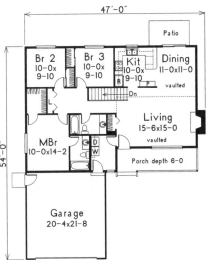

Plan 574-0265

Country Kitchen Center Of Living Activities

Total Living Area:	**1,556 sq. ft.**
Blueprint Price Code:	**B**
Garage:	439 sq. ft.
Front porch:	44 sq. ft.

FEATURES

- A compact home with all the amenities

- Country kitchen combines practicality with access to other areas for eating and entertaining

- Two-way fireplace joins the dining and living areas

- Plant shelf and vaulted ceiling highlight the master bedroom

- 3 bedrooms, 2 1/2 baths, 2-car garage

- Basement foundation

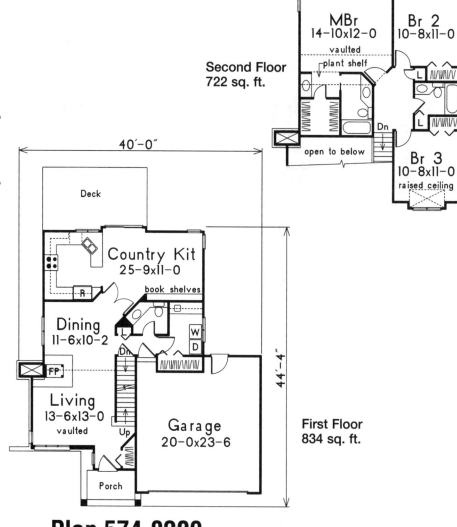

Second Floor 722 sq. ft.

MBr 14-10x12-0 vaulted
plant shelf
open to below

Br 2 10-8x11-0

Dn

Br 3 10-8x11-0 raised ceiling

40'-0"

Deck

Country Kit 25-9x11-0
book shelves

R

W D

Dining 11-6x10-2

Dn

FP

Living 13-6x13-0 vaulted

Up

Garage 20-0x23-6

44'-4"

First Floor 834 sq. ft.

Porch

Plan 574-0209

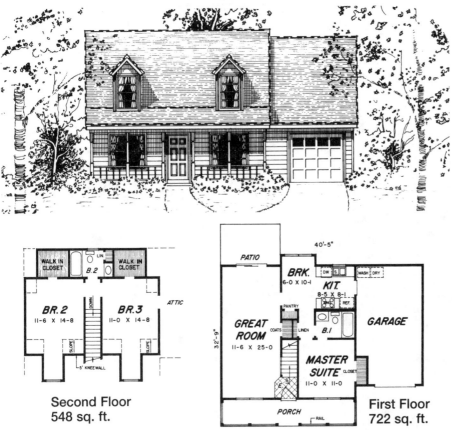

Lovely Front Dormers

Total Living Area:	1,270 sq. ft.
Blueprint Price Code:	A
Garage:	298 sq. ft.
Front porch:	135 sq. ft.

FEATURES

- Convenient master suite on first floor

- Two secondary bedrooms on second floor each have a large walk-in closet and share a full bath

- Sunny breakfast room has lots of sunlight and easy access to great room and kitchen

- 3 bedrooms, 2 baths, 1-car garage

- Slab or crawl space foundation, please specify when ordering

Second Floor 548 sq. ft.

First Floor 722 sq. ft.

Plan 574-RJ-B123

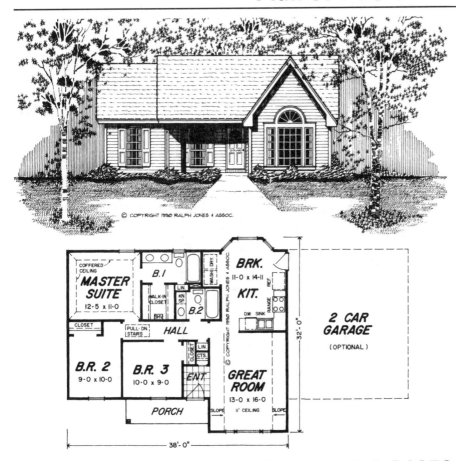

Arched Window Is A Focal Point

Total Living Area:	1,021 sq. ft.
Blueprint Price Code:	AA
Optional garage:	502 sq. ft.
Front porch:	56 sq. ft.

FEATURES

- 11' ceiling in great room expands living area

- Combination kitchen/breakfast room allows for easy preparation and cleanup

- Master suite features private bath and oversized walk-in closet

- 3 bedrooms, 2 baths, optional 2-car garage

- Slab or crawl space foundation, please specify when ordering

Plan 574-RJ-A1079

Quaint Porch
Adds Charm

Total Living Area: 1,735 sq. ft.
Blueprint Price Code: B
Side entry garage: 515 sq. ft.
Front porch: 192 sq. ft.

FEATURES

- Angled kitchen wall expands space into the dining room

- Second floor has cozy sitting area with cheerful window

- Two spacious bedrooms on second floor share a bath

- 3 bedrooms, 2 1/2 baths, 2-car drive under garage

- Basement foundation

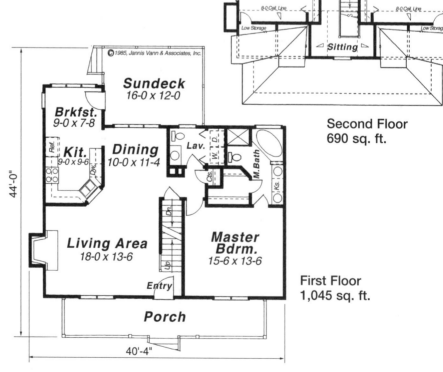

Second Floor
690 sq. ft.

First Floor
1,045 sq. ft.

Plan 574-JV-1735A

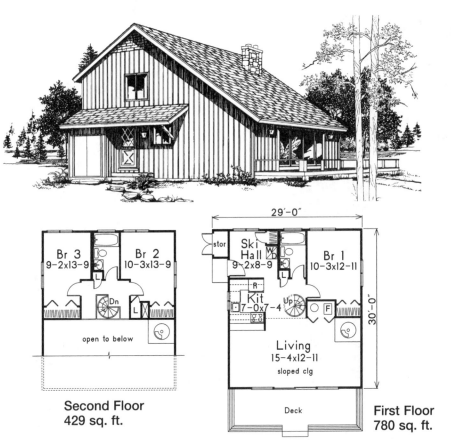

Mountain Retreat

Total Living Area: 1,209 sq. ft.
Blueprint Price Code: A

FEATURES

- Bracketed shed roof and ski storage add charm to vacation home
- Living and dining rooms enjoy a sloped ceiling, second floor balcony overlook and view to large deck
- Kitchen features snack bar and access to second floor via circular stair
- Second floor includes two bedrooms with sizable closets, center hall bath and balcony overlooking rooms below
- 3 bedrooms, 2 baths
- Crawl space foundation

Second Floor
429 sq. ft.

First Floor
780 sq. ft.

Plan 574-N006

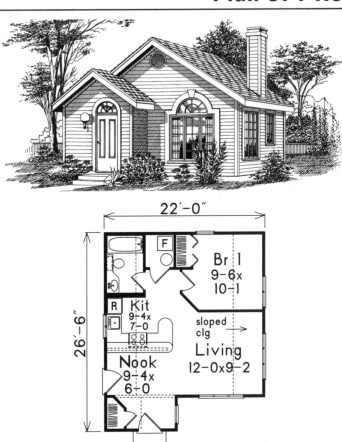

Graciously Designed Refuge

Total Living Area: 527 sq. ft.
Blueprint Price Code: AAA

FEATURES

- Cleverly arranged home has it all
- Foyer spills into the dining nook with access to side views
- An excellent kitchen offers a long breakfast bar and borders the living room with free-standing fireplace
- A cozy bedroom has a full bath just across the hall
- 1 bedroom, 1 bath
- Crawl space foundation

Plan 574-N118

Large Bay Graces Dining And Master Bedroom

Total Living Area:	**1,818 sq. ft.**
Blueprint Price Code:	**C**
Carport:	259 sq. ft.
Front porch:	132 sq. ft.

FEATURES

- Spacious living and dining rooms

- Master bedroom features large bay, walk-in closet, dressing area and bath

- Convenient carport and storage area

- 3 bedrooms, 2 1/2 baths, 1-car carport

- Crawl space foundation, drawings also include basement and slab foundations

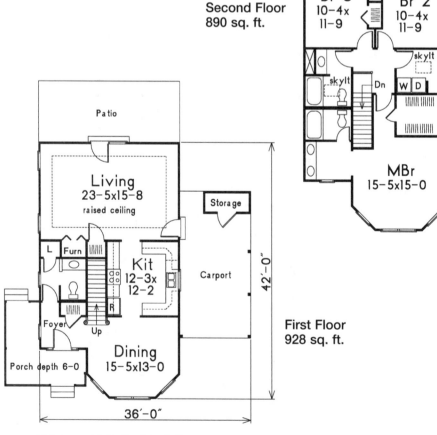

Second Floor 890 sq. ft.

Br 3 10-4x 11-9

Br 2 10-4x 11-9

skylt

skylt

Dn

W D

MBr 15-5x15-0

Patio

Living 23-5x15-8 raised ceiling

L Furn

Kit 12-3x 12-2

Storage

Carport

Foyer

Up

Dining 15-5x13-0

Porch depth 6-0

42'-0"

First Floor 928 sq. ft.

36'-0"

Plan 574-0522

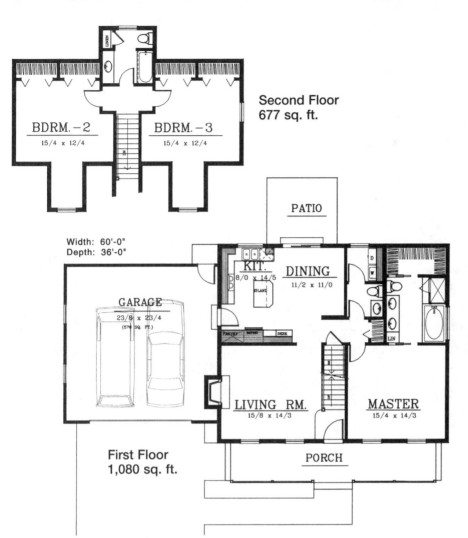

Second Floor
677 sq. ft.

BDRM.–2
15/4 x 12/4

BDRM.–3
15/4 x 12/4

Width: 60'-0"
Depth: 36'-0"

PATIO

KIT.
8/0 x 14/5

DINING
11/2 x 11/0

GARAGE
23/8 x 23/4
(576 SQ. FT.)

LIVING RM.
15/8 x 14/3

MASTER
15/4 x 14/3

First Floor
1,080 sq. ft.

PORCH

Inviting Country Home

Total Living Area:	**1,757 sq. ft.**
Blueprint Price Code:	**B**
Garage:	576 sq. ft.
Front porch:	192 sq. ft.

FEATURES

- Energy efficient home with 2" x 6" exterior walls

- First floor master bedroom has privacy as well as its own bath and walk-in closet

- Cozy living room includes fireplace for warmth

- 3 bedrooms, 2 1/2 baths, 2-car garage

- Crawl space or slab foundation, please specify when ordering

Plan 574-DDI-100-215

Unique
A-Frame Detailing
Has Appeal

Total Living Area: 1,272 sq. ft.
Blueprint Price Code: A

FEATURES

- Stone fireplace accents living room

- Spacious kitchen includes snack bar overlooking living room

- First floor bedroom roomy and secluded

- Plenty of closet space for second floor bedrooms plus a generous balcony which wraps around second floor

- 3 bedrooms, 1 1/2 baths

- Crawl space foundation

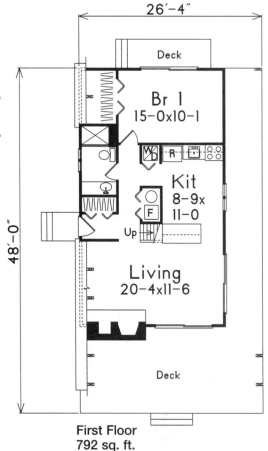

26'-4"

Deck

Br 1
15-0x10-1

W D   R

Kit
8-9x
11-0

F

Up

Living
20-4x11-6

48'-0"

Deck

First Floor
792 sq. ft.

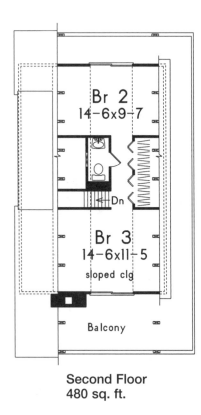

Br 2
14-6x9-7

Dn

Br 3
14-6x11-5
sloped clg

Balcony

Second Floor
480 sq. ft.

Plan 574-N048

Terrific Use Of Space

Total Living Area:	**1,436 sq. ft.**
Blueprint Price Code:	**A**
Garage:	498 sq. ft.
Front porch:	145 sq. ft.

FEATURES

- Corner fireplace in great room warms home

- Kitchen and breakfast room combine for convenience

- Centrally located utility room

- 3 bedrooms, 2 baths, 2-car garage

- Slab foundation

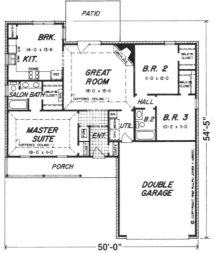

Plan 574-RJ-A1485

Traditional Ranch Styling

Total Living Area:	**1,167 sq. ft.**
Blueprint Price Code:	**AA**
Garage:	473 sq. ft.
Front porch:	76 sq. ft.

FEATURES

- Master suite with private bath

- Handy coat closet in foyer

- Lots of storage space throughout

- 3 bedrooms, 2 baths, 2-car garage

- Slab foundation

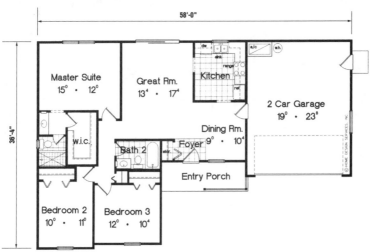

Plan 574-HDS-1167

Bayed
Breakfast Nook

Total Living Area:	**1,442 sq. ft.**
Blueprint Price Code:	**A**
Carport:	437 sq. ft.
Front porch:	164 sq. ft.

FEATURES

- Utility room includes counter-space and closet

- Kitchen has useful center island with double-vanity and workspace

- Vaulted master bedroom has unique double-door entry, private bath and walk-in closet

- 3 bedrooms, 2 baths, 2-car carport

- Slab foundation

2 Car Port

Utility

Storage

Nook

Kitchen

Bedroom 2
12⁰ · 11⁴

Bath

Bedroom 3
10⁰ · 11⁴

Master
Bath

Family
22⁰ · 15⁸

Master
Bedroom
17⁴ · 12⁰

W.I.C.

Foyer

Covered Porch

Entry

Width: 51'-0"
Depth: 70'-8"

Plan 574-HDS-1442-2

©Alan Mascord Design Associates, Inc.

Second Floor
670 sq. ft.

©Alan Mascord Design Associates, Inc.

First Floor
731 sq. ft.

Charming
Two-Story Design

Total Living Area:	**1,401 sq. ft.**
Blueprint Price Code:	**A**
Garage:	276 sq. ft.
Front porch:	85 sq. ft.

FEATURES

- 9' ceilings on first floor

- Energy efficient home with 2"x 6" exterior walls

- Conveniently located laundry area on second floor

- 3 bedrooms, 1 1/2 baths, 1-car garage

- Crawl space foundation

Plan 574-AMD-2188

Formal And Informal Gathering Rooms

Total Living Area:	1,314 sq. ft.
Blueprint Price Code:	**A**
Garage:	413 sq. ft.
Front porch:	130 sq. ft.

FEATURES

- U-shaped kitchen joins cozy dining area
- Family room has direct access into garage
- Roomy closets serve the second floor bedrooms
- 3 bedrooms, 1 1/2 baths, 2-car garage
- Basement foundation, drawings also include crawl space foundation

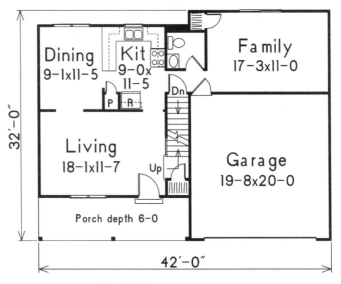

Second Floor
552 sq. ft.

First Floor
762 sq. ft.

Br 2 13-1x10-1

MBr 11-2x12-7

Br 3 9-10x9-3

Dining 9-1x11-5

Kit 9-0x 11-5

Family 17-3x11-0

Living 18-1x11-7

Garage 19-8x20-0

Porch depth 6-0

32'-0"

42'-0"

Plan 574-0196

Designed For Seclusion

Total Living Area:	**624 sq. ft.**
Blueprint Price Code:	**AAA**

FEATURES

- Combine stone, vertical siding, and lots of glass; add low roof line and you have a cozy retreat

- Vaulted living area features free-standing fireplace that heats adjacent stone wall for warmth

- Efficient kitchen includes dining area and view to angular deck

- Two bedrooms share a hall bath with shower

- 2 bedrooms, 1 bath

- Pier foundation

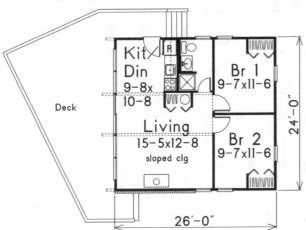

Plan 574-N010

Contemporary Elegance With Efficiency

Total Living Area:	**1,321 sq. ft.**
Blueprint Price Code:	**A**
Rear entry garage:	280 sq. ft.
Front porch:	32 sq. ft.

FEATURES

- Rear garage and elongated brick wall adds to appealing facade

- Dramatic vaulted living room includes corner fireplace and towering feature windows

- Kitchen/breakfast room is immersed in light from two large windows and glass sliding doors

- 3 bedrooms, 2 baths, 1-car rear entry garage

- Basement foundation

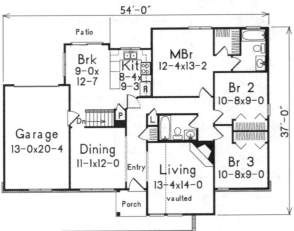

Plan 574-0660

Gable Roof And Large Porch Create A Cozy Feel

Total Living Area:	1,375 sq. ft.
Blueprint Price Code:	A
Carport:	430 sq. ft.
Storage:	95 sq. ft.
Front porch:	102 sq. ft.

FEATURES

- Master bedroom has private bath and walk-in closet
- Kitchen and dining room located conveniently near utility and living rooms
- Cathedral ceiling in living room adds spaciousness
- 3 bedrooms, 2 baths, 2-car carport
- Slab foundation

Plan 574-BF-1314

Inviting Covered Verandas

Total Living Area:	1,830 sq. ft.
Blueprint Price Code:	C
Side entry garage:	772 sq. ft.
Front porch:	409 sq. ft.
Rear covered patio:	250 sq. ft.

FEATURES

- Inviting covered verandas in the front and rear of the home
- Great room has fireplace and cathedral ceiling
- Handy service porch allows easy access
- Master suite has vaulted ceiling and private bath
- 3 bedrooms, 2 baths, 3-car side entry garage
- Basement, crawl space or slab foundation, please specify when ordering

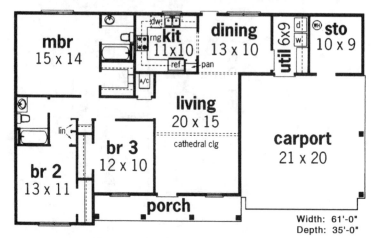

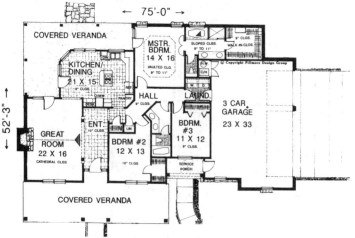

Plan 574-FDG-7963-L

Vaulted Ceiling Frames Circle-Top Window

Total Living Area:	**1,195 sq. ft.**
Blueprint Price Code:	**AA**
Garage:	447 sq. ft.
Front porch:	25 sq. ft.

FEATURES

- Kitchen/dining room opens onto the patio
- Master bedroom features vaulted ceiling, private bath and walk-in closet
- Coat closets located by both the entrances
- Convenient secondary entrance at the back of the garage
- 3 bedrooms, 2 baths, 2-car garage
- Basement foundation

Plan 574-0485

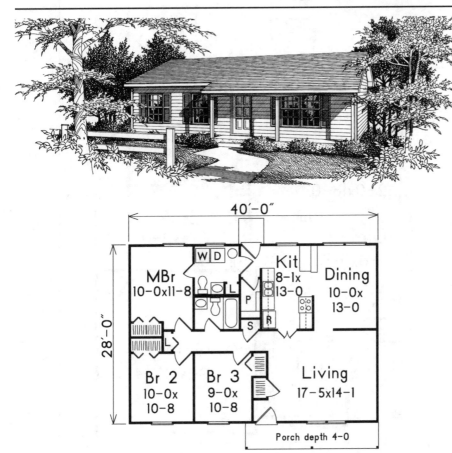

Convenient Ranch

Total Living Area:	**1,120 sq. ft.**
Blueprint Price Code:	**AA**
Front porch:	85 sq. ft.

FEATURES

- Master bedroom includes a half bath with laundry area, linen closet and kitchen access
- Kitchen has charming double-door entry, breakfast bar and a convenient walk-in pantry
- Welcoming front porch opens to large living room with coat closet
- 3 bedrooms, 1 1/2 baths
- Crawl space foundation, drawings also include basement and slab foundations

Plan 574-0587

Perfect Fit
For A Narrow Site

Total Living Area: 1,270 sq. ft.
Blueprint Price Code: A
Garage: 393 sq. ft.

FEATURES

- Spacious living area features angled stairs, vaulted ceiling, exciting fireplace and deck access

- Master bedroom includes a walk-in closet and private bath

- Dining and living rooms join to create an open atmosphere

- Eat-in kitchen with convenient pass-through to dining room

- 3 bedrooms, 2 baths, 2-car garage

- Basement foundation

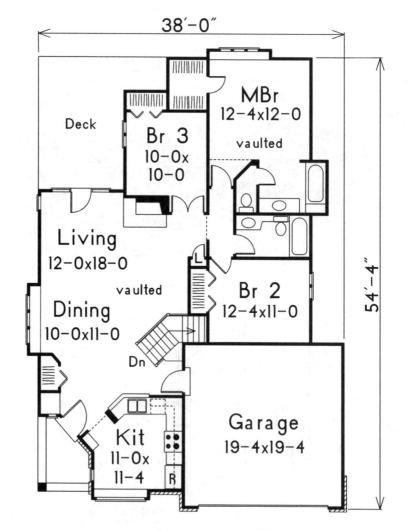

38'-0"

54'-4"

Deck

MBr
12-4x12-0
vaulted

Br 3
10-0x
10-0

Living
12-0x18-0
vaulted

Dining
10-0x11-0

Br 2
12-4x11-0

Dn

Kit
11-0x
11-4

Garage
19-4x19-4

Plan 574-0275

Second Floor
500 sq. ft.

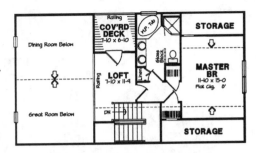

First Floor
1,062 sq. ft.

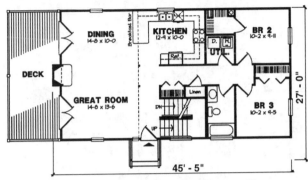

45' - 5"

27' - 0"

Optional
Lower Level

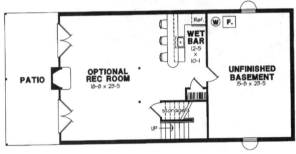

Three-Level Design Has It All

Total Living Area: 1,562 sq. ft.
Blueprint Price Code: B
Front porch: 19 sq. ft.

FEATURES

- Enormous deck off great room and dining area fills home with sunlight
- Kitchen with breakfast bar allows for additional dining space
- Unique second floor loft is open to first floor and has a private covered deck
- 678 square feet of optional living area on the lower level
- 3 bedrooms, 2 baths
- Basement foundation

Plan 574-GH-24705

Covered Front Porch

Total Living Area:	**1,966 sq. ft.**
Blueprint Price Code:	**C**
Side entry garage:	548 sq. ft.
Front porch:	316 sq. ft.

FEATURES

- Private dining room remains focal point when entering the home

- Kitchen and breakfast room join to create a functional area

- Lots of closet space in second floor bedrooms

- 3 bedrooms, 2 1/2 baths, 2-car side entry garage

- Basement foundation

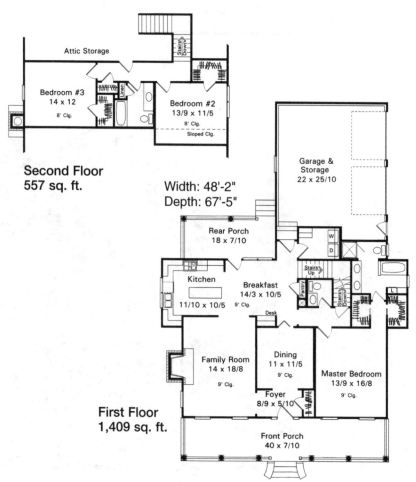

Second Floor
557 sq. ft.

Attic Storage

Bedroom #3
14 x 12
8' Clg.

Linen

Bedroom #2
13/9 x 11/5
8' Clg.
Sloped Clg.

Stairs Down

Width: 48'-2"
Depth: 67'-5"

Garage & Storage
22 x 25/10

Rear Porch
18 x 7/10

W
D

Kitchen
11/10 x 10/5

Breakfast
14/3 x 10/5
9' Clg.

Stairs Up

Pantry

Stairs Down

Desk

Family Room
14 x 18/8
9' Clg.

Dining
11 x 11/5
9' Clg.

Master Bedroom
13/9 x 16/8
9' Clg.

Foyer
8/9 x 5/10

First Floor
1,409 sq. ft.

Front Porch
40 x 7/10

Plan 574-GM-1966

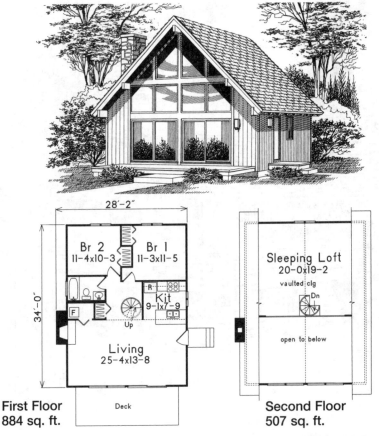

Cozy
Vacation Retreat

Total Living Area:	**1,391 sq. ft.**
Blueprint Price Code:	**A**

FEATURES

- Large living room with masonry fireplace features soaring vaulted ceiling

- A spiral staircase in hall leads to huge loft area overlooking living room below

- Two first floor bedrooms share a full bath

- 2 bedrooms, 1 bath

- Pier foundation, drawings also include crawl space foundation

First Floor
884 sq. ft.

Second Floor
507 sq. ft.

Plan 574-N049

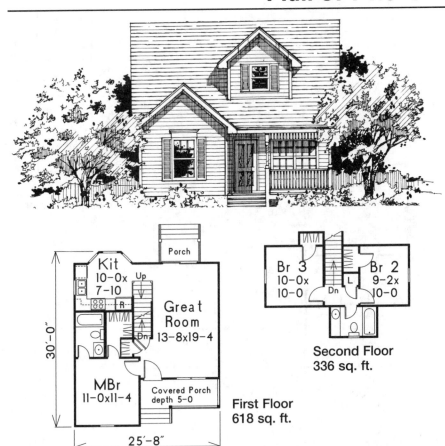

Dormer
And Covered
Porch Add To
Country Charm

Total Living Area:	**954 sq. ft.**
Blueprint Price Code:	**AA**
Front porch:	**70 sq. ft.**

FEATURES

- Kitchen has cozy bayed eating area

- Master bedroom has a walk-in closet and private bath

- Large great room has access to the back porch

- Convenient coat closet near front entry

- 3 bedrooms, 2 baths

- Basement foundation

Second Floor
336 sq. ft.

First Floor
618 sq. ft.

Plan 574-0498

Rustic Feel With Stone Accent

Total Living Area:	1,648 sq. ft.
Blueprint Price Code:	B
Drive under garage:	382 sq. ft.
Front porch:	707 sq. ft.

FEATURES

- Enormous country kitchen has fireplace and a snack bar

- Four sets of sliding glass doors fill this home full of light and make the deck convenient from any room

- Secondary bedrooms both located on second floor along with a full bath

- 3 bedrooms, 2 baths, 2-car drive under garage

- Basement, crawl space or slab foundation, please specify when ordering

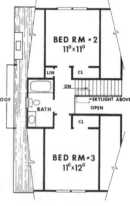

Second Floor
457 sq. ft.

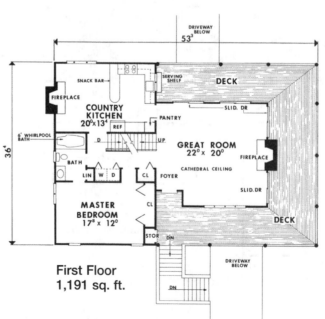

First Floor
1,191 sq. ft.

Plan 574-AX-7944

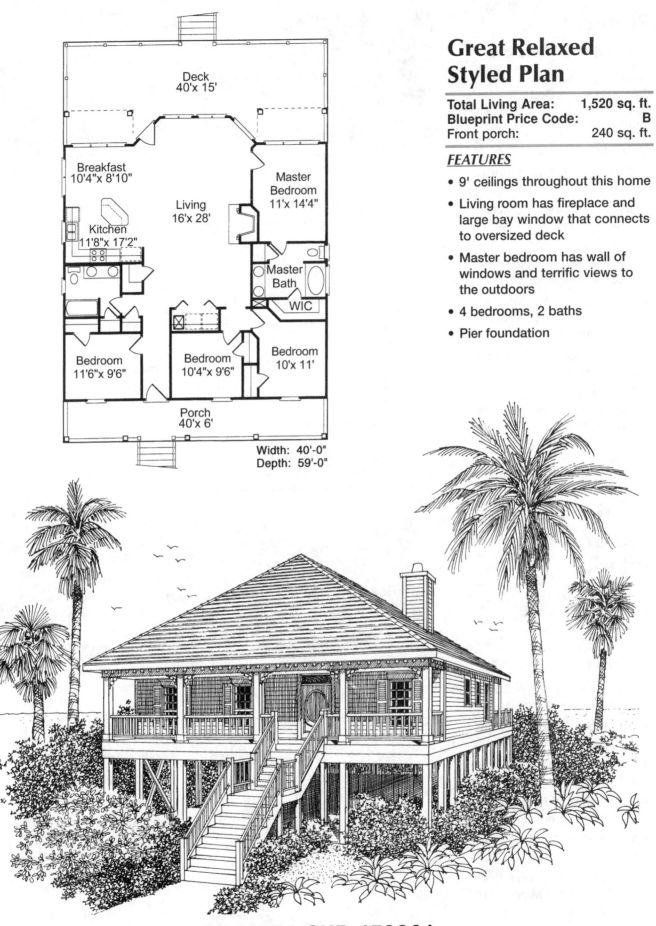

Deck
40'x 15'

Breakfast
10'4"x 8'10"

Master
Bedroom
11'x 14'4"

Living
16'x 28'

Kitchen
11'8"x 17'2"

Master
Bath

WIC

Bedroom
11'6"x 9'6"

Bedroom
10'4"x 9'6"

Bedroom
10'x 11'

Porch
40'x 6'

Width: 40'-0"
Depth: 59'-0"

Great Relaxed Styled Plan

Total Living Area: 1,520 sq. ft.
Blueprint Price Code: B
Front porch: 240 sq. ft.

FEATURES

- 9' ceilings throughout this home
- Living room has fireplace and large bay window that connects to oversized deck
- Master bedroom has wall of windows and terrific views to the outdoors
- 4 bedrooms, 2 baths
- Pier foundation

Plan 574-CHP-1532A1

Perfect Country Haven

Total Living Area:	**1,232 sq. ft.**
Blueprint Price Code:	**A**
Optional garage:	484 sq. ft.
Front porch:	264 sq. ft.

FEATURES

- Ideal porch for quiet quality evenings

- Great room opens to dining room for those large dinner gatherings

- Functional L-shaped kitchen includes broom cabinet

- Master bedroom contains large walk-in closet and compartmented bath

- 3 bedrooms, 1 bath, optional 2-car garage

- Basement foundation, drawings also include crawl space and slab foundations

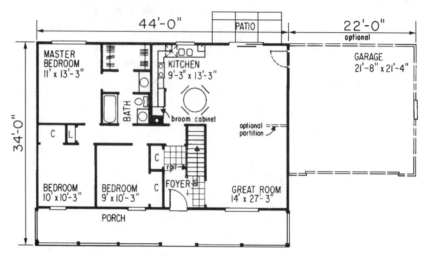

Plan 574-1120

Rustic Facade Features Cozy Interior

Total Living Area:	**1,550 sq. ft.**
Blueprint Price Code:	**B**
Side entry garage:	506 sq. ft.
Front porch:	169 sq. ft.

FEATURES

- Convenient mud room between garage and kitchen

- Oversized dining area allows plenty of space for entertaining

- Master bedroom has private bath and ample closet space

- Large patio off family room brings the outdoors in

- 3 bedrooms, 2 baths, 2-car side entry garage

- Basement foundation, drawings also include crawl space or slab foundations

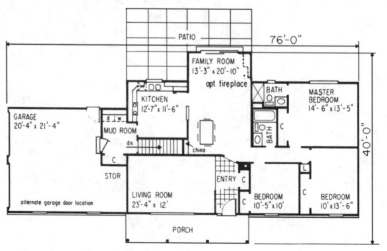

Plan 574-1118

Small And Cozy Cabin

Total Living Area:	676 sq. ft.
Blueprint Price Code:	AAA
Front porch:	156 sq. ft.

FEATURES

- See-through fireplace between bedroom and living area adds character
- Combined dining and living areas create an open feeling
- Full-length front covered porch perfect for enjoying the outdoors
- Additional storage available in utility room
- 1 bedroom, 1 bath
- Crawl space foundation

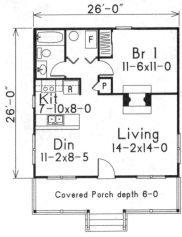

Plan 574-0696

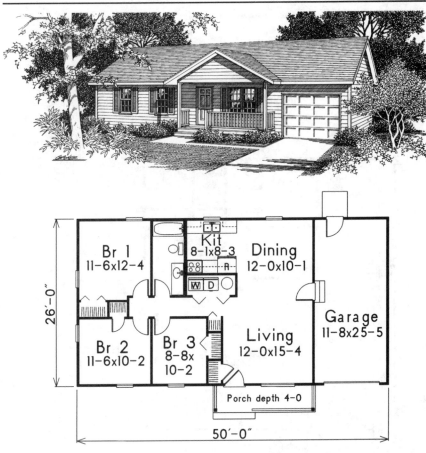

Front Porch And Center Gable Add Style To This Ranch

Total Living Area:	988 sq. ft.
Blueprint Price Code:	AA
Garage:	312 sq. ft.
Front porch:	64 sq. ft.

FEATURES

- Pleasant covered porch entry
- The kitchen, living and dining areas are combined to maximize space
- Entry has convenient coat closet
- Laundry closet is located adjacent to bedrooms
- 3 bedrooms, 1 bath, 1-car garage
- Basement foundation, drawings also include crawl space foundation

Plan 574-0195

Enticing
Wrap-Around Deck

Total Living Area:	**1,295 sq. ft.**
Blueprint Price Code:	**A**
Front sun deck:	336 sq. ft.
Left side:	236 sq. ft.
Carport:	242 sq. ft.

FEATURES

- Compact kitchen includes snack counter for convenience

- Both bedrooms have sliding glass doors leading to spacious sun deck

- Vaulted living area is sunny and bright with double sliding glass doors accessing the outdoors

- 2 bedrooms, 1 bath, 1-car carport

- Crawl space foundation

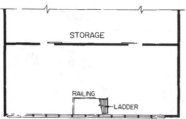

Second Floor
358 sq. ft.

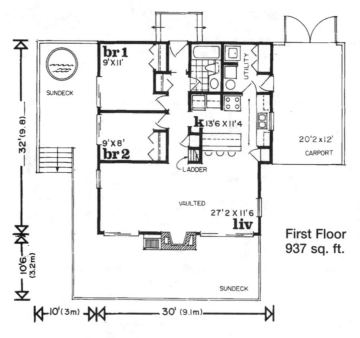

First Floor
937 sq. ft.

Plan 574-SH-SEA-002

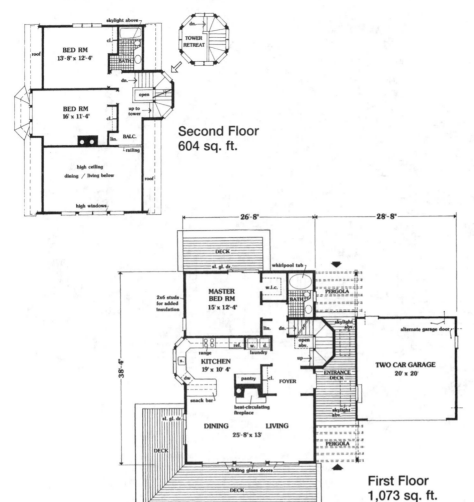

Second Floor
604 sq. ft.

BED RM
13'-8" x 12'-4"

BED RM
16' x 11'-4"

TOWER RETREAT

skylight above

cl.

BATH

dn.

open

up to tower

BALC.

lin.

railing

high ceiling
dining / living below

high windows

roof

roof

DECK

MASTER BED RM
15' x 12'-4"

2x6 studs for added insulation

whirlpool tub

w.i.c.

BATH

PERGOLA

KITCHEN
19' x 10'4"

range

ref.

w.

d.

laundry

lin.

dn.

skylight abv.

open abv.

up

alternate garage door

TWO CAR GARAGE
20' x 20'

pantry

cl.

FOYER

ENTRANCE DECK

skylight abv.

snack bar

dw

heat-circulating fireplace

DINING   LIVING
25'-8" x 13'

sl. gl. dr.

DECK

sliding glass doors

DECK

26'-8"

28'-8"

38'-4"

First Floor
1,073 sq. ft.

Unique
Tower Retreat

Total Living Area:	**1,677 sq. ft.**
Blueprint Price Code:	**B**
Garage:	428 sq. ft.
Front porch:	217 sq. ft.

FEATURES

- Energy efficient home with 2" x 6" exterior walls

- Master bedroom on first floor for convenience

- Skylights enhance second floor bath and covered outdoor deck

- 3 bedrooms, 2 baths, 2-car garage

- Basement, crawl space or slab foundation available, please specify when ordering

Plan 574-AX-1500

This Home Has Alpine Appeal

Total Living Area:	1,735 sq. ft.
Blueprint Price Code:	B
Front porch:	114 sq. ft.
Left covered porch:	110 sq. ft.
Right covered porch:	53 sq. ft.
Covered sun deck:	134 sq. ft.

FEATURES

- Living and dining areas combine making an ideal space for entertaining

- Master bedroom accesses rear verandah through sliding glass doors

- Second floor includes cozy family room with patio deck just outside of secondary bedrooms

- 3 bedrooms, 2 baths

- Crawl space foundation

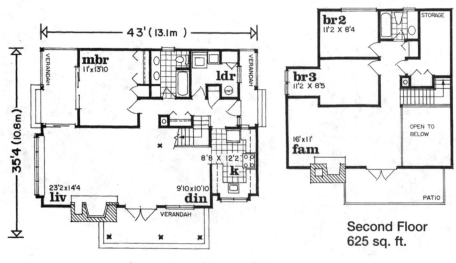

Living and Dining Room Interior View

First Floor
1,110 sq. ft.

Second Floor
625 sq. ft.

Plan 574-SH-SEA-001

Riverside Views From Covered Deck

Total Living Area:	792 sq. ft.
Blueprint Price Code:	AAA

FEATURES

- Attractive exterior features wood posts and beams, wrap-around deck with railing and glass sliding doors with transoms

- Living, dining and kitchen areas enjoy sloped ceilings, cozy fireplace and views over deck

- Two bedrooms share a bath just off the hall

- 2 bedrooms, 1 bath

- Crawl space foundation, drawings also include slab foundation

24'-0"

42'-0"

Br 2
9-1x11-1

Br 1
11-6x11-1

Kit/Dining
11-8x15-9

Living
11-8x22-0
vaulted clg

Covered Deck
24-0x8-0

Plan 574-N114

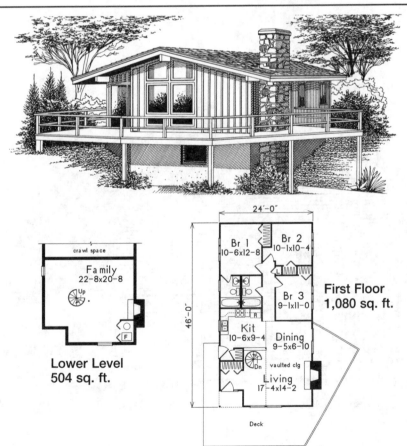

Nestled Oasis Romances The Sun

Total Living Area:	1,584 sq. ft.
Blueprint Price Code:	B

FEATURES

- Vaulted living/dining room features stone fireplace, ascending spiral stair and separate vestibule with guest closet

- Space saving kitchen has an eat-in area and access to the deck

- Master bedroom adjoins a full bath

- 3 bedrooms, 2 baths

- Basement foundation, drawings also include crawl space and slab foundations

crawl space

Family
22-8x20-8
Up

Lower Level
504 sq. ft.

24'-0"

46'-0"

Br 1
10-6x12-8

Br 2
10-1x10-4

Br 3
9-1x11-0

Kit
10-6x9-4

Dining
9-5x6-10
vaulted clg

Living
17-4x14-2
Dn

Deck

First Floor
1,080 sq. ft.

Plan 574-N130

Handsome Double Brick Gables

Total Living Area:	**1,553 sq. ft.**
Blueprint Price Code:	**B**
Garage:	482 sq. ft.
Front porch:	22 sq. ft.

FEATURES

- Kitchen counter extends into great room with space for dining

- Extra storage provided in garage

- Sloped ceiling in master bedroom adds a dramatic feel

- 3 bedrooms, 2 baths, 2-car garage

- Crawl space or slab foundation, please specify when ordering

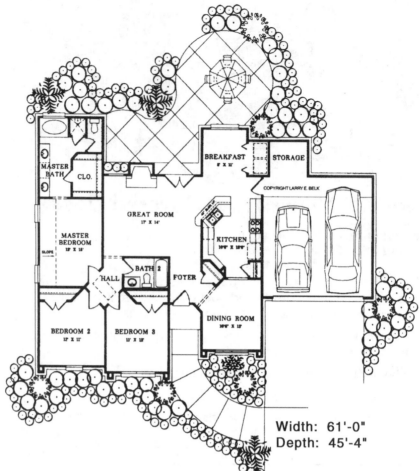

Width: 61'-0"
Depth: 45'-4"

Plan 574-LBD-15-2A

Tall Windows, Sweeping Roof Lines Make A Sizable Impression

Total Living Area:	**1,351 sq. ft.**
Blueprint Price Code:	**A**
Garage:	**480 sq. ft.**
Porch:	**29 sq. ft.**

FEATURES

- Roof lines and vaulted ceilings make this home appear larger than its true size

- Central fireplace provides a focal point for dining and living areas

- Master bedroom suite is highlighted by a roomy window seat and a walk-in closet

- 3 bedrooms, 2 1/2 baths, 2-car garage

- Basement foundation

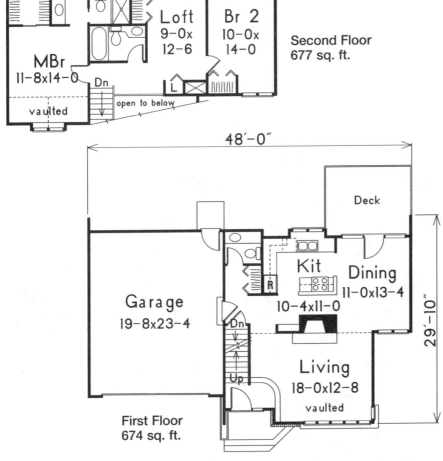

Second Floor
677 sq. ft.

Loft
9-0x
12-6

Br 2
10-0x
14-0

MBr
11-8x14-0

Dn

vaulted

open to below

L

48'-0"

Deck

Kit
10-4x11-0

Dining
11-0x13-4

Garage
19-8x23-4

Dn

Up

R

Living
18-0x12-8
vaulted

29'-10"

First Floor
674 sq. ft.

Plan 574-0103

Innovative Design For That Narrow Lot

Total Living Area:	**1,558 sq. ft.**
Blueprint Price Code:	**B**
Rear entry garage:	484 sq. ft.
Front porch:	76 sq. ft.

FEATURES

- Illuminated spaces created by visual access to outdoor living areas

- Vaulted master bedroom features private bath with whirlpool tub, separate shower and large walk-in closet

- Convenient first floor laundry has garage access

- Practical den or third bedroom

- U-shaped kitchen adjacent to sunny breakfast area

- 2 bedrooms, 2 baths, 2-car rear entry garage

- Basement foundation

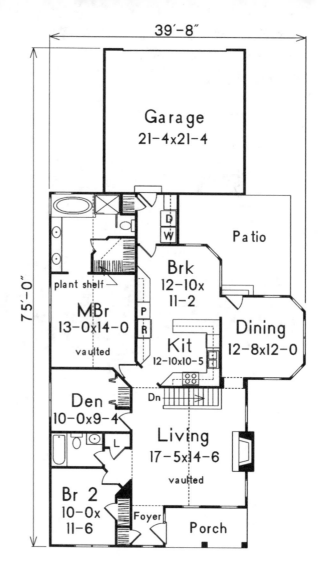

Plan 574-0394

TO ORDER BLUEPRINTS USE THE FORM ON PAGE 256 OR CALL **TOLL-FREE 1-800-367-7667**

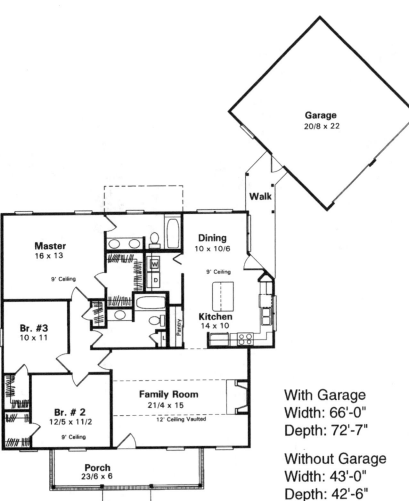

Garage
20/8 x 22

Walk

Master
16 x 13
9' Ceiling

Dining
10 x 10/6
9' Ceiling

Br. #3
10 x 11

Kitchen
14 x 10

Pantry

Family Room
21/4 x 15
12' Ceiling Vaulted

Br. # 2
12/5 x 11/2
9' Ceiling

Porch
23/6 x 6

With Garage
Width: 66'-0"
Depth: 72'-7"

Without Garage
Width: 43'-0"
Depth: 42'-6"

Abundance Of Walk-In Closets

Total Living Area:	1,474 sq. ft.
Blueprint Price Code:	**A**
Detached garage:	454 sq. ft.
Front porch:	142 sq. ft.

FEATURES

- Kitchen and dining area include center eat-in island and large pantry

- Laundry facilities and hall bath are roomy

- Secondary bedrooms both have walk-in closets

- 3 bedrooms, 2 baths, 2-car detached garage

- Slab or crawl space foundation, please specify when ordering

Plan 574-GM-1474

Comfortable Vacation Retreat

Total Living Area:	**1,073 sq. ft.**
Blueprint Price Code:	**AA**
Front porch:	107 sq. ft.
Back porch:	80 sq. ft.

FEATURES

- Home includes lovely covered front porch and a screened porch off dining area

- Attractive box window brightens kitchen

- Space for efficiency washer and dryer located conveniently between bedrooms

- Family room spotlighted by fireplace with flanking bookshelves and spacious vaulted ceiling

- 2 bedrooms, 1 bath

- Crawl space foundation

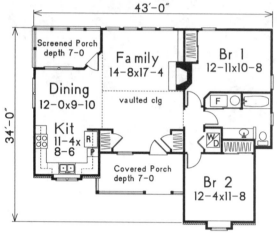

Plan 574-0699

Great Room Window Adds Character Inside And Out

Total Living Area:	**1,368 sq. ft.**
Blueprint Price Code:	**A**
Garage:	433 sq. ft.

FEATURES

- Entry foyer steps down to open living area which combines great room and formal dining area

- Vaulted master suite includes box bay window, large vanity, separate tub and shower

- Cozy breakfast area features direct access to the patio and pass-through kitchen

- Handy linen closet located in hall

- 3 bedrooms, 2 baths, 2-car garage

- Basement foundation

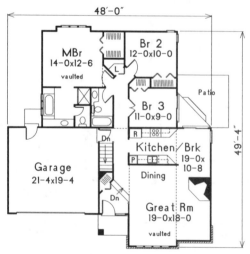

Plan 574-0271

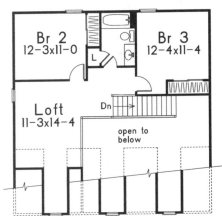

Second Floor
565 sq. ft.

Br 2
12-3x11-0

Br 3
12-4x11-4

Loft
11-3x14-4

Dn

open to
below

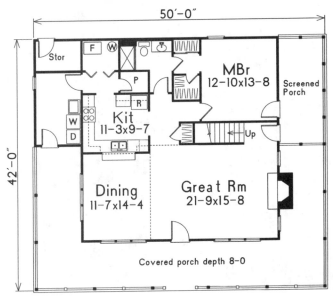

50'-0"

42'-0"

Stor

Kit
11-3x9-7

MBr
12-10x13-8

Screened
Porch

Dining
11-7x14-4

Great Rm
21-9x15-8

Up

Covered porch depth 8-0

First Floor
1,314 sq. ft.

Charming Wrap-Around Porch

Total Living Area:	1,879 sq. ft.
Blueprint Price Code:	C
Front porch:	864 sq. ft.

FEATURES

- Open floor plan on both floors makes home appear larger

- Loft area overlooks great room or can become an optional fourth bedroom

- Large walk-in pantry in kitchen and large storage in rear of home with access from exterior

- 3 bedrooms, 2 baths

- Crawl space foundation

Plan 574-0768

Symmetrical Design Pleasing

Total Living Area:	**1,380 sq. ft.**
Blueprint Price Code:	**A**
Side entry garage:	420 sq. ft.
Front porch:	124 sq. ft.

FEATURES

- Built-in bookshelves flank fire-place in great room

- Lots of storage space near laundry room and kitchen

- Covered porch has views of the backyard

- 3 bedrooms, 2 baths, optional 2-car side entry garage

- Basement, crawl space or slab foundation, please specify when ordering

- 372 square feet of optional living area on the second floor

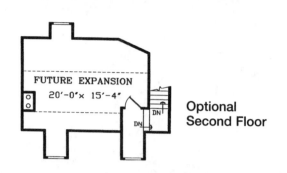

FUTURE EXPANSION
20'-0" x 15'-4"

Optional
Second Floor

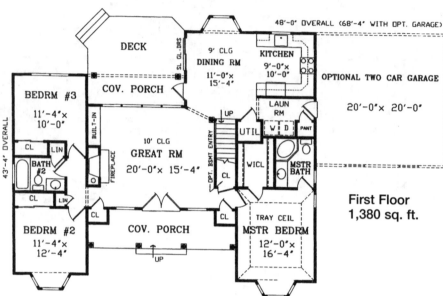

First Floor
1,380 sq. ft.

Plan 574-AX-97359

TO ORDER BLUEPRINTS USE THE FORM ON PAGE 256 OR CALL **TOLL-FREE 1-800-367-7667**

Second Floor
580 sq. ft.

Casual Country Home With Unique Loft

Total Living Area: 1,673 sq. ft.
Blueprint Price Code: B

FEATURES

- Great room flows into the breakfast nook with outdoor access and beyond to an efficient kitchen

- Master suite on second floor has access to loft/study, private balcony and bath

- Covered porch surrounds the entire home for outdoor living area

- 3 bedrooms, 2 baths

- Crawl space foundation

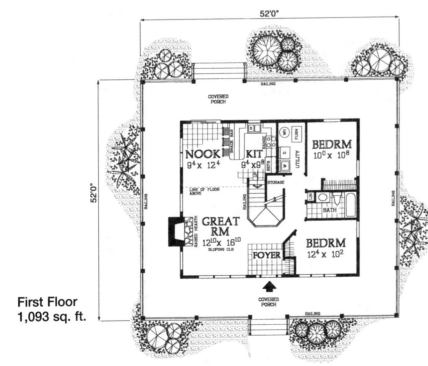

First Floor
1,093 sq. ft.

Plan 574-HP-C675

Country Retreat For Quiet Times

Total Living Area: 1,211 sq. ft.
Blueprint Price Code: A

FEATURES

- Extraordinary views are enjoyed from vaulted family room through sliding doors

- Functional kitchen features snack bar and laundry closet

- Bedroom and bunk room complete first floor while a large bedroom with two storage areas and balcony overlook, complete the second floor

- Additional plan for second floor creates 223 square feet of additional bedroom space

- 3 bedrooms, 1 bath

- Crawl space foundation, drawings also include basement foundation

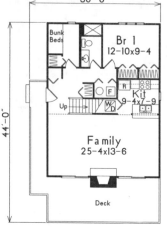

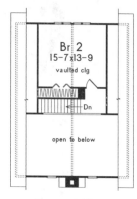

First Floor
884 sq. ft.

Second Floor
327 sq. ft.

Plan 574-N057

Compact Home Maximizes Space

Total Living Area: 987 sq. ft.
Blueprint Price Code: AA
Front porch: 63 sq. ft.

FEATURES

- Galley kitchen opens into cozy breakfast room

- Convenient coat closets located by both entrances

- Dining/living room combined for expansive open area

- Breakfast room has access to the outdoors

- Front porch great for enjoying outdoor living

- 3 bedrooms, 1 bath

- Basement foundation

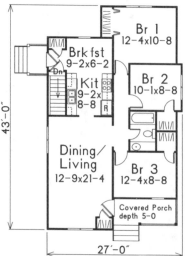

Plan 574-0495

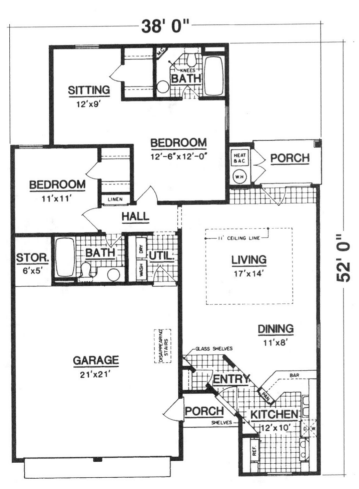

SITTING
12'x9'

BATH

BEDROOM
12'-6"x12'-0"

PORCH

BEDROOM
11'x11'

LINEN

HALL

STOR.
6'x5'

BATH

UTIL.

LIVING
17'x14'

11' CEILING LINE

GARAGE
21'x21'

DISAPPEARING STAIRS

GLASS SHELVES

DINING
11'x8'

ENTRY

PORCH

SHELVES

KITCHEN
12'x10'

BAR

REF

38' 0"

52' 0"

Unique Angled Entry

Total Living Area:	1,150 sq. ft.
Blueprint Price Code:	AA
Garage:	434 sq. ft.
Front porch:	22 sq. ft.

FEATURES

- Master suite has its own T.V. viewing/sitting area

- Living and dining rooms have 11' high box ceiling

- Ornate trim work accents the wood sided exterior

- 2 bedrooms, 2 baths, 2-car garage

- Slab or crawl space foundation, please specify when ordering

Plan 574-BF-DR1108

Relax On The Covered Front Porch

Total Living Area:	1,543 sq. ft.
Blueprint Price Code:	B
Garage:	484 sq. ft.
Front porch:	260 sq. ft.

FEATURES

- Fireplace serves as the focal point of the large family room

- Efficient floor plan keeps hallways at a minimum

- Laundry room connects the kitchen to the garage

- Private first floor master bedroom has walk-in closet and bath

- 3 bedrooms, 2 1/2 baths, 2-car detached side entry garage

- Slab foundation, drawings also include crawl space foundation

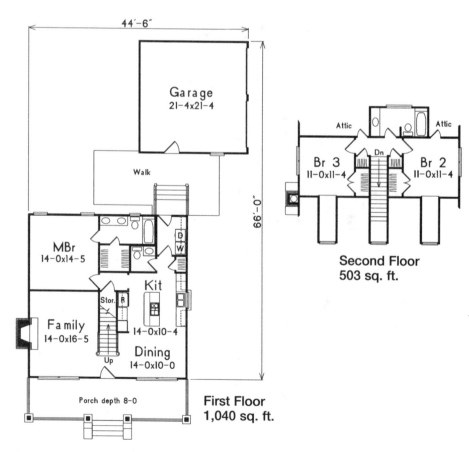

First Floor
1,040 sq. ft.

Second Floor
503 sq. ft.

Plan 574-0489

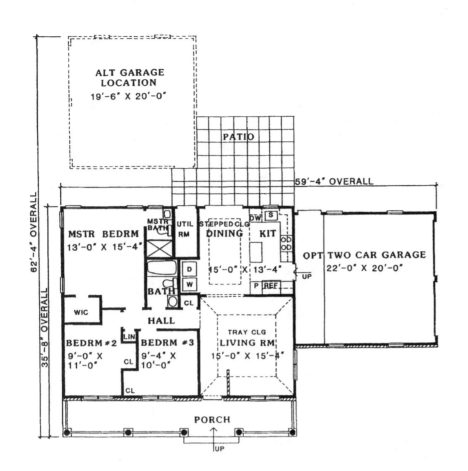

ALT GARAGE
LOCATION
19'-6" X 20'-0"

PATIO

59'-4" OVERALL

62'-4" OVERALL

35'-8" OVERALL

MSTR BEDRM
13'-0" X 15'-4"

MSTR BATH

UTIL RM

STEPPED CLG
DINING
15'-0" X 13'-4"

DW S

KIT

OD OD

OPT TWO CAR GARAGE
22'-0" X 20'-0"

UP

D

W

BATH

CL

P REF

WIC

HALL

LIN

CL

CL

BEDRM #2
9'-0" X 11'-0"

BEDRM #3
9'-4" X 10'-0"

CL

TRAY CLG
LIVING RM
15'-0" X 15'-4"

PORCH

UP

Lovely Full-Width Column Porch

Total Living Area:	**1,097 sq. ft.**
Blueprint Price Code:	**AA**
Optional garage:	461 sq. ft.
Front porch:	222 sq. ft.

FEATURES

- U-shaped kitchen wraps around center island

- Master suite includes its own private bath and walk-in closet

- Living room provides expansive view to the rear

- 3 bedrooms, 2 baths, optional 2-car garage

- Basement, crawl space or slab foundation, please specify when ordering

Plan 574-AX-91316

Breakfast Bay Area Opens To Deck

Total Living Area:	**1,020 sq. ft.**
Blueprint Price Code:	**AA**
Garage:	**400 sq. ft.**

FEATURES

- Kitchen features open stairs, pass-through to great room, pantry and deck access

- Master bedroom features private entrance to bath, large walk-in closet and sliding doors to deck

- Informal entrance into home through the garage

- Great room with vaulted ceiling and fireplace

- 2 bedrooms, 1 bath, 2-car garage

- Basement foundation

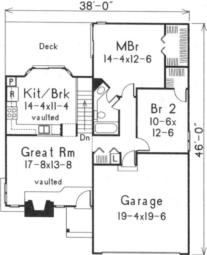

Plan 574-0274

Cozy Ranch Home

Total Living Area:	**950 sq. ft.**
Blueprint Price Code:	**AA**
Garage:	**248 sq. ft.**

FEATURES

- Deck adjacent to kitchen/break-fast area for outdoor dining

- Vaulted ceiling, open stairway and fireplace complement great room

- Secondary bedroom with sloped ceiling and box bay window can convert to den

- Master bedroom with walk-in closet, plant shelf, separate dressing area and private access to bath

- Kitchen has garage access and opens to great room

- 2 bedrooms, 1 bath, 1-car garage

- Basement foundation

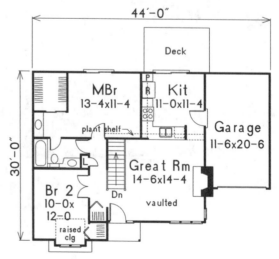

Plan 574-0276

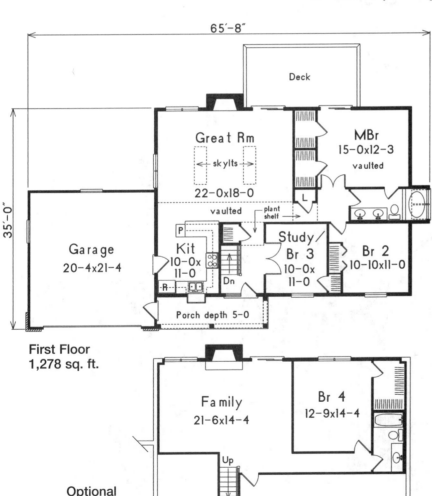

First Floor
1,278 sq. ft.

Great Rm
skylts
22-0x18-0
vaulted

MBr
15-0x12-3
vaulted

Deck

65'-8"

35'-0"

Garage
20-4x21-4

Kit
10-0x
11-0

Study/Br 3
10-0x
11-0

Br 2
10-10x11-0

Porch depth 5-0

plant shelf

P

R

Dn

L

Optional Lower Level

Family
21-6x14-4

Br 4
12-9x14-4

Up

Storage

Grandscale Great Room In A Country Ranch

Total Living Area:	1,278 sq. ft.
Blueprint Price Code:	**A**
Garage:	462 sq. ft.
Front porch:	94 sq. ft.

FEATURES

- Excellent U-shaped kitchen with garden window opens to an enormous great room with vaulted ceiling, fireplace and two skylights

- Vaulted master bedroom offers double entry doors, access to a deck and bath and two walk-in closets

- The bath has a double-bowl vanity and dramatic step-up garden tub with a lean-to greenhouse window

- 805 square feet of optional living area on lower level with family room, bedroom #4 and bath

- 3 bedrooms, 1 bath, 2-car garage

- Walk-out basement foundation

Plan 574-0751

Dining
With A View

Total Living Area: 1,524 sq. ft.
Blueprint Price Code: B
Garage: 407 sq. ft.
Front porch: 80 sq. ft.

FEATURES

- Delightful balcony overlooks two-story entry illuminated by oval window

- Roomy first floor master suite offers quiet privacy

- All bedrooms feature one or more walk-in closets

- 3 bedrooms, 2 1/2 baths, 2-car garage

- Basement foundation

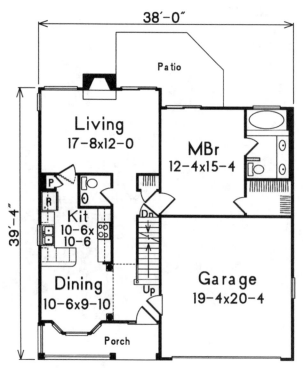

38'-0"

39'-4"

Patio

Living
17-8x12-0

MBr
12-4x15-4

P
R

Kit
10-6x
10-6

Dining
10-6x9-10

Dn

Up

Garage
19-4x20-4

Porch

First Floor
951 sq. ft.

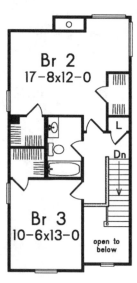

Br 2
17-8x12-0

L

Dn

Br 3
10-6x13-0

open to below

Second Floor
573 sq. ft.

Plan 574-0652

Covered Breezeway To Garage

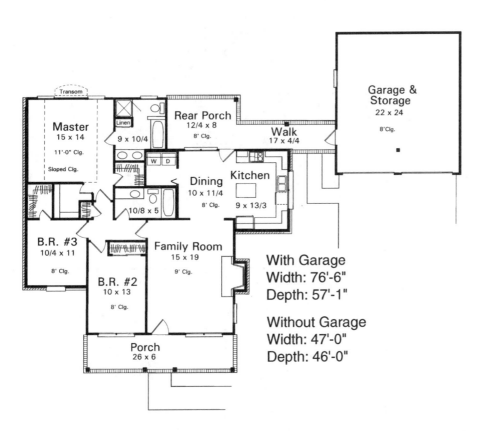

Total Living Area:	**1,406 sq. ft.**
Blueprint Price Code:	**A**
Detached garage:	528 sq. ft.
Front porch:	156 sq. ft.
Rear porch:	107 sq. ft.

FEATURES

- Master bedroom has sloped ceiling

- Kitchen and dining area merge becoming a gathering place

- Enter family room from charming covered front porch and find fireplace and lots of windows

- 3 bedrooms, 2 baths, 2-car detached garage

- Slab or crawl space foundation, please specify when ordering

Plan 574-GM-1406

An A-Frame For Every Environment

Total Living Area:	618 sq. ft.
Blueprint Price Code:	AAA
Front porch:	120 sq. ft.

FEATURES

- Memorable family events are certain to be enjoyed on this fabulous partially covered sundeck

- Equally impressive is the living area with its cathedral ceiling and exposed rafters

- A kitchenette, bedroom and bath conclude the first floor with a delightful sleeping loft above bedroom and bath

- 1 bedroom, 1 bath

- Pier foundation

First Floor
480 sq. ft.

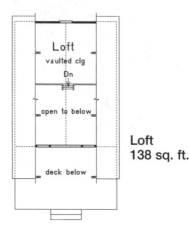

Loft
138 sq. ft.

Plan 574-N145

Spacious Vaulted Great Room

Total Living Area:	1,189 sq. ft.
Blueprint Price Code:	AA
Garage:	440 sq. ft.
Front porch:	73 sq. ft.

FEATURES

- All bedrooms are located on the second floor

- Dining room and kitchen both have views of the patio

- Convenient half bath located near the kitchen

- Master bedroom has private bath

- 3 bedrooms, 2 1/2 baths, 2-car garage

- Basement foundation

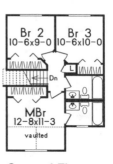

First Floor
615 sq. ft.

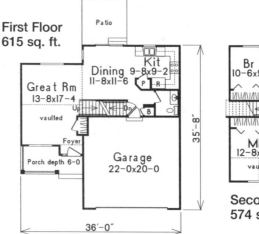

Second Floor
574 sq. ft.

Plan 574-0487

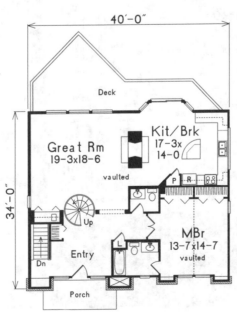

Rear View

Ideal Home For Lake, Mountains Or Seaside

Total Living Area:	**1,711 sq. ft.**
Blueprint Price Code:	**B**
Front porch:	235 sq. ft.

FEATURES

- Colossal entry leads to a vaulted great room with exposed beams, two-story window wall, brick fireplace, wet bar and balcony

- Bayed breakfast room shares the fireplace and joins a sun-drenched kitchen and sundeck

- Vaulted first floor master suite with double entry doors, closets and bookshelves

- Spiral stair and balcony dramatizes a loft that doubles as a spacious second bedroom

- 2 bedrooms, 2 1/2 baths

- Basement foundation

Second Floor
397 sq. ft.

open to below

plant shelf

Dn

MBr below

Loft/Br 2
19-3x12-0
vaulted

First Floor
1,314 sq. ft.

40'-0"

Deck

Kit/Brk
17-3x
14-0

Great Rm
19-3x18-6

vaulted

34'-0"

P R

Up

Entry

Dn

MBr
13-7x14-7
vaulted

Porch

Plan 574-0475

Rustic Home With Large Windows For Views

Total Living Area: 1,516 sq. ft.
Blueprint Price Code: B

FEATURES

- Energy efficient home with 2" x 6" exterior walls
- Warm fireplace adds coziness to living areas
- Dining area and kitchen are convenient to each other making entertaining easy
- 3 bedrooms, 2 baths
- Basement foundation

Second Floor
454 sq. ft.

First Floor
1,062 sq. ft.

Plan 574-DR-2903

TO ORDER BLUEPRINTS USE THE FORM ON PAGE 256 OR CALL **TOLL-FREE 1-800-367-7667**

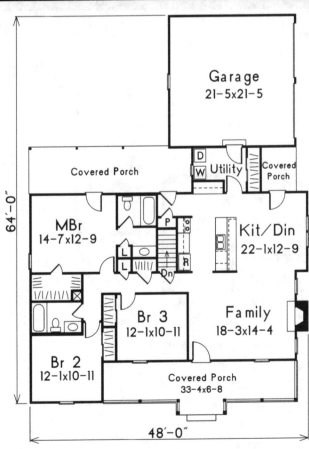

Garage
21-5x21-5

Covered Porch

D
W | Utility | Covered Porch

MBr
14-7x12-9

P

L
L

R

Dn

Kit/Din
22-1x12-9

64'-0"

Br 2
12-1x10-11

Br 3
12-1x10-11

Family
18-3x14-4

Covered Porch
33-4x6-8

48'-0"

Country-Style Home With Large Front Porch

Total Living Area:	1,501 sq. ft.
Blueprint Price Code:	**B**
Garage:	477 sq. ft.
Front porch:	238 sq. ft.

FEATURES

- Spacious kitchen with dining area is open to the outdoors

- Convenient utility room is adjacent to garage

- Master suite with private bath, dressing area and access to large covered porch

- Large family room creates openness

- 3 bedrooms, 2 baths, 2-car side entry garage

- Basement foundation, drawings also include crawl space and slab foundations

Plan 574-0249

Charming Wrap-Around Porch

Total Living Area: 1,700 sq. ft.
Blueprint Price Code: B
Front porch: 303 sq. ft.

FEATURES

- Energy efficient home with 2" x 6" exterior walls

- Cozy living area has plenty of space for entertaining

- Snack bar in kitchen provides extra dining area

- 3 bedrooms, 1 1/2 baths

- Basement foundation

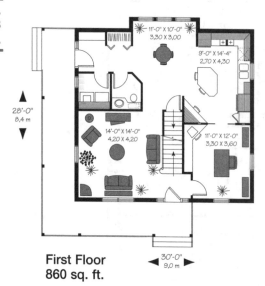

First Floor
860 sq. ft.

Second Floor
840 sq. ft.

Plan 574-DR-2590

10'-0" X 11'-4"
3,00 X 3,40

24'-4"
7,3 m

18'-0" X 11'-4"
5,40 X 3,40

13'-0" X 11'-4"
3,90 X 3,40

32'-4"
9,7 m

First Floor
787 sq. ft.

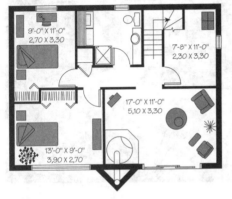

9'-0" X 11'-0"
2,70 X 3,30

7'-8" X 11'-0"
2,30 X 3,30

17'-0" X 11'-0"
5,10 X 3,30

Lower Level
787 sq. ft.

13'-0" X 9'-0"
3,90 X 2,70

Enormous Fireplace Is The Focal Point

Total Living Area:	1,574 sq. ft.
Blueprint Price Code:	**B**
Front porch:	280 sq. ft.

FEATURES

- Energy efficient home with 2" x 6" exterior walls

- Private bedroom on first floor has plenty of privacy

- Lower level has an additional living area which is convenient to secondary bedrooms

- 3 bedrooms, 2 baths

- Basement foundation

Plan 574-DR-2908

Rambling Country Bungalow

Total Living Area:	**1,475 sq. ft.**
Blueprint Price Code:	**B**
Garage:	455 sq. ft.
Front porch:	234 sq. ft.

FEATURES

- Family room features a high ceiling and prominent corner fireplace

- Kitchen with island counter and garden window makes a convenient connection between the family and dining rooms

- Hallway leads to three bedrooms all with large walk-in closets

- Covered breezeway joins main house and garage

- Full-width covered porch entry lends a country touch

- 3 bedrooms, 2 baths, 2-car side entry garage

- Slab foundation, drawings also include crawl space foundation

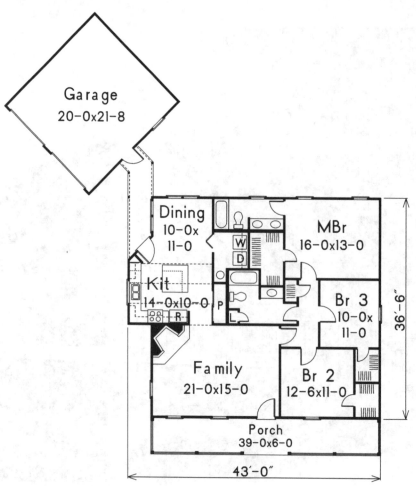

Plan 574-0203

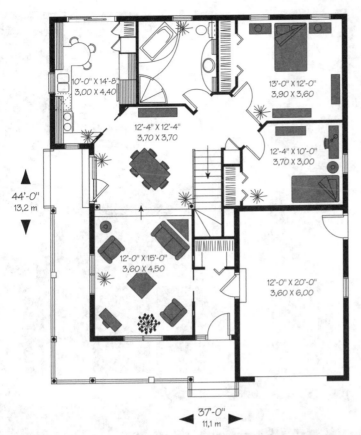

10'-0" X 14'-8"
3,00 X 4,40

13'-0" X 12'-0"
3,90 X 3,60

12'-4" X 12'-4"
3,70 X 3,70

12'-4" X 10'-0"
3,70 X 3,00

44'-0"
13,2 m

12'-0" X 15'-0"
3,60 X 4,50

12'-0" X 20'-0"
3,60 X 6,00

37'-0"
11,1 m

Eye-Catching Luxurious Bath

Total Living Area:	**1,124 sq. ft.**
Blueprint Price Code:	**AA**
Garage:	274 sq. ft.
Front porch:	230 sq. ft.

FEATURES

- Energy efficient home with 2" x 6" exterior walls
- Wrap-around porch creates an outdoor living area
- Large dining area easily accommodates extra guests
- Sunken family room
- 2 bedrooms, 1 bath, 1-car garage
- Basement foundation

Plan 574-DR-2290

Large Patio Adds Outdoor Appeal

Total Living Area: 1,056 sq. ft.
Blueprint Price Code: AA
Front porch: 234 sq. ft.

FEATURES

- Energy efficient home with 2" x 6" exterior walls

- Unique fireplace becomes focal point in living and dining areas

- Three-season room off living area is cheerful and bright

- Galley-style kitchen is efficiently designed

- 2 bedrooms, 1 1/2 baths

- Basement foundation

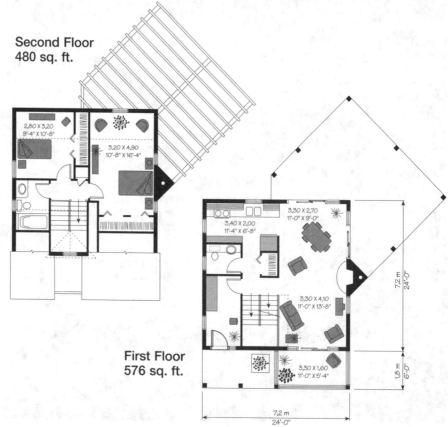

Second Floor
480 sq. ft.

2,80 X 3,20
9'-4" X 10'-8"

3,20 X 4,90
10'-8" X 16'-4"

3,30 X 2,70
11'-0" X 9'-0"

3,40 X 2,00
11'-4" X 6'-8"

3,30 X 4,10
11'-0" X 13'-8"

3,30 X 1,60
11'-0" X 5'-4"

First Floor
576 sq. ft.

7,2 m
24'-0"

1,8 m
6'-0"

7,2 m
24'-0"

Plan 574-DR-2936

Second Floor
533 sq. ft.

9'-0"x 11'-0"
2,70 x 3,30

14'-0"x 11'-0"
4,20 x 3,30

First Floor
587 sq. ft.

24'-0"
7,2 m

10'-0"x 12'-0"
3,00 x 3,60

8'-0"x 11'-0"
2,40 x 3,30

11'-0"x 14'-0"
3,30 x 4,20

26'-0"
8,0 m

Cozy
Farmhouse Style

Total Living Area: 1,120 sq. ft.
Blueprint Price Code: AA

FEATURES

- Energy efficient home with 2" x 6" exterior walls

- Dining and cooking island in kitchen makes food preparation easy

- All bedrooms on second floor for privacy from living area

- Convenient laundry closet on first floor

- 2 bedrooms, 1 1/2 baths

- Slab foundation

Plan 574-DR-2588

Quaint Exterior, Full Front Porch

Total Living Area:	1,657 sq. ft.
Blueprint Price Code:	B
Drive under garage:	481 sq. ft.
Front porch:	228 sq. ft.

FEATURES

- Stylish pass-through between living and dining areas

- Master bedroom is secluded from living area for privacy

- Large windows in breakfast and dining areas

- 3 bedrooms, 2 1/2 baths, 2-car drive under garage

- Basement foundation

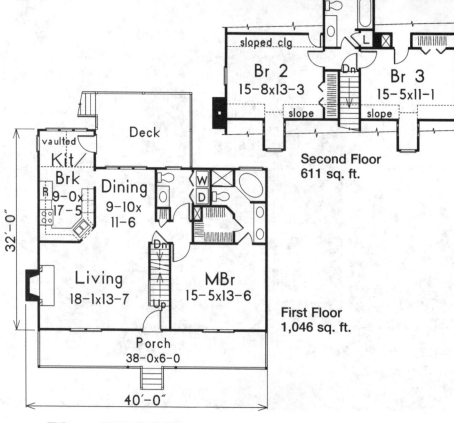

Second Floor
611 sq. ft.

First Floor
1,046 sq. ft.

Br 2
15-8x13-3

Br 3
15-5x11-1

Deck

vaulted

Kit/
Brk
9-0x
17-5

Dining
9-10x
11-6

Living
18-1x13-7

MBr
15-5x13-6

Porch
38-0x6-0

32'-0"

40'-0"

Plan 574-0174

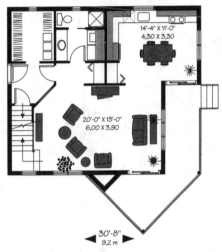

Second Floor
570 sq. ft.

11'-0" X 11'-4"
3,30 X 3,40

11'-8" X 19'-4"
3,50 X 5,80

First Floor
715 sq. ft.

14'-4" X 11'-0"
4,30 X 3,30

20'-0" X 13'-0"
6,00 X 3,90

26'-0"
7,8 m

30'-8"
9,2 m

Lots Of Windows Creates A Cheerful Home

Total Living Area:	**1,285 sq. ft.**
Blueprint Price Code:	**A**
Front porch:	160 sq. ft.

FEATURES

- Energy efficient home with 2" x 6" exterior walls
- Dining and living areas both access a large wrap-around porch
- First floor bath has convenient laundry closet as well as a shower
- 2 bedrooms, 2 baths
- Basement foundation

Plan 574-DR-2929

Charming Country Styling In This Ranch

Total Living Area:	**1,600 sq. ft.**
Blueprint Price Code:	**C**
Garage:	616 sq. ft.
Front porch:	295 sq. ft.

FEATURES

- Impressive sunken living room has massive stone fireplace and 16' vaulted ceilings

- Dining room conveniently located next to kitchen and divided for privacy

- Energy efficient home with 2" x 6" exterior walls

- Special amenities include sewing room, glass shelves in kitchen and master bath and a large utility area

- Sunken master bedroom features a distinctive sitting room

- 3 bedrooms, 2 baths, 2-car side entry garage

- Slab foundation, drawings also include crawl space and basement foundations

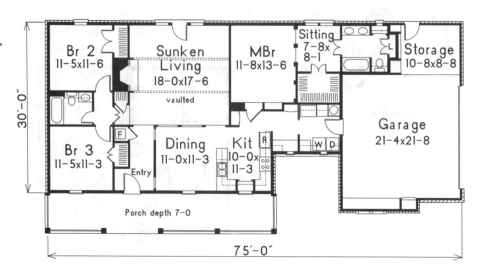

Plan 574-0190

Second Floor
604 sq. ft.

3,10 X 3,90
10'-4" X 13'-0"

3,10 X 3,90
10'-4" X 13'-0"

2,70 X 3,00
9'-0" X 10'-0"

First Floor
946 sq. ft.

3,30 X 3,90
11'-0" X 13'-0"

8,00 X 4,00
26'-8" X 13'-4"

9,2 m
30'-8"

11,1 m
37'-0"

Dramatic Cathedral Ceiling In Living Area

Total Living Area:	1,550 sq. ft.
Blueprint Price Code:	B
Front porch:	248 sq. ft.

FEATURES

- Energy efficient home with 2" x 6" exterior walls

- Master bedroom has walk-in closet

- Separate entry with closet is a unique feature

- 3 bedrooms, 2 baths

- Basement foundation

Plan 574-DR-2542

HOME PLANS INDEX